KORLE MEETS THE SEA

KORLE MEETS THE SEA

A Sociolinguistic History of Accra

M. E. Kropp Dakubu

New York   Oxford
OXFORD UNIVERSITY PRESS
1997

Oxford University Press

Oxford   New York
Athens   Auckland   Bangkok   Bogota   Bombay   Buenos Aires
Calcutta   Cape Town   Dar es Salaam   Delhi   Florence   Hong Kong
Istanbul   Karachi   Kuala Lumpur   Madras   Madrid   Melbourne
Mexico City   Nairobi   Paris   Singapore   Taipei   Tokyo   Toronto

and associated companies in
Berlin   Ibadan

Published by Oxford University Press, Inc.
198 Madison Avenue, New York, New York 10016

Oxford is a registered trademark of Oxford University Press

Library of Congress Cataloging-in-Publication Data
Kropp Dakubu, M. E. (Mary Esther)
Korle meets the sea : a sociolinguistic history of Accra / M.E.
Kropp Dakubu.
p.   cm.
ISBN 0-19-506061-X
1. Multilingualism—Ghana—Accra.   2. Accra (Ghana)—Languages.
I. Title.
P115.5.G4K758   1997
306.4'46'09667—dc20   96-42391

1 3 5 7 9 8 6 4 2

Printed in the United States of America
on acid-free paper

*For Laurel Choquette Kropp, my mother,
and Mumuni Dakubu, my husband.*

PREFACE

This book is about language in Accra, the sprawling capital city of Ghana, a country of something over 13 million people on the West Coast of Africa (Ghana Government 1987). These 13 million speak not fewer than forty-four languages—counts range from thirty-four to fifty-four—but the exact number depends on the criteria used for counting. The average Ghanaian language is therefore spoken by fewer than 300,000 people. However, most languages are not average. Some have far more speakers, and others far fewer. But this is not a case of one speaker–one language: a large proportion of the population speaks several. This is most obviously true in the capital city, with its mushrooming migrant suburbs, but it soon becomes obvious that in varying degrees it applies to the whole country, and that this is by no means a new situation. The pervasive multilingualism has two important results: a few languages have very many more speakers when their second-language speakers are included, and speakers of less widespread languages are not by virtue of that fact alone isolated from the rest of the country.

In the course of many years of linguistic investigation in and around Accra, two problems of multilingualism have come to seem particularly worth investigating. The first is the meaning of answers to the superficially straightforward question "What language(s) do you speak?" and the related "Do you speak (x language)?" It became apparent to me that answers depended on the situation in which the questions were asked and could mean different things for different speakers, but that the answers certainly signified something and that a pattern of some kind was present. This pattern seemed to have something to do with the speakers' idea of what a language included, that is, with their idea of where the boundaries around any particular language lay, with respect to similar and related varieties. This is, of course, a practical problem for anyone who wants to conduct surveys of multilingualism.

The other problem grew out of dissatisfaction with the current ahistoric approach to sociolinguistic treatment of patterns of language choice. It seemed to me that most analyses described particular situations, often with considerable insight and accuracy, but that they did not explain them, nor could they ever explain them, without far more attention to the historical background of the current situation. Fundamentally diachronic phenomena such as migration, colonialism, and stability might be invoked but were generally left unexamined, and the appearance of a particular language in the system was taken for granted. This is the problem on which the present work mainly focuses—the explanation for multilingualism maintained over time—but it is closely related to the first, for a person's idea of a language is to a large extent conditioned by the social history of the use of that language in the community. One suspects, furthermore, that the failure to consider these problems in sufficient depth—specifically, a lack of sensitivity to the forces that have governed language choice in the past—is implicated in the apparent loss of momentum in efforts at language planning in Ghana and in Africa generally. Detailed criticism of the considerable literature on language planning is beyond the scope of this work: the reader is referred to Apronti (1974), Chinebuah (1977), and Smock (1975), specifically on Ghana, and Bamgboṣe (1991) on sub-Saharan Africa.

The approach used in this book certainly does not address all aspects of these problems; probably no single book could. It attempts to answer the question of how a particular set of choices among languages came to exist in Accra in the first place and to explore, tentatively, what difference that historical "how" makes to the array of choices it has created. Reconstructions of how usage domains and user networks have changed are attempted, or at least suggested, in an effort to explain changing linguistic choices. Sociolinguists have, of course, recognized the relevance of change in these parameters of language use, but it has not often been explicitly investigated in any great time depth, certainly not in West Africa.

The first two chapters are introductory. Chapter 1 begins with an account of a linguistic dispute that nicely demonstrates, both symbolically and overtly, the historical rootedness of relations among the four main languages of Accra: Ga, the Kwa language of its traditional community; Akan, another Kwa language, spoken by the largest ethnic grouping in the country, or about 40% of the population; Hausa, the Chadic language that dominates northern Nigeria; and English, the Germanic language of the former colonial power. This is followed by some remarks on general sociolinguistic theory as it is applied in this book. Chapter 2 outlines the history and present state of urban multilingualism in West Africa and proposes a historical orientation for sociolinguistic theory, with reference to the literature on multilingualism in West African cities.

Chapters 3 and 4 present the situation to be explained in this book. Methodologically based on questionnaire surveys, they describe recent multilingualism in Accra by dividing the city into the older inner city, with a relatively local population, and the outer city of more distant migrants. The operative choice systems in these divisions, as well as assimilative tendencies, are found to be partly different.

The next three chapters discuss the historical background of chapters 3 and 4. Chapter 5 traces the development and consolidation of the Ga-speaking community, from some time before the sixteenth century to the twentieth. Chapter 6 discusses the introduction and spread of the two very different major West African second languages, Akan and Hausa, and chapter 7 discusses the introduction and spread of European language use, focusing on the processes whereby Portuguese gave way to English on the Gold Coast. The eighth and final chapter redefines Accra as a field of communication, in the light of the study, commenting briefly on the relationship between Accra's history of multilingualism and its modern urban registers; the chapter proposes the patron-client relationship as the historically salient social vector for language spread in Accra and in the linguistic culture area to which it belongs.

The argument of the book depends heavily on the findings and methodologies of history, ethnography, and sociology, as well as of historical and anthropological linguistics, sociolinguistics, and pidgin and creole studies. I am not expert in most of these disciplines, and those who are will inevitably find much to criticize in my excursions into their fields. I hope that any solecisms I have committed will not seriously detract from the main argument, which is that the methodological horizons of sociolinguistics can and should be widened in time and in ethnographic space.

I also hope that practitioners of other disciplines will find it useful to look at things from a linguistic perspective. Historians, sociologists, and even anthropologists frequently take the vehicles of communication for granted. When they do not, their arguments may be weakened by underestimation of the complexities of a linguistic situation, particularly among historians unfamiliar with techniques for discussing its subtler aspects. From any perspective, social activity is inseparable from communication, for which language provides both the model and the principal means. We observe today that it makes a difference, and also signals a difference, whether or not people speak each other's languages. It was certainly so in the past. This book is offered in the belief, on the one hand, that people speak the languages they do, as they do, as a result of whom they spoke to in the past and why and, on the other hand, that how people speak to each other or spoke to others in the past can provide insight into what they do or once did to each other.

Atlanta   M.E.K.D.
January, 1995

ACKNOWLEDGMENTS

This book draws on research carried out intermittently over almost thirty years, which has depended on the kindness, cooperation, and expert services of a large number of people in several countries. I have previously expressed my gratitude to the members of Ajorkor Okai We, but I would like to take the opportunity to do so again, in memory of Otobiache Ofei Dodoo, who is much missed.

Mary Bodomo and Seth Allotey were research assistants for the surveys of Accra market and kiosk sellers, reported in chapter 3. Both did excellent jobs. I am grateful to them, as well as to the many busy traders who took the time to answer our questions. I also wish to thank members of the field team of the Institute of African Studies' Dangme Project, who collected data on multilingualism in Dangmeland, and the many Dangme people who patiently responded; and Nathan Budu, field assistant for the Kyerepong survey, which also benefited from the kind encouragement of the late Nana Otutu Bagyire IV. The surveys reported in chapter 4 owe their success to James Agalic, research assistant for the Bulsa surveys; Adams Bodomo, research assistant for the Dagaaba survey; Nachinaba Bugri, research assistant for the Bawku community surveys; and the leaders and members of these communities who so graciously responded. Nachinaba Bugri and Hamma Abudulaye ably assisted me in work with the Accra Dogon community, among whom I particularly thank Ahmadu Anakila and Baba Karembey. I am grateful to the late Mahama Isaka for introducing me to the Belko family and sad that he could not live to see the result. I wish to express my appreciation to the entire family, especially Bari, and to M. D. Sulley for their willing help.

For opportunities to consult libraries in Germany I am indebted to the Goethe Institute and to Dr. Bernd Pirrung, then its Accra director, for two months in Bremen in 1985 and to the Deutscher Akademischer Austauschdienst and the English Department of the University of Tübingen for another month in 1993. I am grateful to the Norddeutsch Missionsgesellschaft (North German Evangelical Society); its director, Dr. Dieter K. Lenz; and the Bremen City Archive for access to the library and archive of the mission. I am also grateful to Hamburg University's seminar for African languages and cultures for kindly providing me with a number of photocopies and to the African linguistics department of the University of Frankfurt/Main for its hospitality. In 1993 aspects of the material were presented at seminars of the ethnography department of the University of Münster and the English philology department of the University of Tübingen, which were both enjoyable and useful. On a more personal level, I am particularly grateful to Elsa Lattey, Rosemarie Tracy, Mabel Asante, Rudolf Leger, Franz Kröger, and Professor and Mrs. Rüdiger Schott for making my stays in Germany so fruitful and pleasant.

Parts of this book in various stages of development were presented to classes and to staff and student seminars at the Institute of African Studies, linguistics department, and Language Centre of the University of Ghana. I would like to thank the many Ghanaian colleagues, and especially my students, who helped with critical discussions and information. I could not have written the book without them. Professor K. Odoom kindly advised on the handling of the statistical data. Staff of the computer science department patiently processed the data for the larger surveys. Most of the field research was funded by the Institute of African Studies of the University of Ghana, except for the Dangmeland surveys, which were partly supported by the West African Linguistics Society, and the 1992 Accra market survey, which was supported by the Language Centre.

I am also very grateful to Professor J. S. Nabila and the Geography Department of the University of Ghana for assistance with the maps.

Development of the material was also aided by presentation to a seminar of the linguistics department of the University of Toronto. In the United States, two short teaching appointments at Indiana University in Bloomington helped to make the final writing possible. This was mostly accomplished during a year at the Bunting Institute of Radcliffe College, which provided a working environment that could hardly have been bettered in any respect and for which I am very grateful. A semester's attachment to the Institute of African Studies at Emory University was also very useful. My particular thanks to the library staffs of all these institutions, especially Nancy Schmidt in Bloomington.

I am grateful to Raj Dua and Carol Myers-Scotton for responding to my requests for copies of papers. P. E. H. Hair and Albert Van Dantzig also sent me papers, lent me books, and provided much useful comment. Judith Irvine and Victor Manfredi kindly took time to read and comment on early versions of the first two chapters. They were all very helpful and not, of course, responsible for remaining deficiencies. An anonymous publisher's reader made some very useful criticisms and suggestions, most of which I have adopted.

I am in debt to many people for sheer survival—intellectual, moral, and physical—especially in the later stages of the writing. To Lawrence Boadi, Henry Hoenigswald, Odette Blum, Jonatha and Bob Ceely, Thelma and Salifu Dakubu, Cathe Read, David Locke, Judith Irvine, Florence Ladd, Bill Harris, Eleanor Cawthorne, Beverly Stoeltje, Dick Bauman, Michelle Gilbert, and John Middleton, thanks and thanks again.

Many people besides those named have made a difference in Ghana and elsewhere, deepening my appreciation of the marvelous complexities of language and of Ghanaian life and reminding me that things are rarely as they seem. I hope they will not take it amiss if they have not been mentioned, for their contributions, too, are appreciated. As the Ga say, *wɔtsɛɛɛ moko wɔshiii moko* ("We don't invoke some and leave out others"). Responsibility for the result is, of course, entirely mine. *Tswa! Omanye aba.*

NOTE ON SPELLING AND TERMINOLOGY

Except where quoted from another writer, language names and their spellings follow the practice of Dakubu (1988b) and Bendor-Samuel (1989). Where they differ from ethnonyms, as with Dagbani, the language of the Dagomba people, the connection is indicated as the occasion arises. Asante is treated as a special case: "Asante" is used for reference to both language and people, but "Ashanti" (in the Ga pronunciation) is used for the historical state.

Words in Ga and Akan are spelled in accordance with current orthographic practice in those languages, unless otherwise stated, and except for the occasional addition of tone marks. Well-established English spellings for geographical names are maintained, however.

Transcriptions in square brackets [ ] give a more precise guide to pronunciation. I use Christaller's (1875) system of tone marking: a word-initial sequence of one or more low tones is unmarked; the first high tone in a sequence is marked with ´ over the syllabic segment; and the first low after high is marked with `. A sequence of two high tone marks indicates that the second marks the onset of a lowered (down-stepped) high tone pitch level. A tilde over a vowel (ṽ) indicates that it is nasalized. If both a tilde and a tone mark are required, the tilde is placed on the vowel and the tone mark follows. The Dangme mid tone is indicated by a macron over the vowel (v̄).

CONTENTS

Korle Meets the Sea

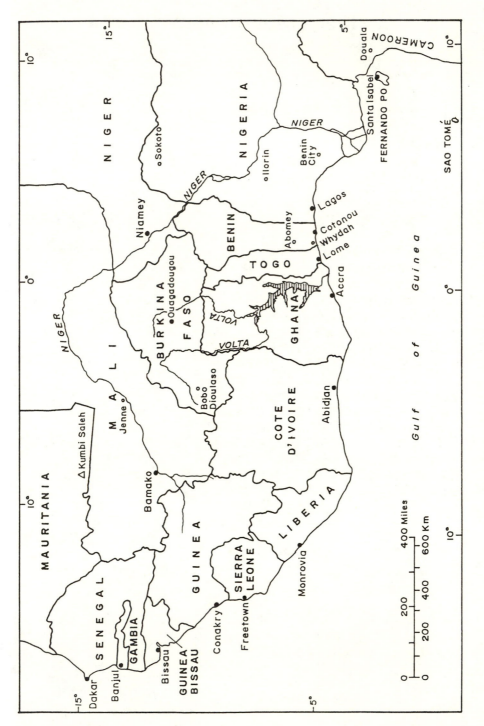

West Africa. Department of Geography and Resource Development, University of Ghana.

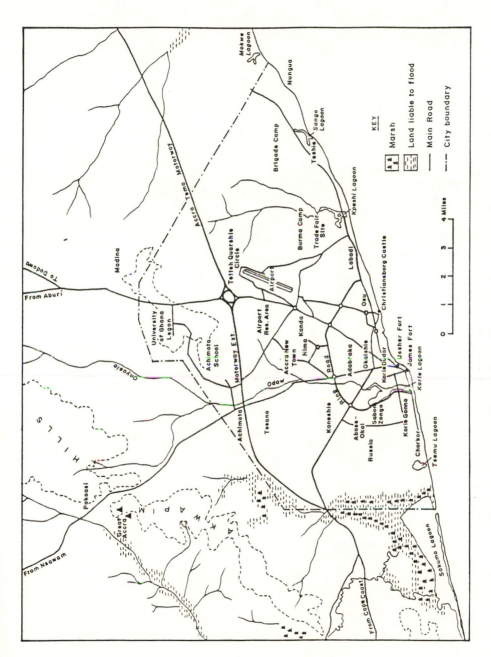

Accra, Ghana. Department of Geography and Resource Development, University of Ghana.

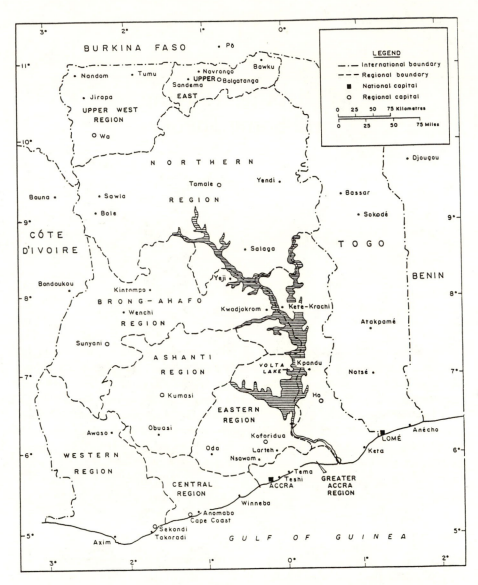

Ghana. Department of Geography and Resource Development, University of Ghana.

1

A Dispute, a Saying, and Some Theory

Ga, the language of Accra, arose in a multilingual context and has existed in one ever since. The split between Ga and its only close relative, Dangme, was undoubtedly triggered mainly by the influence of other languages, some of them spoken by much larger and more powerful groups, and many of whose speakers were assimilated into the Ga-speaking society. The way in which this occurred is explored in chapter 5. Such a situation of continual pressure from outside can be expected to provoke defensive reactions. Although Accra has been generally free of serious ethnic conflict, tensions naturally exist. These sometimes give rise to texts of various kinds that reveal much about their narrators' views of their linguistic universe and of the salient linguistic others.

The Dispute

Such a series of texts appeared in the course of a recent (1990–93) dispute over two place-names, Labadi and Madina. Briefly, the leaders of the La traditional state, one of the six tiny states within the Ga paramount state, declared that the name of Labadi, the La capital, which is now a small enclave within the Accra urban area, was an offensive corruption and that it should henceforth be known as La. They also decreed that Madina, a settlement a few miles north of Accra on land traditionally belonging to the La state, should be known as La Hee, "New La." The first change has won general public acceptance, but the second has been largely ignored. The public discussion is of some interest.[1]

On 27 February 1991, an article appeared in the *People's Daily Graphic* on the installation of Ga chiefs. In a preface to the article it was stated that "La is one of the largest Ga states and its main township has erroneously been referred to as Labadi.

This name, quite derogatory, is being corrected. The right appellation, therefore, is La. The present administration of the La State is doing everything to get the right name used by all." This change of name was reported in the *Mirror* of 12 October 1991 (p.7), and the La Mantse ([mantʃɛ] "chief, king") Nii Kpobi Tettey Tsuru III was quoted to the effect that

> "Labadi" is a corrupted form of La, the original name of the town and its people, coined by the early Europeans in the then Gold Coast.
> According to an oral tradition, the La people migrated from a place called Bonne [*sic*], in between present day Benin and Nigeria.
> At one point in time, after migrating to the then Gold Coast, they were said to be referring to their resettlement as La Bonne, fashioned from the name of the tribe and ancestral home.
> The Europeans with their faint knowledge of the language and history of the people, misconstrued the "Bonne" of the La people to mean "bone" (bad) in Twi and concluded to call the place "Labad" which later metamorphosed into "Labadi."

The association with colonial oppression was reiterated in a column that appeared in the *Mirror* on 21 December 1991, which recalled the British bombardment of Labadi (and Teshi and Osu) in 1854. In compliance with the demand, most public notices around the town have been changed from "Labadi" to "La" by simply obliterating the last four letters, and "La" is now used by the newspapers in place of "Labadi."

Even assuming sufficient familiarity with the Akan word, association by English people of "Bɔne" with "bad" is hardly credible in view of the English meaning of "bonny." In any case, spellings similar to "Labadi" were recorded by people who did not speak English, long before English was used on the Gold Coast and more than three hundred years before colonial times. The first citation comes from just after the first contact of Europeans with this part of the coast, when the Portuguese sent a mission from Elmina to Accra in 1517. In 1520, it is recorded that the "Labida" who "resided in the region just east of Akara" sent a return mission to start trading relations (Vogt 1979: 86). Eighty years later the Hollander De Marees reported, "A mile below [Senya Beraku] lies Labedde, a fine clean place surrounded by walls and bulwarks" ([1602] 1987: 86). Writers throughout the seventeenth and eighteenth centuries spelled the name variously as Labady, Labade, Labbade (Van Dantzig 1978: 65, 85, 96, 355), Labadde (Dudley 1646/47), Labeddé (Dapper 1686), Labode (Rømer 1760), and Labodei (Isert [1788] 1992: 35). Except for the difference between the first and second vowels, which presents problems for people accustomed to Dutch and English orthographic practices, the consistency of the record is impressive.[2]

There is little doubt that these spellings of Labadi reflect an older Ga pronunciation and that, like other instances of proto–Ga-Dangme *d* between nasal vowels, the sixteenth-century [d] has been nasalized, giving the modern La Bɔne. There is systematic evidence for this in Protten (1764). In the introduction to his work, Protten states that some vowels in Ga are nasal, which he will indicate by spelling them with an *n* before the consonant that precedes the nasal vowel. It is not always clear that he followed his own rule consistently, but if we take him at his word we have the correspondence series between modern and eighteenth-century Ga displayed in table 1.1.

TABLE 1.1   Correspondence series between modern
and eighteenth-century Ga

Protten (1764)		Modern Ga	
nSande	/*sãdẽ/	/sãne/	"thing"
Dinde	/*didẽ/	/nĩne/	"arm"
Nande	/*nãdẽ/	/nãne/	"leg"
Fiande	/*fiadẽ/	/ʃwãne/	"afternoon"

There is no [ẽ] in modern Ga. It seems that in these forms, nasality spread to the left and was then lost from the final vowel. With this model, given the evidence of the sixteenth- through eighteenth-century spellings, we may reconstruct the modern /bõne/ as sixteenth-century (and earlier) */bɔdẽ/.[3] The change was complete by the time Zimmermann (1858) recorded these forms in the middle of the nineteenth century. From a phonetic point of view, then, the derivation of Bɔne from "Bonny," which is itself an anglicization of Ịbanị: [ɪbanɪ], the name of an Ijaw language and its speakers (Alagoa and Fombo 1972: ix), while not impossible is not especially attractive.

Therefore, in point of technical historical fact, far from being a foreign corruption, the *d* in "Labadi" is actually a relic of an earlier pronunciation that has been preserved in a foreign language, English, just as Ga preserves the formerly unpalatalized velar consonants of words borrowed from Akan, such as the names Taki and Nsaki (compare modern Akan Takyi and Nsakyi; the Akan orthographic *ky* is pronounced [tɕ]). This has not prevented "Labadi" from serving as a symbol of foreign intrusion, which can be opposed in order to validate the present La State Council and Stool and demonstrate their historic authenticity.

The case of Madina is quite different and must be understood in its historical context.[4] This township lies about ten miles northeast of Accra, two miles beyond the University of Ghana campus. Madina, the University of Ghana, and the Kotoka International Airport all stand on land belonging to the La stool (state). The town was effectively founded on 14 June 1959, under the leadership of Alhaji Seidu Kardo after he and his people had to leave an earlier village on La land near Shiashi, close to the airport and the motorway.[5] Since the first land had been properly acquired according to customary law, through the La *mantse* of the time, Nii Adjei Onano and his successor Nii Anyetei Kwakwaranya II, Alhaji Seidu was given the land at mile 10, very close to the existing La village Nkwantanang. The total initial population was 849 persons, including 81 from Nkwantanang: 30% Ga and Dangme, 12.8% Ewe, 0.7% Akan (1 individual), 23.6% northern Ghanaian, and 32.9% non-Ghanaian (from the Ivory Coast, Burkina Faso, and Nigeria). Only a very small proportion of the Ga, Dangme, and Ewe, but all the northern Ghanaians and non-Ghanaians, were in Alhaji Seidu Kardo's group.[6] There was originally an elaborate plan for the town to develop as an expansion of Nkwantanang, but because relations between these two groups were from the outset very bad, Alhaji Kardo eventually developed Madina without Nkwantanang.

The new town was formally named Madina at the request of Alhaji Seidu Kardo, with the approval of the La *mantse* and his council, at a function on 22 October 1959, chaired by the La *mantse* (Nii Anyetei Kwakwaranya II). There were objections to the name in some quarters, particularly from the Klanaa division of La, which has several times since the beginning of this century unsuccessfully challenged the rights of the La stool over this land. The name was upheld by the Paul Tagoe Commission, which investigated the claims of the Klanaa division at this time, referring to the precedent of places in and around Accra, like Adabraka, Malam, and Fadama, that had also been named (in Hausa or Hausaized Arabic) by their founders. As a concession to local feelings, however, the spelling "Madina" was adopted instead of "Medina" because this was perceived as less obviously Muslim.[7]

In 1964, Alhaji Seidu Kardo was formally installed as headman of Madina by the First Parliamentary Secretary (Paul Tagoe), again with the approval of the La council and the La *mantse*. By the 1990s, each ethnic group had its own community head, and Alhaji Seidu's son, Baaba, was recognized as Chief of Madina by at least some of them.

By 1966 it was evident that there was a certain amount of disaffection among the various ethnic groups, particularly between the Ewes and the northerners. But there has never been any doubt that allodial rights in the land are held by the La *mantse* and the La state. From the beginning, a portion of the land was reserved for the use of Labadi people. At some point a chief of Madina was appointed by the La state, under Nii Anyetei Kwakwaranya II, but he was not effective.[8]

The population in 1966 was over three thousand, and the ethnic, and therefore linguistic, composition had altered considerably. The proportions of non-Ghanaians, northern Ghanaians, and Ga plus Dangme had fallen to 14%, 5%, and 12%, respectively, while the proportions of Akans and Ewes had risen equally dramatically, to 31% and 38%, respectively. These figures are roughly consistent with the findings of a linguistic survey conducted by Gilbert Ansre and Jack Berry in 1969, who found that Ewe and Akan were each the first language acquired of a third of the two thousand residents they interviewed. Dangme was the first language of almost 10%, and Ga, of a mere 1.3% (Apronti 1974: 10). (This has been the only survey, including censuses, to enumerate Ga and Dangme separately.) The rest must have been extremely diverse, for in all the surveyors found seventy community languages, an average of fewer than thirty speakers per language. No northern or non-Ghanaian language was spoken by more than 4.1% of the total (Kotokoli), and Hausa was the first language of only 2.4%. Not surprisingly in the circumstances, Madina was also polyglot: 96%, or nearly everyone, spoke two or more languages, and 70% spoke at least three (Smock 1975: 171). By the census of 1970, the population was well over seven thousand. Non-Ghanaians were down to about 12%, but the proportion of Ga plus Dangme may have risen slightly, to almost 19%.[9] No more recent data are available, but the township is obviously very much larger than in 1970.

Residents say that the Ga language is rarely heard in Madina except in Nkwantanang, which has always remained apart, and that there is no feeling of ethnic "Ga-ness." Indeed, some sections, especially those of the original founder and of the Ewe, are said to actually resent the idea that their land is Ga land. Nevertheless, there is little interethnic tension in daily life.

Against this background, a cyclostyled letter to the La *mantse*, dated 12 April 1991, from a La citizen residing at Nkwantanang congratulated the Traditional Council on the recent change from Labadi to La and also mentioned a current rumor, that the name Madina was to be changed to La Hee "New La." However, nothing was made public until the *Mirror* article of 12 October, already mentioned, in which the La *mantse* was reported as confirming this change, stating that "Madina is not Ghanaian." It was also stated that "The La Mantse is very apprehensive of the attitude of some community heads at La Hee (Madina) who are trying to brew trouble by arrogating to themselves the authority as land owners."

Indeed, the people of Madina objected strongly. Both the *People's Daily Graphic* and the *Ghanaian Times* of 21 October 1991 carried accounts of a meeting on 19 October at which residents of Madina rejected the name change. This was followed by an article in the form of an open letter in the *Ghanaian Times* of 25 November 1991, under the headline "Madina Residents Reject Name—a Rejoinder," signed by the president and secretary of the La Youth Association, referring to the people of La Hee as tenants of La and implicitly accusing them and others of fraudulent land deals. Finally, the maiden issue of a newspaper called *Madina today*, dated 20 December 1991, gave the text, dated 26 November, of a resolution apparently proposed by the Madina community heads and passed by the people of Madina that reiterated the rejection of the name change, together with the proposal—not mentioned in the *Mirror* article of 12 October but apparently announced at a meeting at about that time—that a La chief of Madina should be appointed by the Traditional Council.

It is clear that the underlying issues are political, but this has several faces. The continued hostility of Nkwantanan is one. Another is the political situation within the La state. Nii Anyetei Kwakwaranya II, under whom Madina first developed, was eventually destooled. It is probably relevant that Nii Anyetei came from a quarter of La that had joined the state and begun to provide chiefs relatively recently (Field 1940: 201, succession chart). The Klanaa claim on the land, which he had opposed, is part of a wider, ongoing struggle over the control of land among the La *mantse*, the La Traditional Council, and the various La clans. This is clear from a series of public notices published in the *People's Daily Graphic* during 1992 and 1993 in which conflicting claims were made.[10] There is thus division within the state itself, which is expressed in innuendoes about the past behavior of opposing factions. One may suspect that this is also a factor in the change of the name of La itself. That is, the current stool faction may wish to be seen as the one to establish the true, pure La, cleansed of colonial corruptions, unlike the earlier one, which is thus tainted with some of that corruption.

Another aspect, of course, is the relationship of La with Madina, which accepts the legal status of the land under the La stool but admits no other kind of allegiance. In particular, the Madina people as represented by their community heads rejected any legal obligation to present gifts to the La stool at the Ga annual Homowo festival, a traditional symbol of political subordination, and the right of the Traditional Council to give them a chief. The "Resolution of the Madina Community Heads" also pointedly refers to Madina as an urban community. The main first-page story of *Madina today* was actually the inauguration in November of the Madina Urban Council. The letter of the La Youth Association had called it "one of the rural settlements of La."

Although the argument seems to be fundamentally about politics, as represented by the power to appoint a chief and demand tribute, it was invariably presented as a linguistic issue. The publication in the *Mirror* of the interview with the La *mantse* gave the first six and one-half of a total of ten column inches to the issue of names and then referred to the chieftaincy issue only very indirectly. Both the *Graphic* and the *Times* of 21 October used the name issue in their headlines, and the *Graphic* account, which was only an extended caption to a photograph of the meeting, did not mention the chieftaincy or land issues at all. The La rejoinder of 25 November also headlined the name issue and discussed it first, although most of it was devoted to the right of La to appoint a chief, and the same pattern obtains in the *Madina today* story ("Residents Vote Against Change of Name: Residents of Madina have voted unanimously to reject a new name 'La Hee' and a chief being imposed on the town . . .").

According to the La Youth Association, "[T]he installation of a La citizen as chief of La Hee as well as the change of name of Madina are all part of a program designed to reflect the heritage of the La people," but they obviously do not reflect the heritage of the residents of Madina. In this case, the competing names both have constituencies. That is, although no group is strongly motivated to support "Labadi" against "La," some people do feel strongly about "Madina." The La state seems to have created a competition that it cannot win. The name Madina originally served to distinguish the town from the Ga already there, whose village, ironically, had and still has an Akan name (*nkwantanan* "crossroads"), but it did nothing to unite the various groups it did not exclude. In competition with La Hee, however, it seems to have done exactly that. *Madina today* reported that the meeting of 19 October began with a minute's silence in Alhaji Seidu Kardo's memory.

It must be remembered that in both cases, the argument is not over what the towns are to be called in Ga but what they are to be called in English. Labadi has always been called [laa] in Ga, and there has never been anything to prevent the Ga from referring to Madina as La Hee, although in fact they did not.[11] What is at issue is official and public reference, which is most often in English; there seems to be no interest at all in what names are used in other languages. At stake is the power to control how the community is referred to by others, at the highest available political level.

The symbolism at work derives from the fact that inevitably a settlement's name is a historical text. At some level, it implies a theory of how the settlement came to be, its constitution. In referring to the habitation group by name, others affirm a theory of its history or a definition of it. If the name used differs from the community's own name for itself, that use appears to impose an external theory of that group onto its definition in the eyes of the world. If the community can cause others to use the community's own name, it thereby causes (or may believe that it causes) the others to affirm its own theory of its historical self. This prevents others from appropriating the group's history into their own, and it also excludes them from the community, thereby giving it boundaries.

The insistence on replacing the hitherto publicly accepted "Labadi" and "Madina" with "La" and "La Hee," however it is rationalized, clearly expresses tensions arising from urbanization, especially urbanization accompanied by increasing interethnic contact; this is a result of increasing population density within a limited geographical area and is symbolized as competition among languages. Multilingualism in the Ga-speaking area is not declining. Furthermore, it is generally believed that the Akan language is growing in strength, at the expense of Ga. After centuries of surviving by absorbing and adapting, so it is thought, the Ga language actually seems to be declining in some of its traditional strongholds, especially in Accra.

Further, Accra is growing physically and swallowing some of its smaller neighbors. Sandwiched between the wealthy suburbs of Osu and the elite North Labadi residential areas and the Trade Fair site, on La land that the La state has effectively lost, it is not surprising that the La traditional state feels itself under pressure and in danger of marginalization. In such a situation people quite commonly look for a symbol to assert group identity. In this case, the competition between the indisputably ancient Ga name "La" and the English "Labadi" provided an excellent icon for the group's struggle to assert itself. It was given substance by a supposed historical relationship with colonialism, that is, the subjection of the La state by a historical power that, being of the past, need not be confronted in terms of present-day political realities. The contest therefore had the virtue of being winnable. Although this historical power was in objective fact too recent to be responsible for this name, it was certainly more recent than the preferred name and is sufficiently far in the past to be outside most individuals' experience, giving it a mythic quality.

The Akan cultural and linguistic threat, in contrast, is current as well as historical and far more intractable, and therefore it is addressed only very indirectly. The Akan are tacitly accused of playing a hostile part in the colonial misnaming, which suggests that other grievances may lurk in the background, but no attempt to remove the linguistic traces of Akan is made. Such an attempt would be highly unlikely to succeed, if only because many Akan loanwords have been so thoroughly naturalized. The relationship with Hausa, however, is both less intimate and more recent, and its speakers (or those people associated with the language in the eyes of the Ga, whether or not they actually speak it) are less ambiguously other.

The Saying

These four languages, Ga, English, Akan, and Hausa, stand out as the most important languages of present-day Accra, coexisting in a complex and shifting structure of multilingual communication. Historically speaking, the structure has been built up in layers, the Ga foundation closely followed by Akan, with the Hausa and English presences gaining strength in the course of the nineteenth century. If the objection to "Labadi" is relatively recent and to "Madina" obviously so, the Ga language itself bears witness to the presence of comparable tensions before English was a crucial factor in Ga consciousness.

There is a well-known Ga expression that, in language deliberately indirect and richly ambiguous, underlines both intergroup tensions and the modes of accommodation by which such tensions were (and are) dealt with, simultaneously asserting that community identities, symbolized by language, are uppermost in people's conscious responses. In interpreting it in this way we are indulging in a kind of linguistic archaeology, in which conventional expressions are treated as monuments from the past, which can be excavated and analyzed as pointers to the social forces that created them. At least two versions occur in the literature on proverbs. *Ekɔɔle yaa ŋshɔŋ* (Ankrah 1966: 36), literally "His/her Korle goes to the sea," indicates that someone understands the current discussion, especially in the linguistic sense, that is, speaks Ga. It is a warning from one Ga to another in the presence of a third (the referent of *e* "his/her") who is not Ga. A version recorded more than a century earlier (Zimmermann 1858: 158) is even less direct, being grammatically focused on the event, not the person: *Kɔɔle ŋya ŋshɔŋ* "Korle is going to the sea." Zimmermann does not mention the linguistic interpretation, only that the saying is used to warn people not to reveal any secrets. Its surface opacity is undoubtedly intended to mask this intent from the person against whom the warning is issued.

Even if a specifically linguistic interpretation is historically secondary, it is certainly now important and may well have been implicit from the beginning. A symbolism of "them and us" is plainly at work, whether or not "our" language signifies or is only secondarily implied. *How* the symbolism works is not immediately clear to the cultural outsider—naturally, since opacity is its purpose and strategy. The key is in the opposition of Korle, the lagoon, to the sea. To use this key to open a door on the character of multilingualism in Accra culture, some basic geography is required.

The coast of Ghana, as of much of West Africa, is only slightly above sea level, and the surf is very strong. Rivers and streams generally do not empty directly into the sea but spread out in shallow lagoons that form behind a sandbar and empty into the sea at points where the beach is particularly low, or when they are very full at the end of the rainy season. If the bar builds up, the lagoon may not empty at all but become extremely large. Even the mouth of the Volta River must be periodically dredged to keep it open. Except for the Keta lagoon, the lagoons of the coast of Ghana are now not as vast as the Lagos lagoon, for example, or those around Abidjan; but all of them are venerated as natural shrines, each the home of a deity whose worship is the responsibility of a resident lineage of the nearest coastal town. Accra is especially associated with the Korle [kɔɔle] lagoon, which ends the Odaw [odɔ] River and borders the old city on the west. Korle is a female deity, wife of Sakumo (whose lagoon is the western boundary of the Ga coast) (Kilson 1971: 127) and special protector of Accra (specifically, Ga Mashi) in times of crisis.[12]

Water is an extremely important image in Ga culture (Dakubu 1987a; Kilson 1969). Ga-speaking territory is bounded by water, with the sea to the south, major rivers east and west, and a high-rainfall forest belt to the north. Yet, the Accra plain is a very low-rainfall area, and in Accra itself water has historically been a problem. This saying links two bodies of water, both of which are in some way associated with Accra. In Ga metaphor the Ga people are frequently linked with the sea, in opposition to inland people. Sea fishing is regarded as a prototypical Ga activity, some sections of the people believe their founder arrived from the sea, and there are stories about visits to people who live under the sea. The significance of Korle, also a body of water, for the Ga of Accra has been indicated. Yet we seem to have an identification of Korle with what is foreign.

In the Ga lexicon there is a fundamental opposition between the open sea and inland waters, represented by *ŋshɔŋ* "sea" and *faa*, which is usually translated as "river" but may also refer to inshore waters, or the lagoon, as well as the river behind it. Although in English the name Korle is limited to the lagoon, in Ga it may include the Odaw River. The oppositions between *faa* "river"; and any of *mukpó* "lagoon"; *kpaakpó* "pond, lake, spring"; and *bú* "spring, well" are secondary.[13] Korle as *faa* signifies the non-Ga other as inland, in contrast to the Ga sea.

The paradox is largely resolved if we consider what the Korle River has meant in the history of Accra. Before 1679, the main political and trading center of the western Ga is believed to have been Great Accra (now completely ruined), inland near Ayawaso at the western edge of the Accra plain near the source of the Odaw or Korle River. After defeat by the Akan-speaking Akwamu, the nucleus of Great Accra moved down to Little Accra by the sea, which implies that it traveled the course of the river and of today's Nsawam-Accra road. As chapter 5 demonstrates, there is reason to believe that Great Accra had a mixed Ga, Guang, and Akan population and that only by moving down the river to the sea did Accra become "truly Ga."

Since the crucial migration, many other groups, at first Akan-speaking and later from farther north, have followed that route into Accra. Some have become entirely assimilated, but others, more recently, have not. The verb (*ya* "go") that links the two bodies of water is therefore crucial, for the second (being for most of its course a stream) is not so much a *body* of water as a movement, which has been characteristic of the city since its very foundation. The inflow of people and their strange languages has been continual. Assimilation is not automatic; significantly, even Korle, protector of Ga Mashi, is not the most senior deity in Accra but the third. First place belongs to Nai, god of the sea, who was there first. Second in rank is Sakumo, Korle's husband, warrior deity of a larger lagoon to the west of Chorkor beach, which seems to have been settled by fishermen earlier than Ga Mashi. There are many degrees of Ga-ness and foreignness.

Water in Ga imagery includes a strong element of danger, often expressed as storm and flood. When a low-lying river arrives at the sea and forms a lagoon, the sandbar that forms is a joint creation, built up by the action of the sea, on the one hand, and silt carried down by the river, on the other. This is a continuing process, so that it cannot be assumed that the lagoon will ever reach the sea of its own accord. A continually growing lagoon is dangerous to human habitation because, especially in the rainy season, it will spoil the surrounding land for farming and dwelling and the lagoon itself for fishing. The traditional religious cycles of Accra and Teshi include ceremonies in which the sandbar is cut through, to allow the lagoon to drain into the sea (Field 1940: 156, 208). The ceremonies are still performed, although the practical relevance has been removed by modern road construction.

The ceremony itself is regarded as dangerous. Investigating its performance at the barrier between the Kpeeshi lagoon (east of Labadi, at the present Trade Fair site) and the sea, Field was informed that it had to be done in such a way that "the lagoon can go to the sea without killing anyone" (1961: 57). The persons in danger of being killed in the lagoon's successful passage are the chief and high officials of the town responsible for the ceremony.

If the sandbar can be read as the mutually constructed boundary between incoming people, with their strange languages, and the people already there, it is nonetheless a problem. The barrier perhaps provides initial protection, but it can and must be cut; that is, communication must be established across ethnolinguistic boundaries because not to do so would also be dangerous and because, in principle, an influx of new people is desirable. Historically it has been refugees and prisoners of war who have established new sections of Ga towns or swelled old ones. The tension between the La state and Madina can be read as the result of the La desire to integrate the new arrivals on the old model and its inability to do so.

At the same time, establishment of contact that may ultimately lead to assimilation is also dangerous. *Ekɔɔle yaa ŋshɔŋ* is used in the presence of an individual stranger because that individual represents a group and could be a Trojan horse. If mistakes are made it is the host group that will suffer. The town representatives who will be killed by improper cutting of the sandbar might stand for either the town as a whole or the established political power within it, but they are not simply themselves.

The dynamic of the relationship between the lagoon and the sea beautifully represents the historical dynamic of ethnicity and language in Accra. The sandbar that separates them represents constantly shifting, disintegrating, and reconstituted boundaries between groups of people. It may imply a linguistic boundary between the Ga language and all others or the desirability of such a boundary. It does not necessarily reflect multilingualism as a characteristic of the Ga-speaking community itself, but it might be interpreted as advocating it as a safety measure in relations with other groups. This suggests that the use of second languages has provided a filter through which the inland waters can be allowed to approach the sea with minimum danger to all concerned, a safe channel for linguistic communication that does not obviously threaten the carefully constructed protection of ethnic boundaries until they can be rebuilt in different places.

Theoretical Considerations

This book attempts to contextualize and organize in historical perspective the symbolic struggle among languages. It begins with an examination of patterns and trends in contemporary multilingualism, in which languages are treated as broad, even crude wholes, according to the self-reported behavior of a combination of economic groups and self-defined communities. It then attempts to project languages, speech communities, and the relations among them back in time, using the evidence of the written record. The remainder of this chapter attempts to place this whole-language, community-based diachronic sociolinguistics within general linguistic theory and especially to outline some of the considerations that underlie the discussion in later chapters.

There is a sense in which "sociolinguistics" is an aberrant term, not because linguistics as a discipline should not take social phenomena into account but because it cannot reasonably do otherwise. Language is a fundamentally social phenomenon in every sense that phrase can have. Whatever the individual's innate physical disposition or potential may be, a language (let alone "language") is not normally experienced and is never initially acquired except in a group of at least two, the learner and another who is already a speaker. Furthermore, whatever generalized structures may eventually exist in a speaker's head, a language is practically acquired through participation in groups defined by both membership and function, as constituted on specific occasions for particular purposes. This surely implies that the language one learns—whether in initial acquisition or later at home, in the classroom, or anywhere else—is shaped and determined from the moment learning begins by what others deem acceptable. It follows that from the point of view of the language-using group, the distinction among formal grammaticality, contextual appropriacy, and acceptability in performance (Hymes 1972) is not always clear-cut.[14]

From this standpoint, the distinction between "linguistics" and "sociolinguistics" is only useful if the aim of the latter is to provide an explanation from a sociocultural point of view of the general linguistic (that is, the sociolinguistic) situation. Socio-linguistics, properly speaking, is then the bringing to bear of methods and insights gained through the social sciences—sociology, anthropology, history, geography— on the relations between language (including performance) structure and social struc-ture as they exist at a given time and place. People speak the way they do, make the linguistic choices that they do, within the range of what is grammatical in the social situation, where "grammar" as formal linguistic acceptability includes everything from phonetics to the choice between language and nonlanguage. It is the job of general linguistics to delimit and describe what is grammatical. Traditionally, his-torical comparative linguistics explains the boundaries of the grammatical as the accumulated results of shifts in the boundaries between linguistic tokens. (Such bound-aries need not match segmental boundaries.) Sociolinguistics explains them as the product of shifts in the boundaries between social groups, as expressed in formal linguistic alternatives. From the point of view being developed here, a general his-torical linguistics must relate shifting boundaries between linguistic tokens to shift-ing social boundaries, and a historical sociolinguistics will put these events into social-historical context.

The original purpose of this book is descriptive, not theoretical. However, since any description is necessarily constructed within a frame of theoretical reference and assumption, it may be regarded as an essay in historical macro-sociolinguistics; by "macro-sociolinguistics" we mean the explanation of the character of permissible language choices from the perspective of communities, of groups that communicate with other groups *as groups*, rather than from the differentiated points of view of the individuals who make up those groups. Without communication between individu-als, there would be no group and no group communication; the fact and the crucial importance of individuals and their roles is not in question. But the converse is also true: above and beyond the instrumentality of language in forming groups in the first place, individuals do not communicate except in groups. For two people to begin to talk to each other, however superficially, there must be at least an inch or two of common ground: they must have a reason to communicate and some shared or at least complementary physical means of doing so. That is, there must be something, no matter how trivial, that can be regarded as common knowledge, and wherever knowledge is shared, a social group exists. The reason and the medium for commu-nication are logically and, we must suppose, historically antecedent to the act of communication itself; hence there can be no language in the ordinary sense of the term, let alone a linguistic act, except within the framework of a group.[15]

Linguistic choices are made along a wide scale, from the crude decision to speak one language or another through the adoption of dialect features and gross status conventions to the subtlest of lexical distinctions and phonetic signaling of innuendo.

The origins of these decisions can be studied by considering the behavior of individuals in relation to one another and within the context of the groups they inevitably represent; this study I take to be the activity of micro-sociolinguistics. Behind those choice-making individuals there lies a long history of other choices, made by very many other individuals, also acting as members of groups. Neither the groups of individuals nor the linguistic tokens that represent the systems of available choices have existed unchangingly since social groups and their languages began; their mutual history is a vastly complicated, kaleidoscopic series of structured decisions in many dimensions, which have lead continually to formations and dissolutions of groups and associated linguistic systems, at all degrees of delicacy. The study of the dynamics of this process—the principles and behavior of the kaleidoscope itself—I take to be the province of macro-sociolinguistics. Crudely put, the term denotes a focus on reasons for choices that affect all members of a group, instead of the reasons for personal choices by individual members.

Approached from this angle, the groups that are the objects of sociolinguistic study can neither be defined as collections of individuals nor as sets of linguistic encounters between individuals. A feature of the nonfiniteness of language is that for both a language and a community that speaks it, there are no truly stable boundaries. The set of potentially creatable sentences in a language is not only infinite but also always changing, as the rules of its structure and the social and psychological circumstances of its use change. The potentially infinite set of sentences in the Ga language in the year 1600 C.E. could not possibly include any of the sentences that might be created in 2000 C.E. by a speaker or writer of Ga who is reviewing, say, the perceived state of Accra's commercial transportation system, even supposing that someone in 1600 C.E. could have foreseen the presence of motor cars. The fact of changing extralinguistic circumstances points to the non-finiteness of the language-using group: not only do old members die as new ones are born or otherwise created, so that membership is not constant, but also the social and material fortunes of groups wax and wane, and those of their languages along with them. Both the number of speakers of a language and the number and kinds of things they use it for alter over time, at variable rates. Not only are the possible numbers and kinds of potential encounters among members of a sociolinguistic grouping continually altering, but also the numbers and kinds of sociolinguistic groupings are themselves in a constant state of flux. Cooper's definition of language spread, as "an increase, over time, in the proportion of a communication network that adopts a given language or language variety for a given communicative function" (1982: 6), is therefore not quite satisfactory, for network, language (variety), and communicative function are not static, and none can be held constant or regarded as "given."

To continue a banal example, the groups that speak Ga or English as their community language in August 2000 C.E. will be utterly different from the groups that spoke them in August 1600 C.E.: their social structures will be extremely different, and rather few members will trace all their biological ancestors to the earlier group. Yet there have been strong elements of continuity in both cases. This book proceeds on the principle that any attempt at explanatory sociolinguistics, especially one that tries to explain a multilingualism, must start from a hypothesis of constant revolution.

The distinction between macro- and micro-sociolinguistics lies in the direction from which the data are approached, as indicators of group behavior or as group-induced features of individual behavior. It is not primarily a matter of the data themselves nor of the level of social organization at which questions are asked about them. In terms of practical investigative technique, there may be little difference. The same studies may illuminate the concerns of both or either (or neither). Not all writers work from this point of view; many seem to distinguish macro- from micro-sociolinguistics mainly in terms of research methods. Roughly, questionnaires, examination of official policy documents, and the like are associated with macro studies; the observation of small groups of interacting individuals with micro.[16]

On the one hand, close observation of individuals is probably essential for determining why, given the fact that choices exist and human beings have different personalities and wills, people behave as they do. On the other hand, such a study may not reveal why a specific choice exists in the first place, although it may help in the elucidation of the significance of that choice. In this book I concentrate on discovering how and why a choice has come to exist.

Within either macro- or micro-sociolinguistic behavior, there is a hierarchy in the scope of decision, of the choice to be made. At the very top lie decisions affecting the whole world: which shall be the dominant language(s), for political inequality of languages is as old as politics, and shall one of them become the main lingua franca worldwide (from the macro point of view)? Or which, if any, of the major international second languages shall my child choose to study in school (a micro question)? Choices in the geographical dimension are made at regional, national, provincial, local, neighborhood, and household levels through a range of situations in the social dimension (from international political or academic meetings through market and classroom to scolding one's children) in relation to linguistic choices (from whole languages through social dialects, polite forms, and obscenity to stress accent placement and how emphatically to whisper).

In some social environments, communicative competence, or the ability to use language appropriately (Hymes 1972: 292), may involve the ability to actively deploy more than one language. The saying about Korle going to the sea may indicate that Accra has provided such an environment. Whether or not and to what extent and why given individuals actually acquire that competence is a micro question, but the form of the option, with respect to the relations with other groups that it implies, and why it exists at all within a given group is a macro question. The macro questions around which this book is organized can be formulated as follows: what broadly constitutes linguistic acceptability in the highly multilingual groups, groups of groups, and intersections of groups under consideration? How did it get to be that way? And where, perhaps, is it going? Answers are attempted only fairly high up the organizational hierarchy, at most points of the geographical and social scales but only at the less delicate end of the linguistic scales; that is, they will be concerned with the sources of group choices of language, and sometimes dialect, but hardly at all with style and register and the specific linguistic features they involve.

Although this work does not address the choice of linguistic tokens much below the level of whole languages, questions of competence in the traditional, single-language sense are nevertheless relevant. Since communities are made up of individuals, one possible way of acquiring insight into inter- and intragroup dynamics is to survey many members of the communities concerned in order to extrapolate from sets of individuals to their communities as units of social behavior. Chapters 3 and 4 are based on this research method. Responses to questions about linguistic repertoire seem to require a means of evaluating them in terms of objective competence. That is, perhaps it is not enough to know whether a person claims to speak a particular language or is thought to do so by others, for "speaking a language" can mean many different things, anything from being able to greet people more or less correctly through full native command in all everyday situations to exceptional ability in manipulating the language for a special purpose, the expertise of the artist in words. How is this to be evaluated when one is studying groups that, as I claim, cannot be defined as sets of participants in internal chains of face-to-face encounters?

The questionnaires employed merely asked people whether they spoke a language well, spoke it a little, or only understood some. Such a scale is not, of course, an objective measure of anything. Yet it is by no means irrelevant in the evaluation of competence. A study of second-language speakers of Ewe in the Volta Region, which is an important source of immigration into Accra, found a close correlation between self-evaluation and the results of a comprehension test (Ring 1981: 18).[17] I suggest, however, that such correlations are not really the point. The response to a self-evalution question tells us what the respondent believes about his or her communicative competence through the medium of that language and within the sociolinguistically relevant parameters, whatever these may be. This is important information.

In the social circumstances in which the surveys discussed in this book were carried out, interviews were rarely private between interviewer and individual speaker. Other members of the responding group were normally present, and all took a degree of multilingualism for granted. It is unlikely, therefore, that individual claims of competence in specific languages were seriously exaggerated or misleadingly modest, but they do not necessarily reflect constant standards. In general, people reported the competence that they believed they had and that people who knew them agreed they had. If a given percentage of, for example, the Dagaaba in Accra say they speak Akan well, it means that those people are confident of their ability to communicate in that language for the purposes for which they need or want to do so, in the fashion expected of members of their community. Since awareness of communicative competence is a matter of experience—one generally knows whether or not the communication aimed at has taken place—they must be largely right.

From this point of view, communicative competence has little to do with technical proficiency as it is usually understood, that is, with how closely the language of a group of second language speakers, say, Akan as spoken by Dagaaba in Accra, approximates to the language of community speakers, say Akan as spoken in Akropong-Akuapem, or even by Akan community speakers resident in Accra.[18] Depending on the situation, a marked degree of deviation from the community language may be tolerated or even encouraged. Consequently, judgments of community speakers themselves are not necessarily helpful in assessing claims since such judgments are also subject to social constraints.

Geography is another possible factor: what counts as speaking a language quite well in a cosmopolitan, urban context might count as speaking it only a little in another context, for example, in a more or less linguistically homogeneous village, where the standards of performance for the community language are more elaborate. Furthermore, it appears that prevailing intergroup circumstances are often such that for a second-language speaker to sound like a native speaker would be regarded as unsuitable, by one side or the other, and so detract from communication. In the Accra case, this is particularly noticeable with respect to languages originating outside southern Ghana.

In any multilingual situation, there will be differences in the language used as a community language; the language adopted for community-language purposes by a group that is not part of the original community but is perhaps in the process of becoming assimilated to it; and versions of it used as a second language by other groups, either with community-language speakers or with other second-language speakers. This book does not explore that problem, except to acknowledge probable differences. It assumes that there is sufficient convergence that people who claim to speak a language identified by the same glossonym can achieve at least a degree of communication, and that where members of two groups claim to be able to speak a given language, communication between those groups is possible and perhaps exists. This means, for example, that for survey purposes "pidgin" forms are classed as radical varieties of "normal" languages of the same name. In Accra, one function of these varieties ("Broken English" and certain locally employed varieties of Hausa and Akan) is to enable communication between their speakers and the speakers of a multidimensional range of more standard varieties, and to a large extent they are successful. In the multilingual urban context, the range of acceptable varieties available to the second-language speaker is different from the range available in a more homogeneous linguistic environment.

Finally, a few remarks to justify focusing on individuals only insofar as they are members of groups and on their behavior and attitudes as indices of group characteristics—the macro-sociolinguistic approach as herein defined. The groups considered are largely self-defined, usually by community language, although, as will be seen in chapter 4, this simple equation is not always valid and additional or alternative criteria may operate. It seems to be a feature of the social psychology of the subregion that most people allot community membership priority over individuation in the definition and presentation of self. In almost any social activity, people accept that they are there as representatives of groups before they are there on their own personal account.[19] When people arrive in a strange city, they think of themselves first as members of their hometown community and a more or less congruent ethnolinguistic unit, in contrast to fellow workers or coresidents who are not members. Beyond the "hometown" group, communication is most intense within groups defined by community language, a pattern that is often reinforced by residential patterns, sometimes by employment, and sometimes by religious practice. Although communication with nonmembers of the "home" group is frequent and in most cases relaxed, there is a profound sense in which nonmembers are encountered not as isolated individuals—a mode of existence that in most people's eyes is hardly human—but as representatives of other communities. One's self then inevitably enters the encounter as a representative of one's own community. Multilingualism in Accra is fundamentally a system for communication among groups of people, not merely the product of many individuals talking to other individuals, and there is no particular trend away from this arrangement.

2

Multilingualism and the West African City

West African coastal cities are not often praised. Mary Kingsley ([1897] 1982: 30) said of colonial Accra in the early 1890s that it was attractive from the sea but otherwise "a mass of rubbishy mud and palm-leaf huts." In contrast, Klose (1899: 17) seems to have been impressed with the European-style buildings. Sanitation is a constant problem: Ioné Acquah ([1954] 1972: 20) mentions complaints about the cleaning of Accra dating from 1858, and they are still commonplace. Unlike the old cities of the Sahel, which are granted a certain originality of architectural style and romantic atmosphere, the coastal cities are considered by modern writers of all political stripes to be colonial creations, owing practically nothing, it would seem, to any indigenous creative drive. They are deprecated as bastions of neocolonialism, with their blatant display of social and economic inequalities and "alien" values—material, social, and spiritual. At the same time, they have been, it would seem, largely unsuccessful as centers for spreading the modernization and development that at least some forms of imperialism and almost all independent governments have sought to introduce, taking a disproportionate share of the national resources by demanding and obtaining for themselves expensive modern infrastructures and facilities that work uneconomically or not at all. The city as a whole and its residents as individuals are frequently accused of being economic parasites on the rest of the country.[1] Yet, many city dwellers live in extremely deprived conditions, in surroundings that are generally perceived by locals and outsiders alike to be dirty, noisy, crowded, and unhealthy. In some cities, moreover, violent crime has become a serious problem. The list of their shortcomings seems endless.

Nevertheless, many of these cities have a flair and vitality that fascinate both residents and visitors. As Kenneth Little (1973: 4) remarked, they possess a "special urban 'atmosphere'" that is hardly conveyed by the "ordinary academic monograph."

20

The setting is rarely dramatic or even distinctive, Freetown being perhaps an exception. Indigenous architectural styles, even if they survived colonial conquest, were rarely highly developed along the coast, and the modern state architecture is occasionally pleasant but usually notable only for size. Late colonial attempts at civic beautification, such as the promenade along High Street in Victoriaborg (an early European residential district) in Accra, have often been allowed to decay, probably because they were carried out with little or no local support and, indeed, were resisted as colonial impositions for which local people had to pay (Crooks [1923] 1973; Reindorf [1889] 1966). What gives such a city personality is not its appearance, which is often ramshackle, but its social style, the style in which the human beings that dwell within it interact.[2]

Any attempt to define so subjectively complex a quality as a local style of living is certain to run into difficulties. Nevertheless, I suggest that the creative impulse of the West African urban community is most typically expressed in broadly characteristic variants of three forms of human behavior whose primary manifestations are not physical (and their visible effects are therefore not always immediately recognized), namely, a highly individualistic form of small- and medium-scale trading entrepreneurship, an obsession with intricate and highly personalized politics, and language.

The interest in trade was remarked on early and often. Fraenkel (1964: 11) pointed out that Freetown and Monrovia were originally planned (by other people) as communities of independent peasant farmers but that this view of their future was firmly rejected by the settlers, who engaged vigorously in commerce from the start. The circumstances under which Freetown and Monrovia were founded are admittedly somewhat special—both were early nineteenth-century settlements of freed slaves and their descendants from overseas or other parts of the coast—but the trading enterprise of the populace is not. In Accra in the 1890s almost every house was also a shop, according to Kingsley (1982: 31,77), who also describes African women trading between Lagos and Calabar, undertaking considerable voyages with their goods.

The engagement of West African women in trade dates from well before the nineteenth century (Little 1973: 46), especially in those parts of the coast where urban centers developed first. West African men have always engaged in trade, too, and in fact have usually dominated it (especially when larger-scale finance and overseas contacts are involved), but it is the prominent role of women in local and medium-scale trade that has usually struck visitors from other continents, no doubt because of the contrast it presents to recent patterns in Western society. Certainly the active participation of women is a characteristic feature of today's markets. The growth and continuing prosperity of virtually every West African city has been based on its function as a commercial center. The involvement of a very high proportion of the populace in trade may be its single most conspicuous social feature.

Moreover, trade has been closely involved with politics in these cities, which have also been centers of influence and patronage before, during, and after colonial times. Some, such as Accra and Banjul, capital of the Gambia, became political centers in the first place because they were trade centers, but others, such as Lomé and Abidjan, are trade centers only because they were simultaneously built up as politi-

cal and trading centers by a colonial power. However, it would be a mistake to dis-
count the internal political life of the city before or after independence as purely
contingent and derivative. Although Lagos and Accra may largely owe the intricacy
of their sociopolitical structures to their positions as major trade centers, neither the
structures themselves nor the cultural and religious principles that underlie them are
imported. The political history of Accra goes back continuously to the sixteenth century (Reindorf [1889] 1966) and that of Lagos to the seventeenth (Adefuye 1987;
Agiri and Barnes 1987), both involving fairly large proportions of the populace.

Culturally pervasive multilingualism that involves a high degree of individual
participation is one of the most distinctive characteristics of urbanism in West Africa.
It is also closely bound up with trade (as will appear) and with politics (as seen in the
previous chapter). However, it is important to recognize that the distinction between
urban and rural society is not always sharp or absolute; not only is there usually free
and frequent communication between the two but also, in many of the most popu-
lous areas, specifically including western Nigeria (O'Connor 1983: 28) and central
Ghana (Ewusi 1977), the same people are likely to be urban dwellers and rural dwellers
at different times of their lives. This has implications for linguistic patterns, including the rural-urban contrast. In addition, the characteristic urban multilingualism is
by no means a recent development. In later chapters we examine how it developed
in Accra. First, it will be useful to reconsider urban multilingualism in general, particularly in relation to the West African town.

The topic is evidently a dual one. Its "urban" aspect will be considered presently.
The term "multilingualism" has two possible referents: the linguistic repertoire of
a social group and the repertoires of individual members of the group. Sometimes
the terms "multilingualism" and "polyglotism" are opposed to distinguish the two
referents. In this book, we describe a state, town, community, or other social-geographic
unit in which several languages are used as "multilingual" and an individual who speaks
several languages as "polyglot." In terms of the preceding chapter, it is a macro-
sociolinguistic job to explain a multilingual situation, which characterizes a social
group, and a micro-sociolinguistic task to explain polyglotism, which describes individual behavior as it reflects specified features of the social context.

What is particularly interesting and possibly distinctive about the West African
situation, and what seems to require explanation, is not the occurrence of multilingualism in itself nor even the existence of polyglotism, since these are normal phenomena, but a particular relationship between the two. Several sorts of relationship
between multilingualism and polyglotism are logically possible and empirically
observable in the world. Obviously multilingualism, as the use of many languages
within some formally defined social-geographical unit, does not necessarily entail
widespread polyglotism; that is, the possession of a degree of competence in many
languages by large numbers of people.[3] On the one hand, multilingualism within a
physically defined area with no polyglotism whatever implies no communication (at
any rate, no communication via language) between members of the different language
communities in the area, and it is difficult to see in what sense such a collection of
groups could be regarded as a social entity or how it could have any sort of stability.
On the other hand, a multilingual state need not have a large proportion of polyglots
to be politically viable. Ultimately it requires only a few bilingual individuals in key

but not necessarily exalted positions. In the days before education in a metropolitan language was widespread, such a situation must have been more common than it is now, but even today something like it can be observed. In Canada, for example, it seems that even though there is more than one recognized, official language, it is only rather recently that many political leaders have found it expedient to speak more than one, and especially in the larger (English-speaking) group the great majority of the inhabitants are probably functionally monoglot. They may once have studied the other language (French) in school, but they hardly use it.

The proportion of polyglots varies considerably among multilingual states, and the dynamics of the situation, with its long-term tendencies, also varies. In North America, it is observable that while younger speakers of nonofficial, "minority" languages generally acquire an official or socially dominant one, they rarely acquire a second nonofficial or minority language, and acquisition of the dominant language need not lead to bilingualism. Many elderly American speakers of English spoke another language in childhood, say Yiddish or French, which they no longer use. Presumably there is still latent competence, but if over a long period the occasion to exercise it rarely arises, that competence must be considerably diminished. In acquiring another language, such speakers seem to have shifted functionally from monoglotism in one language to monoglotism in another. The dynamic of the multilingual situation in much of North America does not usually impel individuals in the direction of increasing polyglotism but toward the exchange of one language for another. Unlike the rest of the world, the tendency in America has historically been toward the elimination of the multilingual situation itself (Fishman 1970: 71).

In continental Europe, relatively large numbers of languages continue to coexist within a geographically limited area, in different political states and also within states. The multilingual geography of the region is accompanied in this case by a moderate degree of polyglotism; many Europeans speak more than one European language, but very large numbers do not. In Europe, competence in another language is strongly associated with consciously focused efforts to acquire it, such as a sojourn in another country for that purpose, and with formal education. It is also nonreciprocal: a speaker of the language of a relatively small community such as Danish or Dutch is far more likely to speak French or German than a French or German speaker is to speak Danish or Dutch. This is even more clearly the case with languages like Basque or Romansch, which are not only spoken in relatively small communities but also are not the dominant language of any state.

Multilingualism in the first place is a geographic fact: the use of more than one language within the same physical boundary. Modern mass communications over very long distances undoubtedly make a difference as far as the major world languages are concerned, but for most people the languages of their environment are still the languages they hear spoken by people who are physically present. Most people, after all, especially in countries where the mass media are most readily available, do not tune in to languages they do not already understand. Individual adjustments to this geographical fact are heavily influenced by the aspect of social relations known as politics, that is, by power relations between language communities.

The sort of power relations that affect polyglotism are no different from those that operate in other areas of life. However much they may resent the fact, people tend to learn the languages of those with whom their economic relations are crucial or of those who have conquered and colonized them. At the same time, sheer numbers seem to count very heavily, for a small occupying force has often adopted the language of the people it dominated in almost every other way. Whether or not the situation becomes permanent and the politically dominant group is absorbed into the group that is weaker, except in sheer numbers, is obviously affected by varying circumstances. In North Africa and southern Europe, for instance, the languages of Arabic-speaking and Latin-speaking invaders, respectively, have almost completely overwhelmed the languages of those they invaded, but in West Africa the Mande conquerors of the Gonja became Gonja-speaking, and the Normans in England eventually shifted to English.

The foregoing generalities are as true of sub-Saharan West Africa as of anywhere else. What seems to be distinctive about this geographical area is a combination of extreme multilingualism (more languages in less space) with an unusually high degree of polyglotism (a high frequency of relatively large individual repertoires of not mutually intelligible languages). That is, on the one hand, there does not appear to be a general tendency toward a reduction of multilingualism, and the historical American phenomenon of wholesale exchange of one language for another—or a shift in individual linguistic competence—is not obvious. On the other hand, reciprocity is as lacking in Africa as elsewhere: the small and weak learn the languages of the big and powerful, and not the other way around. Since some language communities are very much larger than others and all the other variables of linguistic power also pertain, we shall consider whether the situation is indeed as stable as has sometimes been claimed.

Polyglotism as adaptation to a multilingual environment is not so strongly correlated with formal education in West Africa as it is in Europe, partly because few of the languages involved are taught in schools and partly because the school environment (where it exists) is often less, or differently, multilingual than the surrounding society. It is also less dependent on travel and concentrated effort at acquisition, although these facts of personal history are also relevant. Instead, in the course of ordinary daily activities many people acquire a rudimentary working knowledge of several languages, not unconsciously or without effort but unsystematically. Some people make a deliberate effort and so acquire a better knowledge of one language or of several.[4]

The phenomenon of widespread adaptive polyglotism is most clearly visible in the urban context. In many cities of the world, a large number of languages are to be heard within a small space. In West African towns, especially the towns on the coast, not only is the number of languages particularly large relative to the population but also a particularly large proportion of the urban population speaks several of them. In some Senegalese towns it seems there is a fairly strong tendency to language exchange, although it is not clear whether exchange is being accompanied by a reduction in multilingualism (Calvet 1988). However, this does not seem to be the most common situation. The language of one ethnic community is often clearly dominant, and members of others often learn it, but they do not necessarily make it their own. A good example of such a language is Yoruba in Lagos, as described by Scotton

(1975). On the coast generally, urbanization does not seem at the present time to imply linguistic assimilation, if by assimilation is meant homogenization, or the convergence and reduction of individuals' repertoires.

Accra presents a particularly good example. In many respects it seems to be a typical West African city, with both social and linguistic features that are characteristic of most.[5] It may therefore provide as good a laboratory as any for investigating the dynamics of West African urban multilingualism. At the same time, it is not possible to discuss the dynamics of the linguistic situation in Accra itself apart from the city's position within the social, political, economic, and linguistic systems of the region. For both purposes, some background is required. I therefore look more closely at the linguistic history of West African towns in general, with the resulting contemporary configurations, and then propose a generalized working model before narrowing the field to one particular West African coastal city: Accra.

A Historical Overview

For our purposes, West African states may be divided roughly into two categories, with important implications for every aspect of communications: those within or bordering on the Sahel and those with a South Atlantic coastline. In the history of states in the first category, the Sahara desert has been likened to an inland sea, guiding and defining the corridors of communication.[6] Their contacts with one another and the world beyond have been conducted around and across the desert, and their important cities almost all arose originally as "ports" on that sea. They were entrepôts in the trade in gold, ivory, kola, beads, iron, salt, cloth, paper, and slaves among North African (and ultimately European) peoples, other Sahelian states, and the lands to the south. The earliest of these states, Ancient Ghana between the eighth and twelfth centuries and Mali in the thirteenth and fourteenth, and more particularly their capitals, arose on the western side of the sub-Saharan Sahel. Ancient Ghana was known as a center of the gold trade by the eighth century at the latest (Levtzion 1973: 3). The fourteenth and fifteenth centuries saw the rise of the Hausa states, situated to the east in present-day Nigeria (Bovill 1968: 225). The Songhay built an empire on the Niger in the fifteenth century (Hunwick 1973: 52). Its capital was Gao, on the eastern side of the Niger bend, but it incorporated important towns of Ancient Ghana and Mali (by now much declined) such as Walata, in the southeast corner of modern Mauritania, and Jenne and Timbuktu, in present-day Mali. The last of the West African Sahelian empires to appear was the Fulani empire, which had its initial impetus from the jihad of Uthman dan Fodio in the first decade of the nineteenth century and eventually extended over almost all of present-day northern Nigeria and beyond, its capital being in the west at Sokoto (Bovill 1968: 230).

As might be expected, these are the countries—including present-day Mauritania, Senegal, Mali, Niger, and northern Nigeria—where the influence of North Africa, Arabia, Islam, and Islamic culture has been strongest and is most in evidence today. Some of their cities, particularly in northern Nigeria, are still of political and economic importance because they have found functions in the political and economic constitutions of the modern states that have inherited them. Others, such as Gao, Jenne, and Timbuktu have drastically declined in national significance if not always in size. Kumbi Saleh, capital of Ancient Ghana, and Niani, capital of Mali at its height, are in ruins, significant only to archaeologists and historians.

The broad linguistic configurations of those ancient (as well as the not so ancient) Sahelian cities are known. The first commercial towns of sub-Saharan West Africa date at least from the seventh century, and the first language of international trade was Berber (Dunn 1986: 291). Hunwick (1964) provides evidence that Arabic was used as the language of the court and also for written correspondence in twelfth-century Ghana and fourteenth-century Mali and for religious and legal teaching in fifteenth-century Songhay. The impact that Arabic has had on the major languages of the Sahel and northern savannah is consistent with fairly widespread bilingualism in Arabic among culturally influential people over a considerable period of time.[7] Today, a variety of Arabic is the first language of a small group in northeastern Nigeria called the Shuwa Arabs, and varieties regarded as pidgins are spoken as second, "market" languages in some centers, including Niamey, the capital of Niger, and Maiduguri in extreme northeastern Nigeria (Blanc 1971: 503, 505). Historically, however, the language of the economically and culturally influential Arabic-speaking traders from Egypt and the Maghreb and the written language of culture and religion they carried with them have been the important contact languages (Greenberg 1945: 85) and therefore the major terms in the sociolinguistic configuration of towns.[8] In the Mali empire, Arabic was the language of foreign relations, but in later Sahelian empires (and also in Mali) its most important roles were in commerce and the Islamic religion (Alexandre 1971: 656). The other major town languages, first and second, were undoubtedly the languages that are most widespread across the region today: Berber languages, particularly Tamascheq, and various closely related dialects of northern Manding, as well as Fula, Songhay, and Hausa.[9]

Although North Africans by their trading enterprise may have catalyzed town formation, and incidentally urban bilingualism, West Africans took over the process very quickly. The Mande became a major trading people, developing trade networks and establishing towns and trading posts throughout the Sahel to the forest edge and even beyond. The fact of empire favored Malinke-speaking traders,[10] and trade (and politics) favored the spread of their language; thus when the Portuguese arrived on the coast in the fifteenth century they met Malinke in several places from which it has since retreated, including the Senegal-Gambia area and even at Mina on what became the Gold Coast (Baesjou 1988; Wilks 1993: 5). A little later, the Hausa began to expand to the west and south as a trading power, so that today the western boundary of Ghana (marked in the north by the Black Volta River) roughly coincides with the boundary between the areas of currency of the two great trade languages of West Africa: Jula,[11] a Manding dialect (or dialect cluster) to the west of the line, and Hausa to the east.

The rise of trading towns and trading languages often brought about a linguistic difference between town and countryside that could hardly have existed before. Hunwick (1973: 52) suggests that in several important towns of the western Songhay empire in the sixteenth century, the language of local administration was Songhay, the language of trade and scholarship was Arabic, and the ordinary locals spoke a Mande language: Bozo in Jenne and Azer in Walata. In the heyday of the Mali empire and that of Ancient Ghana before it, the language of administration was presumably Mande (Malinke in the former and Soninke in the latter), but Arabic, as well as Berber languages such as Tamascheq, must have been as important for scholarship and trade as they were later. Administration, trade, and scholarship are all activities associated with town life, so Arabic, Berber languages (where these were also languages of traders and a scholar class), and Songhay in Mali (but not in Niger, where it was indigenous) must also have been especially associated with towns. Note that these languages could hardly be more disparate, both linguistically and in the geographical area of origin. In fact, they represent three of Africa's four great linguistic phyla: Songhay is the westernmost representative of the Nilo-Saharan phylum, which otherwise is located east of Lake Chad; Arabic, of course, belongs to the Semitic branch of Afroasiatic and is ultimately an intrusion from the northeast, whereas Berber languages belong to a different, northern branch of Afroasiatic; and the Mande languages constitute a branch of Niger-Congo, which is firmly sub-Saharan. Thus one important feature of the pattern was set very early: bilingualism (or multilingualism) in West African towns is essentially a function of economic and political relations and not, at least in the first instance, of the kind of social ties (kinship, for example) that are likely to be a function of crude geographical proximity. The irrelevance of geographical proximity underlines the general absence of a close genetic relationship among the languages involved.

As the Mande trading network moved farther south, a string of towns grew up across the northern Ivory Coast and southwestern Burkina Faso—including Odienné, Seguela, Touba, and Bobo-Dioulasso, in which Jula is the language of the community—but in the surrounding villages the community language is either an entirely different Mande language or a Gur language, with Jula, the language of the town, widely used as a second language (Derive 1976; Wilks 1968).[12] At the southeastern extreme of the Mande trading area the pattern is especially complicated. In the northwest corner of the Brong-Ahafo Region of Ghana, now rather remote, several towns inhabited by people whose forefathers were involved in the gold trade between Ashanti and Mande (Wilks 1993: 17) are in fact twin towns, with two spatially and ethnically distinct sectors that speak different languages. Twinned or neighboring villages may speak one of several varieties of Ligbi,[13] a Northern Mande language closely related to Jula, or Kulango, Degha (also called Mo), Nafaanra, Gonja, or the Brong dialect of Akan.[14] In Manji and Brawhani, for example, the politically dominant language is Ligbi, whose speakers probably represent a wave of Mande traders who preceded the Jula, but an equally ancient and smaller section of each town speaks Nafaanra, the easternmost representative of the Senufo subgroup of Gur (Dakubu 1976; Persson 1980). A similar situation evidently exists in Banda (Kondor 1989). Variations on the pattern occur throughout the Banda region of western Brong-Ahafo, complicated by a considerable influx of refugees from the west during the nineteenth century and local trends in linguistic assimilation.[15] The linguistic pattern in this part of Brong-Ahafo is apparently continued in the pattern in Bonduku (a trading town just across the border in the Ivory Coast that is the capital of the Abron state called Gyaman), which has close, long-standing ties with this part of Brong-Ahafo and which counts at least three major languages—Kulango, Jula and Brong (Akan)—and numerous smaller ones—including Nafaanra and the Huela and Numu dialects of Ligbi—within its borders, each spoken in a geographically distinct section of the town (Tauxier 1921: 40).

It is likely that a comparable pattern once existed in ancient Begho, a town now visible only as mounds, which in the fifteenth century was a major trading center for kola and gold (Levtzion 1973: 156). The town included artisan and Muslim quarters, as well as a quarter of people whose culture seems to have been very similar to that of the Akan of Hani, the nearest modern village, and a market quarter where people of all the quarters met (Posnansky 1987). These quarters are clearly distinguishable archaeologically, and we may suppose they were also distinguished linguistically, with a Manding variety functioning as market language, although by the end of the town's decline toward the end of the eighteenth century, this may have been replaced by Akan (Goody 1964: 195, Posnansky 1979: 24, Wilks 1993: 18). The "quarters" are well separated, about a kilometer apart.

A pattern emerges of a type of trading town in which ethnically and linguistically different groups come together to carry out different economic functions and maintain their separateness geographically, despite close proximity and economic interdependence. In present-day Brong-Ahafo, the Ligbi and the Nafana[16] rarely speak each other's languages but communicate in an Akan dialect, either Brong or Asante. Kulango[17] is the dominant language of Bonduku today. The modern village closest to the site of old Begho, Hani, is Brong-speaking, but it is not clear what the language of intergroup communication would have been in the past. It is reasonable to suppose that Jula was initially the language of trade but that as the power of Bono Manso—the local Akan state that preceded the rise of Ashanti (Arhin 1979: 10)—increased, so did the general currency of the Akan language.

Begho and now Manji display a linguistic pattern that has been a feature of West African towns since earliest times. The capital of Ancient Ghana is thought to have consisted of two towns, one royal and one for foreign traders, several miles apart. The former was no doubt mainly Soninke-speaking. The traders' town, Kumbi Saleh, in turn consisted of two sharply distinguished quarters, one strongly Muslim and presumably inhabited by merchants from the Maghreb, and the other local Mande (Levtzion 1973: 23–25; Mauny 1968: 481). It is likely that Arabic was particularly important in the former. Soninke is more likely to have been used in the latter. Berber might have been used in both.

Farther east, within the Hausa trading area, there is a variation on the pattern. We do not find towns in which the dominant language is different from that of the surrounding villages, as in the Ivory Coast and Brong-Ahafo, possibly because by the time the Hausa became active to the west, during the fifteenth century (Levtzion 1968: 17), there were already local towns, or at least centers of political power, strong enough to prevent outright colonization. That is, the Mosi, Mamprusi, and Dagomba states existed in nearby (but not quite adjacent) regions of modern Burkina Faso, Ghana, and Togo in the early fifteenth century at the latest (Iliasu 1971: 106; Levtzion 1968: xiv). In what is now northern Ghana, chiefs insisted that traders' camps (generally known as *zongos*, from the Hausa) be established near, but at a respectful distance from, political capitals. The result was often twin towns, recalling the pattern reconstructed for Kumbi Saleh, each twin being the scene of quite distinct activities and presenting a correspondingly different linguistic profile. Several of these camps became the nuclei of modern towns, as is said to be the case in Ghana with Gambaga outside the Mamprusi capital, Nalerigu; Salaga near Kpembe, the capital of Gonja (Levtzion 1973: 25); and Tamale several miles from the Dagomba capital, Yendi. Although the main language of these camps was certainly Hausa, and a large proportion of the people in them came from Hausaland, they did not become towns of Hausa people but rather Mamprusi, Gonja, or Dagomba towns with an important Hausa quarter (also called, in Ghana, a *zongo*). That is, the language of the countryside is also the language of the local political establishment, in these cases Mampruli, Ngbanya (Gonja), or Dagbani, and is considered to be the language of the town; Hausa is the language of a group of economically important but politically marginalized residents of exotic origin ("strangers"), which a number of indigenes engaged in trade (beyond strictly local trade) also use. Even in these cases, however, the principle still holds, that trade and familiarity with the trade language have been and continue to be associated with towns.

With the exception of Senegal, which is historically and geographically on the extreme western edge of the Sahel, the Sahelian states are landlocked. The capital cities of the modern states of the Guinea coast—Conakry in Guinea, Freetown in Sierra Leone, Monrovia in Liberia, Abidjan in the Ivory Coast, Accra and earlier Cape Coast in Ghana, Lomé in Togo, Whydah and then Cotonou in the Republic of Benin, and Lagos and the cities of the River states in Nigeria—also arose in response to international trade, this time as ports on a watery, not a sandy, sea and rather more recently. The circum- and cross-Atlantic trade, which gave the impetus for the establishment and expansion of these cities, began as the Portuguese explored eastward along the coast in the fifteenth century, when many of the Sahelian and savannah towns were flourishing and few coastal towns were yet of any size or importance. Accra can be counted as a major center from about the middle of the seventeenth century, just before it became the capital of the Ga-speaking people, although it was still small. Most of the others, such as Dakar, Freetown, and Lagos, are more recent still; but in contrast to the older cities of the Sahel and the northern forest edge, they have central functions in the modern state and its economy. Some, such as Abidjan, which hardly existed before the 1920s, were created expressly to perform such functions. In all of them, a European language has always played a role, paralleling that of Arabic in the early cities of the Sahel; but again, as in those cities of another era, this implies nothing about the capacity for expansion of the indigenous languages.

Between these essentially trading cities of the Sahel and of the coast there is a third category, what we might call (following Levtzion 1968: xiii) a middle belt of African cities, all precolonial. It is actually constructed in two rather different tiers: the northern, savannah tier contains the capitals of the Mosi-Dagomba states of Nupe and of Borgu and represents a southward extension of the political evolution of the Sahel. South of these, the towns of the Guinea states—such as Ife and Benin in Nigeria; Abomey in traditional Dahomey; and the Ashanti capital, Kumasi, in Ghana—were certainly related to and affected by the trading systems of both the Sahel and the Atlantic coast. They arose primarily as political centers, however, protected from the potentially disruptive foreign influences to be found in major market centers further north, and also as military bases from which kings attempted to control those centers and their contacts with the growing trade on the coast. Despite this important (and linguistically relevant) difference in the social circumstances in which they developed, the forest towns arose first in response to trading contacts from the north, predating most of today's seaports as political centers, and thus historically represent a further stage in the general southward trend that ends at the coast.

In the area of present-day Ghana, Akan kings did their best to keep commercial contacts between north and south under tight control. Although northern traders were resident in Kumasi at various times, the forest kingdoms in general kept the outsiders at an even greater distance than did the northern states, perhaps because forest paths are easier to control than routes across open savannah (Wilks 1975: 267–69). Although a *zongo* was eventually established in Kumasi, it was not the traders' half of a twin town of the northern type. Instead, the forest-savannah margin of Ashanti was marked by a line of trading towns, principally Atebubu, Kintampo, and Nkoranza, where traders from the north had to hand over their goods to Ashanti dealers (Arhin 1989). In the trading history of the Akan states we read of the roads being closed rather often. Consequently, while the Asante population was undoubtedly heterogeneous in origin and at various times quite cosmopolitan (Wilks 1975: 84–86), the town of Kumasi and its hinterland seem to have been more ethnically and linguistically homogeneous than most of the states farther north, and certainly more so than the great majority of towns on the coast. Yet even in Kumasi at its most powerful, business and foreign affairs could not be conducted entirely in the language of the country, the Asante dialect of Akan, and in the nineteenth century written correspondence between Ashanti and countries to the north was conducted in Arabic (J. Goody 1968: 242; Wilks 1975: 40).

We find, then, that linguistically the towns of West Africa exist along an east-west axis and on a north-south axis. Not all towns are influenced in equal measure on both. Our primary concern in this book is with towns of the coast (rather than those of the Sahel, savannah, and forest), but it is important to recognize that in many ways the patterns that appear in the "modern" towns of the coast continue patterns already long established farther north. Although most of the coastal towns have not developed as twin towns—one for kings and indigenes, the other for trade and foreigners—areas of residential settlement are almost always broadly divisible into local and "nonlocal" sectors. These in turn are divided into quarters that reflect the settlement history of the locality, a feature that originated in the long-standing tradition of physical separation of strangers, or foreigners, and of economic and political functions and complementary linguistic practices. O'Connor's (1983: 37) type of the "dual city," which incorporates an older traditional city and a new modern city, with many parallel functions, and even his "colonial city"—in those cases where the colonial town was related to an indigenous settlement, however tiny—can be seen as specialized developments of the old twinning model. For example, the "dual city" of Kano, with its relatively homogeneous (and monolingual) old town and its complex and diversified new town, recalls Atebubu, with its core Akan-speaking Brong population (historically a merger of a Guang population with Asante immigrants) and its multilingual Zongo, populated by various groups from northern Ghana and beyond (Arhin 1971). Each section or quarter may be largely self-sufficient, but the specialized functions that brought the various groups together in the first place tend to be spatially and also linguistically associated with those who introduced them. Thus in

Accra the location of a market, the kinds of goods sold in it, and the languages most used in the selling are closely related. English continues to be most heavily used in the residential areas first settled by the English and in governmental and administrative functions, also largely geographically localized, which were originally introduced by English people, even though the inhabitants and participants are now almost entirely non-English.

Virtually all the coastal towns can be seen to have developed linguistically in response to the east-west axis. They were in contact with one another from their beginnings, and they still are, by land, sea, and now air. This has been an important factor in the formation of their populations and has affected language patterns in several respects, including the development of a popular urban style.

Not every coastal town has historically maintained communications on the north-south axis. Freetown and Monrovia, for example, colonized from Great Britain and North America early in the nineteenth century, had very little contact with the interior until quite recently. For most, however, the hinterland to the north has made a crucial difference, according to whether or not it represented a reservoir of speakers of an indigenous language of the town. Thus Lagos, backed by the vast Yoruba-speaking country, presents a Yoruba face, even though in its earliest days other languages were also present—namely, Gun, perhaps Ewe, and certainly Edo (Agiri and Barnes 1987)—and it is now host to very large numbers of migrants who speak other languages. On a much smaller scale, a similar pattern is to be found in the old Akan-speaking town of Cape Coast in Ghana. Accra and Abidjan, in contrast, are in the homelands of small languages, with no hinterland to provide networks of use in external communication and streams of native-speaking migrants to reinforce them. The result in both cases is a more complex pattern of multilingualism, but they are not at all the same. In the case of Accra, the immediate hinterland is dominated by a large language, Akan, which has powerfully affected the situation in Accra. For Abidjan, there is no dominant language in the immediate hinterland, which is linguistically fragmented (Dumestre 1971) and far less densely populated than western Nigeria or even central Ghana. Presumably this is why Jula and more recently pidgin French have become the urban *lingue franche*. It is nevertheless significant that neither the Ebrié language of Abidjan, which in 1965 was spoken by only 50,000 (p. 14), nor the Ga of Accra, spoken by about ten times that number but still less than half the city, seems to be actually disappearing.

To conclude this brief account of the linguistic history of the town in West Africa, it may be observed that over the past thousand years there has been a general trend southward, from Sahel to savannah and then to the southern savannah and into the forest, until today the centers of economic and political power are mainly on the coast. The landlocked countries whose main urban centers are in the savannah do not present exceptions, for they are generally poorer and weaker than the others. To a lesser extent there has also been a shift from west to east, following the greatest concentration of population. This can be observed in the shift from the Mauritania-Mali border area, which was the political and economic focus in medieval times, to the south and west toward Jenne, Gao, and then Sokoto and Kano. Today the largest cities and towns, at all geographical levels but especially the southern, are in Nigeria, to the extreme southeast of our area. The shifting center of trade has meant the gradual spread of certain languages over very wide areas, as second languages and to some extent as community languages. It seems invariably to have involved the appearance of significant numbers of foreigners—first, Arabic speakers in Ancient Ghana and Mali, then Manding and Hausa speakers farther south, and speakers of European languages on the coast—whose languages have become established for specific purposes (usually without displacing local languages for community use). As the process moved southward and new layers of population took up trading activities, new languages acquired geographically extended spheres of use, so that in the area of present-day Ghana, for example, Waale (the Gur language of the Mande-influenced town of Wa) and Asante (the language of Kumasi, which grew in response at first to Mande and later to Hausa and European commercial activities) are both thought to be spreading as languages of trade (at the expense of Hausa, in the case of Asante). In West African trading towns throughout history, at least one exotic language has always been in use for vehicular and other purposes, and very often (perhaps usually) two or more have coexisted with each other and with one or several languages of more local use for extended periods of time. Vehicular languages have tended to spread from north to south and then between east and west. The coastal states and seaport towns are included in this pattern, but they become especially complicated because there the north-south system meets another system made up of exotic languages, mainly European, that spread first from west to east (and back again) along the coast and, much more recently, from south to north as well.

Toward a Dynamic Model of West African Urban Multilingualism

It has been suggested that a trilingual model of multilingualism is particularly applicable to Africa. Abdulaziz-Mkilifi (1972) proposed that modern East Africa is typically "triglossic," with communicative functions shared among three language varieties that need not be (indeed most often were not) closely related or even related at all. The three languages are typically disparate in geographic origin, one being local; one an "indigenous" lingua franca, Swahili; and the third a European language of international currency. The term "indigenous" is relative since Swahili is hardly indigenous to Nairobi. Alexandre (1971: 660) made essentially the same proposal, classifying languages as used in Africa into the local, the national or vehicular, and the European.

The political status of Swahili in Tanzania, and hence the function of local language and Swahili bilingualism, is very different from the status of Akan in Ghana and the nature of the attendant bilingualism there. Nevertheless, Bruce Johnson (1975) used the model to describe multilingualism in Larteh, a small hilltop town a few miles north of Accra, in the Akuapem traditional state. In Larteh, bilingualism in Larteh (Lεtε, a Guang language) and the Akuapem dialect of Akan is universal among nonmigrant adults, and a very high proportion know English as well. Johnson suggested that the three-language configuration is not only frequently encountered but also a state toward which African linguistic patterns naturally tend, and so perhaps inherently stable. He quoted the missionary Andreas Riis to the effect that Akan-

Guang bilingualism was already universal among adults in 1854 (p. 99), so that it must antedate the promotion of Akan in schools and churches by the Basel mission.

"Stable Triglossia" Reconsidered

It is true that in many places in Africa today, observable language practice may be described by a three-term system of languages, among which choices are made on a scale that balances group solidarity against economic efficiency in a rather complex way, for example, English-Swahili-Luganda in Kampala, French-Jula-Ebrié in Abidjan, or English-Akan-Ga in Accra. The most obvious common feature of these systems is geographical: with respect to the town involved, the languages are used in progressively less location-specific domains and have arrived from increasingly more distant places of origin.[18] On closer inspection, it is also obvious that the more distant the origin of a language, and the less specific to the locality are its uses, the greater the power wielded on the world stage by those who introduced it.[19] Such a situation often seems to be the "most natural" response to communication problems under the prevailing postcolonial (or neocolonial) social and political conditions and therefore, presumably, likely to be a stable condition once achieved. "Natural" in this context apparently means cost-effective, at least in the short term, in meeting the goals of communication as proposed by Scotton (1976: 202).

Figure 2.1 represents the trilingual situation for Ghana as a whole, based on this model. As can be seen, one obvious difficulty is the existence of several languages in common use as a second language (L_2), often by the same people. (Only the most widely spoken are listed.) Even when the local community language (L_1) can be classed as an indigenous lingua franca, the number of major languages is not necessarily reduced. In Kumasi, for example, the local community language is Akan, which is also the largest single language in Ghana and is apparently spreading as a second language; but Hausa, too, has long been a major presence there. In Accra and in many

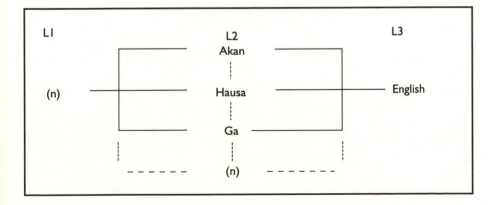

FIGURE 2.1 The Trilingual Configuration in Ghana; *n* indicates that the number of possible languages in a category is indefinite.

other towns, Hausa, Akan, and Ga are in competition as lingua francas among migrants, who speak none of them as their community languages, which they continue
to use in the urban environment. Even in Larteh and other small towns of Akuapem,
a third of the adult population speaks Ga, in addition to Akan and English. This is
surely a significant sociolinguistic fact, even though, unlike the other three languages,
Ga is not normally used within the town itself. In Figure 2.1, the exotic language
(L_3) is the only term represented by just one language, English. This fact may help to
account for the apparently secure position of this language, despite the notorious
inequality of access to it.

Not only is the triadic configuration problematic, but a closer look at the situation in Larteh and comparable towns calls its stability into question. The Larteh language is mutually intelligible with other varieties, including Okere and Anum, grouped
under the name Hill Guang (Painter 1980); but it is isolated from them by steep val-
leys in the case of Okere (which is spoken in several villages on the Akuapem ridge
opposite Larteh) and by the Volta River, in the case of Anum. Larteh is also separated from Anum by Krobo-speaking communities. In Larteh, as we have seen, essentially the entire adult population is actively bilingual in Akan and Guang, and more
than half the town speaks the European language as well. Surveys directed by me in
1978 in the Okere-speaking Akuapem towns of Abiriw and Apirede and in Abonse
(also in Akuapem) produced the same results (Dakubu 1978). The three languages
are used in Larteh (and the other Akuapem Guang towns) in essentially discrete social domains: Larteh is used domestically and locally, Akan is less used in the home
but predominates everywhere else, and school is the primary domain of English.
Children of Guang parents who live in Guang towns still learn Guang first, but our
survey of fifty residents of Abiriw indicated that more than 10% also used Akan with
their children, and some used it with their parents as well. There were also isolated
cases of this incipient intergenerational shift in Apirede and Abonse. In Larteh, Bruce
Johnson (1975: 95) found that although Larteh was the home language, some children were already fluent in Akan before they began school.

Among the Hill Guang communities, only Larteh maintains a Guang-language
oral literature (Ansah 1974; Bruce Johnson 1975). Even Larteh people do not sing in
Larteh, and the formulas employed in tale-telling are in Akan. Ansah came to the
conclusion that the Hill Guang language generally was in the process of extinction.
Since observers agree that all Larteh people (and other Hill Guang speakers) learn
Akan but that migrants resident in Larteh rarely learn Larteh, it seems likely that—
assuming the continuance of the sociopolitical forces that have operated on language
practice for the past 350 years, beginning with the defeat of the Akuapem Guang by
Akwamu in the 1640s (Brokensha 1966: 2)—we have been witnessing the slow con-
traction of the Hill Guang language, which could lead to its ultimate demise. But the
outcome is not a foregone conclusion. For several years, the Guan Historical Society
has been trying to reverse the trend by encouraging the use of Guang languages in
school and church. Its success will undoubtedly depend on the outcome of the current political crisis in Akuapem, which may indeed alter the sociopolitical trends of
four centuries and the relative status of Guang and Akan in towns like Larteh.[20]

The "stable trilingualism" model not only misses the essence of a situation that
is neither strictly trilingual nor inherently stable but also fails to give adequate weight

to the distinction between the social domain in which the language is used, or immediate social function of a language event, and the broader communicative goal, or why language (and a particular language) is being used at all, as well as the relationship between the two. It therefore sheds no light on the common observation that the same individual may use more than one language in the same or very similar domains, sometimes in combination (the phenomena of code switching and mixing). We have seen that a few Guang speakers use Akan with their children, even though they know the Guang language and both are locally in general use. It is difficult to see how a model that relies on a generalized category of synchronic social domain can explain why they choose to do this. Even when the domains of language choice are discrete, as they largely seem to be in Larteh, the model does not really explain why domains should be distinguished by language in the first place. Why do people learn more than one language, only to speak them mainly with one another, depending on the occasion? Such a situation must have a history.

Scotton's work, also carried out in the 1970s, takes the distinction between domain and goal into account.[21] Although she does not refer to it as such, Scotton (1975, 1976) effectively presents a trilingual model of language use in Kampala (English-Swahili-Luganda), Nairobi (English-Swahili-Kikuyu), and Lagos (English–Pidgin English–Yoruba). She introduces the three as potentially alternative lingua francas in urban work situations, but obviously they are not potential on the same level. In each city, English, the language of recently imposed styles of education and government, plainly fills the L_3 slot. Swahili or Pidgin as L_2 is also perceived as nonindigenous although less foreign, being aurally-orally learned from local models and therefore without the kind of status associated with writing and English. The third language is also the community language of each city's nonmigrant population.

This does not mean, however, that the multilingual patterns of the three cities are identical. In the groups Scotton (1976: 212–13) studied, for example, she found that Swahili was more likely to be used at work in Kampala and Nairobi than English, in Lagos Pidgin was not more likely to be used than English, and Swahili was also a more likely choice in Nairobi than in Kampala. Although in all three cities the local community language is apparently least likely to be used if it is not the community language of one or both parties, the use of Kikuyu in Nairobi or especially of Luganda in Kampala reflects interethnic tension, and is aimed at the deliberate exclusion of others, to a much greater extent than the use of Yoruba in Lagos (pp. 208, 215). This is partly due to specific historical and political factors, but it is also surely relevant that Yoruba is a much more diffused language than either Luganda or Kikuyu, with a considerable media presence, and is spoken as a community language by more people, both local and migrant.

We shall concentrate on Scotton's (1975, 1976, 1982) picture of Lagos since, unlike Kampala and Nairobi, it has historically been in constant communication with Accra. Scotton emphasizes that in all the situations she has studied, domain alone (she treats mainly the domain of work, in contrast to domestic and personal domains) cannot account for all language choices. The other factors she emphasizes are "societal norms" (after Hymes 1972) and the language economy, that is, ultimate goals of communication. In Lagos, for example, societal norms determined that Yoruba speakers avoid ethnic confrontation in public domains when non-Yoruba people were or might be present by using a language other than Yoruba, but they did not require the same avoidance in more personal domains, so that non-Yoruba friends, for example, might be expected to speak Yoruba (Scotton 1975: 85). Societal norms require that in certain situations a "neutral" language be used, no matter what other languages the parties have in common. These norms are based on a "cost and reward" evaluation of the outcome of a language transaction (Scotton 1976: 202). Ultimately, language choice is modeled on the relationship between the system of languages potentially available for use in a given domain and the communicative goal of the language event.

Where information is available, the model seems as applicable to towns of the precolonial past as to the postcolonial city. To illustrate, we may apply it to nineteenth-century Ilorin as described by Alexandre (1971: 656). Ilorin was an important town of the Yoruba kingdom of Oyo, which was conquered by the expanding Fulani in the 1820s. According to Alexandre, at the time of the Fulani emirate the town communicated in four languages—Arabic, Fulfulde, Hausa, and Yoruba—plus a number of other languages spoken in neighboring villages. Since the last were perhaps not, strictly speaking, languages of the town, figure 2.2 ignores them. The figure includes a military domain for Hausa since it seems that the Fulani troops, and perhaps some of the Yoruba troops as well, were Hausa people (Smith 1969: 141–42) and that Hausa became a military lingua franca in the course of these wars. It also adds domains for the use of Yoruba. Although the picture is still very much simplified, figure 2.2 illustrates some possible relations among language, domain, and goal, while providing an outline model of multilingualism in Ilorin around 1830.

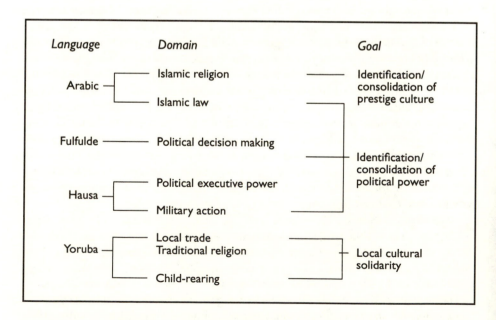

FIGURE 2.2   Multilingualism in nineteenth-century Ilorin.

One way in which the picture is simplified is in the omission of any domain with political goals for Yoruba, for the language must surely have continued in that function in some reduced fashion after the Fulani conquest. The domains actually displayed for Yoruba are assumed in order to flesh out the picture of the probable pattern of linguistic life. Commercial goals for other languages are omitted because neither Alexandre (1971) nor Smith (1969) mentions them, and it is possible that the times were too disturbed to favor trade beyond the strictly local. The result of these omissions is the functional isolation of Yoruba: it appears to share neither domain nor communicative goal with any other language. This may reflect a real functional divide between Yoruba and the three imposed langages.

To judge by the pattern that appeared later in calmer times, if the commercial domains could be added they would almost certainly turn out to be shared between Yoruba and Hausa, reducing the isolation of the former. Even without these extensions, however, the position of Hausa is striking. Via different domains, it shares political goals with Arabic and Fulfulde. Given a residual political domain for Yoruba and eventually a share (with Yoruba) in the functions of commercial life, Hausa appears as an intermediary language, furthering nearly all the operative goals in selected domains. That is, several domains may have been the exclusive preserve of Hausa, but no function was specific to that language; in the political economy of nineteenth-century Ilorin, its use primarily furthered the goals of social groups other than its community, which was not true of either Fulfulde or Yoruba in the circumstances. Such a state-based analysis, of course, simplifies the situation even further, for it ignores, on the one hand, the large numbers of Hausa community speakers who were apparently present and were crucial to the availability and use of the language (Smith 1969: 137) and, on the other hand, the size, extent, and diversity of "local" Yoruba. However, this analyis has the virtue of highlighting a historical precedent for a recurring pattern: a local language (in this case, Yoruba) that serves the purposes of the local community and an external language (or in this case, two languages, Fulfulde together with Arabic) that serves the interests of an invader group and another that is historically external but provides a vehicle for mediation between the other two. In the case of Ilorin, Hausa seems to have acquired these functions, principally political and military, because its speakers, caught originally between the Yoruba and Fulani military powers, were employed by both of them in military and then political functions. Putting it briefly Fulfulde and Yoruba speakers could not communicate directly, but Hausa speakers associated with either side could—with one another and with their respective masters. As we shall see in chapters 6 and 7, vehicular Hausa and vehicular English were to play comparable roles in colonial Accra, and the emergence of the former was in all probability directly connected to the situation in Ilorin.

Domains, Goals, Networks, and Time

An analysis of a local multilingualism must explain whether or not, and if so in what sense, a complex, spatially defined social unit (such as any of the West African towns we have been discussing) can be meaningfully interpreted as speech communities in the sense of Hymes (1986: 54). This can best be done if the historical background, or how things got to be this way, is given much more prominence than it has had in the studies we have considered so far. A truly satisfactory analysis will integrate considerations of shifts in social boundaries over time in relation to changing cultural boundaries (by which we mean changes in what people talk about and talk about doing, and to whom), in relation to shifting linguistic boundaries, and in relation to geographical boundaries. At the least, the dynamic of the sociolinguistic process will not be revealed without considerable deconstruction of the essentially static concepts of domain and goal.

If a domain of language use involves the social relationships among those speakers of the language who use it for a particular activity, then any of these three terms—"language," "social group," and "activity"—may change, and the relationships among them may also change, reconfiguring the domain or altering it beyond recognition. For example, the defeat of the Guang in Akuapem by Akan speakers and the victors' insistence on the use of Akan in their courts caused a split in the political domain for the people of Larteh and Abiriw; the same Guang speakers probably continued to operate politically, but for certain purposes this subgroup of Guang speakers was incorporated into the political group of Akan speakers and had to use Akan in order to accomplish particular purposes and goals, which had not previously existed. This fact will have had implications for the political discourse functions remaining to the Guang language and the status relations among its participants. Similarly, with the establishment of schools and churches that use Akan or Ga, these languages acquired new domains, both written and oral, in which not only were new topics and new activities dealt with but also new social relations—of teacher and pupil, reader and writer, pastor and congregation, traditionalist and Christian—were created. The attitudes of speakers, both Christian and other, to the subject matter and activity of traditional religion also changed, as the very term "traditional" suggests. Alternatively, it could be said that the domains of religion and of practical knowledge expanded into entirely new subdomains, and the old subdomains of cult practices and traditional lore were in turn radically altered by being placed in contrast to the new. Such changes in the social and situational aspects of domain may in turn promote or accompany change in the language itself; those who today use Ga, Akan, or Yoruba in the context of the national political campaign do not use the language exactly as did those who practiced the art of politics before the advent of independence or before colonialism.

The sociolinguistic concept corresponding to the users of a language is the network, borrowed from communications theory. A language or language variety is considered to imply at least one interlinking set or network of users (the individual users who constitute nodes on the network), all communicating with one another directly or through other nodes, either to the complete exclusion of other people (a closed network) or, more likely in the case of natural language, with greater frequency than they communicate with others (Cooper 1982: 19) through the medium of the language variety in question. In theory, the users of the language need not constitute a socially organized group in any other sense. Specific channels, or communicating subsets of nodes, will employ the language in its various domains, communicating among one another much more often than they do with other channels (groups of speakers). Use of the language in the domestic domain, for example, is likely to occur over numerous discrete channels (corresponding to individual households) which often change in size and multiply or decline in number as people are born, die, and reassemble into new households. Another domain, such as a linguistically particular cult practice, might be used on just one channel that changes more slowly. Normally there will be considerable overlap among channels or sets of channels defined by domain. (That is, it is normal that the same people use a language in more than one domain.)

The communication network model of the one-language community has been used effectively for some diachronic purposes, notably by Milroy and Milroy (1992) in modeling the spread of linguistic innovation, that is, changes in formal linguistic boundaries. In an early paper, Fishman ([1965] 1972: 16) extended the model to describe a multilingual situation, referring to the group of speakers of a single language in use as a "speech network," and to the system of networks in a multilingual society to which the individual member has potential access as the "over-arching speech community." The difficulty with this concept is that it is unbounded. Since it includes all the languages spoken by members of the same community, in a cosmopolitan center—where many people have international contacts—it quickly includes the whole world. Hymes's (1986) distinction between speech community, as the primary social unit of analysis, and speech field and linguistic community, which represent potentialities, is clearly necessary. In the present context, it is also necessary to stress the local character of the speech community and the fact that it is not defined by a single community language, although reference to such a language may be an important characteristic. Thus, the Bulsa community of Accra will be defined somewhat differently, both geographically and linguistically, in terms of its second languages and their distribution among speakers from the Bulsa community of the Upper East Region. Furthermore, although networks that use the Buli language will unite most of the Accra Bulsa speech community, and most members may define the community with reference to Buli, it is not absolutely essential to speak that language to be a member of this community.

From a social-historical point of view, a major deficiency of the network model, whether applied to a unilingual or a multilingual community, is that it disregards the social relations among "nodes" that are crucial to the determination of domains. Even if we take nodes to represent classes of participants (such as mothers and children) and not individuals, all nodes are theoretically equal but all speakers (or socially defined types of speakers) certainly are not. A piece of language sent from speaker X to speaker Y does not carry the same information as the identical piece of language going in the other direction, if, for example, X is Y's grandfather or his prisoner. Status differentials might be included through some such metaphor as signal strength, but this does not help us actually to understand the difference. Similarly, to view human language as code fails to capture the inherent multivalency of linguistic semantics, encouraging us to forget that every speech act carries more than one message on many different levels.

The most serious difficulty is with the concept of communicative goal, for even more crucially than "code," it fails to recognize that the unstated goals of language activity are multileveled and symbolic and that language use is itself a symbolic act, not a value-neutral manipulation of signs. That is, with a concept of goals based too closely on communication theory, it is not possible to understand what is really going on in the dispute over the names of Labadi and Madina in English or very much at all about the configuration of multilingualism in Accra. The goals of language use in any domain, especially the indirect goals, are in a continual state of tension with the social relations expressed in that domain, for those goals always involve adjustments, such as the avoidance or provocation of conflict or the consolidation or reversal of the social relations by symbolic means. "Societal norms," and decisions whether to abide by them, are functions of this tension.

A dynamic sociolinguistics cannot be divorced from the culture of symbols that languages support, express, and embody. Even Milroy and Milroy (1992: 13), whose purposes are rather different from ours, found it necessary to introduce the concept of more or less prominent network markers, that is, social symbols, to explain how a phonological innovation spreads. Once this is recognized, it is possible to begin to deal with the sociolinguistic significance of variation in space and time. Clearly, the symbolic functions of language use can change with a geographical shift. For a Larteh-speaking father to choose to speak Akan to his children in Larteh, for example, would signify differently from making that choice in Akan-speaking Aburi or in Accra. Similarly, it is clear from Scotton's (1976) remarks that choosing to speak Hausa in Lagos means something rather different from choosing to speak it in Accra.

The concept of a neutral lingua franca is highly suspect. "Neutrality" presumably means that the choice cannot be construed as signifying any particular relationship among the speakers, but it is doubtful whether this can ever be entirely true of any language choice. In any case, a choice that is neutral in one domain or in that domain in a particular location may not be neutral at all for the same people doing something else or the same things in another place.

If we want to know *why* a given language choice signifies differently in Lagos and Accra, we need to take history into account. It is recognized, of course, that the choices between Yoruba and English or Ga and English exist because of British colonial and commercial domination in the past. Even strictly synchronic work such as Scotton's (1975, 1976, 1982) mentions this fact. The choices between Yoruba and Hausa, Ga and Hausa, and Akan and Larteh also have histories, and if these choices signify differently, that, too, is a consequence of history. To understand the dynamics of multilingualism in Accra, we need to understand how Accra has developed as an arena for linguistic communication.

Social Varieties and the "Pidgin" Problem

One of the most difficult problems in multilingual dynamics concerns the discreteness of the languages in the system. When can we say that the language being used by one or more groups of people in different situations is or is not the same language? It might seem that as long as the languages are extremely different and of clearly diverse origin, such as English, Hausa, and Ga, the problem can be ignored. Then, all but one of the languages must necessarily have moved, probably because groups of speakers, however small, have migrated; as we have seen, relocation means change, both socially and linguistically, as networks, domains, and goals are re-formed. In the Accra context, the most pressing problems arise with English, but they are by no means peculiar to it. Scotton (1975) described Lagos practice as dependent on a three-term system, of English, Pidgin English, and Yoruba. Apparently, her interviewers and informants had no problem in discriminating among three relevant varieties or in agreeing on the application of these labels. In Accra, however, English is perceived as having a very wide range of variation. Some forms may be labeled pidgin under some circumstances, but they do not seem to correspond to a consistent set of differences in linguistic tokens. In the following chapters I shall take the position that although the difference is certainly not value-neutral, it is not formally linguistic but rather a matter of who is speaking and where. I am in general agreement with the position adopted by LePage: "The perceived boundaries around groups, and around 'languages', will depend as much upon political and social factors and on cultural stereotypes as upon linguistic focussing or diffusion" (1992: 146). 'Languages' are abstractions from the linguistic behavior of groups.[22] Comparable problems exist with expatriate and second language varieties of Akan, Ga, and especially Hausa.

Within the shallow time depths we are dealing with, of less than a thousand years, language split is therefore a matter of cumulative perceptions of differences (and their assignment to social differences) more than the accumulation of formal changes themselves. This is why the boundaries between what language names actually name rarely coincide with the language boundaries defined by linguists. Either they are broader, as in the case of Arabic, or narrower, as in the case of speakers who refer to their language by the name of their own village. Sometimes they cut across linguists' boundaries, as in the case of Twi, which refers to some Akan dialects but not to a linguistically definable subgroup of them, and often they employ extra-linguistic criteria, as with Huela, the Ligbi spoken by historically non-Mande converts to Islam. We cannot avoid working with language names, but the boundaries between them are no more constant than the other boundaries to be studied.

3

Modern Multilingual Accra I

Accra is a city of about a million people, almost 8% of the country's population. The administrative region of Greater Accra, which covers the Accra plain, and includes the whole of the Ga-Dangme speaking area except Krobo, has a population of at least 1.5 million, about 12% of the country.[1] After the defeat of Great Accra near modern Ayawaso by the Akwamu in 1677, its successor by the shore grew slowly but fairly steadily, from an estimated 3,000 inhabitants (or 560 active men) in the 1690s to about 20,000 in 1881 (Marion Johnson 1977: 282, 283).[2] The population declined somewhat between 1881 and 1911 (Kilson 1974: 8), but since then the city has visibly grown immensely and has continued to do so at an accelerating rate, especially since the 1940s. Most of this growth has been the result of migration (Acquah [1954] 1972: 30; Ewusi 1977: 14).

Today, the city presents an expanse of building that stretches uninterrupted, except by a park and two cemeteries, from Dansoman between the Chemu lagoon and the sea on the west, to Labadi and the Trade Fair site by the Kpeeshi lagoon on the east, and north from the sea to the Airport Residential Area on the Dodowa road and Achimota village on the Nsawam road. At the peripheries, where the city still has a more open appearance, its quasi-rural character is owed to the fact that large tracts are reserved by the military establishments, the University of Ghana, Kotoka International Airport, and the Achimota Forest Reserve.

Like many urban agglomerations, Accra consists historically of a core settlement that has expanded into outlying areas, plus neighboring settlements that have either been surrounded by the expanding metropolis or grown to meet it. The stretch of coast between the Korle and the Kpeeshi lagoons includes three Ga-speaking towns, Accra, Osu, and Labadi (from west to east), which until this century were separated by unbuilt land and are still culturally and politically distinct. Accra occupied the land above the beach behind James and Ussher forts. Anyone who claims to

be a Ga from Accra belongs to a lineage that is part of one of the seven geographically and politically defined divisions (*akutsei*, sing. *akutso*) of Accra.[3] In the eyes
of Europeans, the seven divisions or quarters, were divided into two towns—called
English Accra (in Ga, Ŋléshì), or James Town, and Dutch Accra, or Kinka, respectively—according to the spheres of influence of the forts before the English took over
Fort Crèvecoeur from the Dutch in 1867 and renamed it Ussher Fort, after the British administrator of the Gold Coast at the time (Ward 1967: 238). As far as the
inhabitants themselves were concerned, however, it was either one town or seven,
depending on the focus. The distinction is now obsolete, although James Town and
Ŋleshi continue to be used as nearly synonymous toponyms for the area between the
Korle lagoon and Bannerman Road.

In 1826, Accra reached north as far as what became Horse Road (now Asafoatse
Nettey Road), three-quarters of a kilometer north of James Fort.[4] Osu occupied a small
area behind Christiansborg Castle and was known to Europeans as Danish Accra, at
least until the castle was bought by the British in 1850 (Ward 1967: 434). By 1883,
after the British had taken over and the colonial era was underway, High Street
extended from Ussher Fort to the Castle. The Christian sector, Salem, had been
established in Osu itself, so that the combined town extended eastward from the
present intersection of Castle Drive with the Labadi road and reached north to about
where Karl Quist Street crosses Salem Road (east of Osu Cemetery) today.

The area between Accra and Osu, which is now entirely taken up by commercial buildings (on the west) and government buildings and installations, including
Black Star Square, was first developed between 1885 and 1900 as a European residential area. Previously, Europeans had rented rooms in town (Acquah [1954] 1972:
23). The name Victoriaborg, presumably devised by the British to counter the Danish Christiansborg, is only occasionally heard today.

Labadi and Osu have acquired the appearance of a continuous settlement in the
past fifty years through the agency of government-sponsored construction. The South
Labadi Estate, along the beach between these towns, was begun after the earthquake
of 1939 (Acquah [1954] 1972: 28). However the Ring Road dual carriageway, begun
in the 1920s but not completed on the eastern side of the city until the 1960s, with
the commercial and industrial establishments around it, ensures that although there
is almost no empty land between them, the two towns are still separated. Labadi is
effectively bounded on the east by Giffard Road, the International Trade Fair site,
Kpeeshi lagoon, and military installations beyond them, so that it cannot merge with
Teshi to the east.

The settlements of Accra (James Town and Ussher Town), Osu, and Labadi still
keep a strongly residential and Ga-speaking character. The spaces between them, as
we have seen, are mainly nonresidential and attract a very mixed population of workers, among whom Ga-speaking people are strongly represented but nevertheless probably constitute a minority. These newer nontraditional, nonresidential areas constitute real barriers to social assimilation and have served to promote the preservation
of the original towns as cultural entities, even though each has undoubtedly changed
in character in the course of the present century. Accra and Osu were united (by the
British) under a single municipal authority in 1896. In 1945 the authority was extended
eastward to include Labadi, as well as the Ga towns Teshi and Nungua, and in 1963,

after independence, to Tema fifteen miles to the east (Kilson 1974: 8). After several subsequent realignments, the Accra Urban Council area now includes Accra, Osu, and Labadi. Physically and perceptually, the city of Accra consists of Accra proper—or what is commonly referred to as Central Accra with its northern suburbs—plus Osu and more recently Labadi and the filled-in spaces between and around them.

With the development of Riponsville (another rarely heard name, used by Kilson 1974) between Horse Road and Derby Avenue, Korle Dudor (*Kɔɔle dudɔ* "Korle's water pot") to the northwest around Knutsford Avenue and Hansen Road, and Okaishi to the northeast on the other side of the Nsawam road, Accra expanded directly to the north. These areas, between Horse Road (Asafoatse Nettey Road) and Kinbu Road (i.e., *kíŋ bu* "government well"),[5] formerly Rowe Road, began to be developed in the early years of this century and were still being built on in the 1930s. They were never as solidly Ga as the original Accra, with settlements of strangers along the eastern edge of Riponsville (Zongo Lane) and in Okaishi—including the "Moham-medan Village" of 1903 (Acquah [1954] 1972: 25), now Cow Lane—bordering what became the major commercial and market district. There were large numbers of Yoruba trading in this part of Accra before 1970, when the abrupt enforcement of immigration regulations caused most of them to leave.

Areas of settlement to the north of Kinbu Road have always been populated by a mixture of Ga and others. Adabraka (from Hausa, ultimately from Arabic *albarka* "blessing"), which was first settled by Hausa and other northerners who kept beef cattle, was developed by the colonial government, in the wake of the bubonic plague in 1907 as a residential suburb in a strip between the Nsawam road (Liberty Avenue) and Boundary Road (now Kojo Thompson Road) and from Castle Road north to Farrar Avenue. Tudu, a mixed residential and commercial area that had many non-Ga from the beginning, developed southward from Adabraka in the 1930s and 1940s. To this day these "strangers" developments on the hill, which are now also home to large numbers of Ga, are separated from the older urban core by Accra Police Headquar-ters, built in 1915 (Gillespie 1955: 50) and the railway station, as well as numerous commercial establishments large and small.[6]

Expansion of the city across the lagoon to the west was also at least partly effected through government agency, following natural or social disaster. There have always been fishing villages along the beach, but the planned suburb Korle Gonno (*Kɔɔle gɔŋ nɔ* "on Korle's hill") was established—like Adabraka, in the second decade of this century, following the 1907 plague—and expanded further when Korle Bu ("Korle's well") Hospital was built to the north of it in the 1920s. Unlike Tudu and Adabraka, Korle Gonno, Korle Bu, and also Mamprobi (which was developed im-mediately to the west after the earthquake of 1939) drew their original populations from Central Accra. In 1953 Korle Gonno was found to be 68% Ga, the rest being mainly Akan and Ewe. North of Korle Bu, the strangers' section of Sabon Zongo (Hausa for "new camp") was developed for the Hausa and associated community in about 1933 to relieve the congestion in Central Accra and Tudu (Acquah [1954] 1972: 40–41).

The city had begun to develop beyond its northern municipal boundary with the establishment of the Police Training Depot on the Nsawam road near Tesano in 1928 (Gillespie 1955: 62) and Achimota College before that. Farther west, Kaneshie (Ga *kané shî* "under the lamp," in reference to its beginnings as a night market) grew into a sizable settlement. Closer to the city but still quite separate, Nima, Kanda, and Maamobi existed as villages of Fulani and Hausa ranchers and began to take their present sprawling forms in the late 1940s and 1950s, when many former soldiers settled around the capital (Burrows 1987: appendix 3). Nima land originally belonged to Osu and Labadi, not Accra, and was first acquired for cattle rearing in the 1920s. The identity of the original lessee is disputed, but according to the Fulani chief of Nima (in 1986) its name is derived from a Fulfulde word [neγema] "fertile land." It was incorporated into the city of Accra in 1953 (Acquah [1954] 1972: 41, 105). The creation of the Ring Road dual carriageway in the 1950s permanently separated the mixed but mainly southern settlement areas like Asylum Down (built up in the 1950s, below the ridge occupied by the Accra Psychiatric Hospital and later also the Roman Catholic cathedral) from the rapidly growing suburbs of mainly northern migrants to the north of it. Meanwhile, settlements along the road to Nsawam, such as Kpehe (Ga *kpee hé* "meeting place") and Alaajo (Ga *alá àjo* "they sing and dance"), some of which began as settlements of former (non-Ga) slaves (Christaller 1889), were engulfed in Accra New Town, which is very mixed both ethnically and economically.

West and East Ridge were established as European residential areas in the 1920s, permanently separated from expanding Accra by the large open space between Kojo Thompson (formerly Boundary) Road and George Padmore (formerly Barnes) Road, now occupied by the National Archives, Social Advance Institute, museums, Accra Technical Institute, and other organizations. The areas are capped by the hospitals on Castle Road to the north and the former Turf Club and the Osu Cemetery to the south. Ringway Estate and North Labone Estate, continuing this affluent, low-density residential belt north of Osu, did not appear until the late 1950s and 1960s, although development of the airport residential area had begun earlier. A relatively large proportion of the residents of these areas come from other countries and continents, but as a whole they are distinguished from residents of other, older parts of the city more by economic status than by ethnic origin; doctors, lawyers, successful business people, and senior officers of the public and civil services from all over Ghana live there, as well as diplomats and representatives of international organizations.

In sum, there are differences of potential linguistic significance between areas of settlement. It is not clear that the Ga remain a majority in Central Accra, but at least they maintain a strong presence, especially in the area below Ussher Fort. The Ga character of the areas of first expansion northward is somewhat dilute, but it is strong across the lagoon to the west; and Chorkor beyond Mamprobi is still in many ways a Ga fishing village, even though surrounded by suburban sprawl. In later settlement to the north and west, the Ga element is merely one among many.

Further, each successive stage has been insulated from the last by a commercial belt, inhabited by non-Ga and often nonsouthern Ghanaian Africans; by a physical barrier (either natural like the Korle lagoon or man-made like the Ring Road); or in the case of more affluent and originally European developments, by public facilities of various kinds. Although the character of some sections is in the process of changing—for example, West Ridge, which is no longer residential (as the first European residential area, Victoriaborg, ceased to be long since) and is gradually being rebuilt—

the basic pattern is being preserved. The affluent sectors apart, the settlement pattern of Accra historically and spatially distinguishes Ga and non-Ga in the first instance, southern Ghanaian (Ga-Akan-Ewe) and other West Africans in the second.

These divisions and separations are far from creating ethnic ghettoes. Nevertheless, we propose that Accra between the Korle lagoon and Independence Avenue and south of Ring Road constitutes an arena of social interaction, in the sense that there are very many frequently operated networks within that area but relatively few that cross to the north. This is the most congested area of the city, and we have seen that there are several important divisions within it. We might expect, for example, that communication within Central Accra is particularly dense, between Central Accra and Adabraka less so. In this chapter, we shall first examine how multilingualism is employed in Central Accra, with a view to what it may reveal about linguistic networks that involve both the traditionally indigenous population and others, mainly migrants from adjoining parts of Ghana, who live and work in the area. In the next chapter, we shall examine multilingualism among migrant groups living in the outer city and consider what our findings imply for networking, both actual and potential, among these urban migrants and between them and the inhabitants of the inner city.

The Languages of the Inner City

Ga [gã`] is the name of the people indigenous to Accra, of their language, and of Accra itself in the Ga language. Accra is also called Ga Mashi [máʃì], in contrast to other names (now obsolescent) such as Ga Wɔɔ, which referred to other parts of the Ga-speaking country (Field 1940: 142). The 1960 census figures gave the population of Accra as 337,828 and of Central Accra, meaning James Town and Ussher Town (Ga Mashi) plus Riponsville, at 25,887, of whom 58% of the total, or 54% of the adults, were Ga (quoted in Kilson 1974: 8). Most of the non-Ga were probably in Riponsville. In 1953, Ussher Town had been 91% Ga (Acquah [1954] 1972: 40).

The population of the city as a whole has almost tripled since 1960, and the old inner city has become noticeably more congested.[7] There are many tales of people who are using rooms in shifts, but this is not a particularly new situation; in 1953 in Ussher Town, which had the highest population density in the city, 82% of households were reported to occupy one room *or less*, the average household consisting of 6.2 persons and the average number of persons per room being 4.3 (Acquah [1954] 1972: 49, 50). As Acquah remarked, this "suggests that the majority of the inhabitants of Accra lack a home life," a situation of potential significance for the dynamics of multilingualism.

Unfortunately, no census since 1960 has collected information on which an estimate of the proportion of Ga in Central Accra or any section of it could be based. Many Ga people believe that it has decreased as Ga who prosper move out and other people are attracted into the area by relatively cheap accommodations. The Ga are still very much a presence, but even in 1960 they were a majority of adults by only 4%.

I have approached multilingualism in Central Accra through surveys made in and around the Salaga market in 1989 and 1992, in which data were collected on the language repertoires, contexts of language acquisition, and patterns of language use of people working in and around the market, both residents of the area and others. The Salaga market, in Ussher Town near Atukpai and the Central Post Office, has long been the major in-town fish and meat market. Virtually everyone selling in the market on the days the interviewer visited was questioned. These data are supplemented by field observations made at various times, by a survey of an Ussher Town lineage made in the early 1970s, and by the data and observations of other writers. The aim is to show the character of language use in Central Accra from the 1970s into the early 1990s.

The purpose of the second Salaga market survey was to provide some sort of check on the first, in view of its nonrandom selection method. Both are regarded as most significant where their results coincide. On the one hand, it seems unwarranted to give any historical significance to the differences between two surveys less than three years apart in the conditions under which they were made. On the other hand, in both years virtually everyone present and willing to talk was interviewed. Trade liberalization in the intervening years had produced a burst of commercial activity in 1992, which may have attracted a more diverse group into the market. This could account for the generally very small but consistent tendency to greater diversity, multilingualism, and polyglotism that, as will be shown, appears in the later group.

The 1989 survey was conducted among 153 people selling in Salaga market (100) and in shops around the market (53) (table 3.1). Fifty people, or just under one-third, were men, but they accounted for almost 74% of those who worked in shops; only 11% of those who sold in the market were men. Over 86% of the women, in contrast, sold in the market. In the 1992 survey of 152 people, which included very few shop sellers, the sex imbalance was even greater: only 20 people, 13% of the total, were male.[8]

In the 1989 group, those selling in shops tended to be somewhat older than the market sellers. Half the women selling in shops were aged forty or over, compared to a little over a third (36%) of the women selling in the market. More than 60% of the men selling in the market were under the age of thirty (seven individuals), as were 51% of the men selling in shops. The men thus tended to be younger than the women, and this is also true of the 1992 group. The figures for the two cohorts are very similar: in 1989, 36% of the women were forty or older, as were 22% of the men; in 1992 the figures were 30% and 20%, respectively. In 1989, the largest age group of men was twenty to twenty-four years old (fifteen individuals, 30%), but in 1992 this was no larger than the group aged twenty-five to twenty-nine (five and six individuals, or 25% and 30%, respectively). In 1989, the largest age group of women was thirty to thirty-four years old (21%), but in 1992 it was thirty-five to thirty-nine (18%). Thus, for both sexes the 1992 group tended to be slightly older than the 1989 group. However, in both groups, approximately 70% of the men and 57% of the women were between twenty and thirty years old. We may surmise that many were assisting an older female relative. Since the relatively small size of the male groups probably reflected the character of the population, it seems that women's trading careers spread out over more of their lives than men's do.

Similar proportions of men and women had had one to nine years of schooling, about 40% in 1989 and 50% or slightly higher in 1992 (table 3.2). However, the sexes differed considerably at the extremes of the educational scale. In 1989, about half

TABLE 3.1   Responses to Salaga Market Survey, according to Sex and Age

| | 1989 | | | | | | 1992 | |
| | Market (n = 100) | | Shop (n = 53) | | Total (n = 153) | | (n = 152) | |
Age	M	F	M	F	M	F	M	F
15–19	1	4	2	1	3	5	2	16
%	9.1	4.5	5.1	7.1	6.0	4.9	10.0	12.1
20–24	4	6	11	1	15	7	5	14
%	36.4	6.7	28.2	7.1	30.0	6.8	25.0	10.6
25–29	2	12	7	3	9	15	6	21
%	18.2	13.5	17.9	21.4	18.0	14.6	30.0	15.9
30–34	1	22	7	0	8	22	2	18
%	9.1	24.7	17.9	0.0	16.0	21.4	10.0	13.6
35–39	1	13	3	2	4	15	1	24
%	9.1	14.6	7.7	14.3	8.0	14.6	5.0	18.2
40–44	1	9	3	5	4	14	1	10
%	9.1	10.1	7.7	35.7	8.0	13.6	5.0	7.6
45–49	1	10	1	0	2	10	0	11
%	9.1	11.2	2.6	0.0	4.0	9.7	0.0	8.3
50–54	0	2	1	1	1	3	1	6
%	0.0	2.2	2.6	7.1	2.0	2.9	5.0	4.5
55–59	0	6	4	0	4	6	1	11
%	0.0	6.7	10.3	0.0	8.0	5.8	5.0	8.3
60+	0	5	0	1	0	6	1	2
%	0.0	5.6	0.0	7.1	0.0	5.8	5.0	1.5
Total	11	89	39	14	50	103	20	132
%	11.0	89.0	73.6	26.4	32.7	67.3	13.2	86.8

the women but only a third of the men had never been to school. In 1992 the numbers of the unschooled were down, to 40% for women, but the difference between the sexes was greater. The numbers of men and women who had had ten or more years of school were small, but in both years they included approximately 22% more men than women.

It is popularly believed that Accra and its markets are shifting to Akan as the main language of trade and of interaction beyond, or even within, ethnolinguistic groups. The variety of Akan most used may be different in different area markets. It is commonly said, for example, that Fante is the main language of the Kaneshie market. It is therefore of interest to know not only how many of these Central Accra market people considered themselves indigenous Ga, and what proportions of Ga and others actually lived in the Ga Mashi area, but also how this was reflected in the linguistic practices of both Ga and other people.

TABLE 3.2   Years of Formal School, 1989 and 1992

Age	None		1–3 Yrs.		4–6 Yrs.		7–9 Yrs.		10–12 Yrs.		More	
	M	F	M	F	M	F	M	F	M	F	M	F
1989												
15–19	2	2	0	1	0	0	0	2	1	0	0	0
20–24	3	4	0	0	1	0	7	3	4	0	0	0
25–29	3	3	0	1	0	0	3	7	2	3	1	1
30–34	3	9	0	1	0	1	1	8	4	3	0	0
35–39	1	9	0	1	0	0	2	5	1	0	0	0
40–44	0	8	0	2	2	2	3	1	1	1	0	0
45–49	1	8	0	0	0	2	0	0	1	0	0	0
50–54	1	1	0	0	0	0	0	1	0	0	0	1
55–59	2	5	0	1	0	0	2	0	0	0	0	0
60+	0	4	0	1	0	0	0	1	0	0	0	0
Total	16	51	0	8	1	5	18	28	14	7	1	2
Males	32.0%		0.0%		2.0%		36.0%		28.0%		2.0%	
Females	49.5%		7.8%		27.2%		4.9%		6.8%		1.9%	
1992												
15–19	0	0	0	0	1	2	0	13	1	1	0	0
20–24	1	3	0	0	1	2	2	9	1	0	0	0
25–29	0	3	0	2	0	0	3	13	3	3	0	0
30–34	0	5*	0	2	0	3	0	5	1	6	1	0
35–39	0	7†	0	2	0	2	1	10	0	4	0	0
40–44	0	4	0	1	0	2	0	3	1	1	0	0
45–49	0	10†	0	0	0	0	0	2	0	0	0	0
50–54	1	4	0	0	0	1	0	1	0	0	0	0
55–59	0	8	0	0	0	0	1	0	0	0	0	0
60+	0	9	0	0	0	0	1	0	0	0	0	0
Total	2	53	0	7	2	12	8	56	6	15	1	0
Males	10.0%		0.0%		10.0%		40.0%		30.0%		5.0%	
Females	40.2%		5.3%		9.1%		42.4%		11.4%		0.0%	

*Includes one woman who attended Koranic school.

†Includes one who attended adult education classes.

Our questionnaire provided two criteria for gauging ethnicity: the place the re-spondent claimed to "come from" (Ga *nèègbɛ ojɛ*, Akan *wófiri hen* "where are you from?") and the language(s) of the respondent's parents. In Ghana, a person's claim to come from a certain place, to claim a "hometown," does not necessarily refer to that person's birthplace nor to a place of protracted residence but rather signals cul-tural and political allegiance to a local polity. A single place may thus be the site of more than one such polity, and it is possible, though not normal, to "come from" a

TABLE 3.3   Regions of Origin

Region	1989	(N = 153)	1992	(N = 152)
Greater Accra*	103	67.3%	91	59.9%
Central Accra	62	40.5%	43	28.3%
Eastern	20	13.1%	15	9.9%
Central	9	5.9%	12	7.9%
Ashanti	3	2.0%	2	1.3%
Western	0	0.0%	3	2.0%
Volta	14	9.2%	20	13.2%
Outside Ghana	4	2.6%	8	5.3%

*Figures for Greater Accra include those for Central Accra.

place in which one has never been. Such allegiance is usually viewed as a natural function of kinship. Among the matrilineal Akan, one "comes from" wherever one's mother "comes from"; but among the Ga and most northern groups, one is usually considered to "come from" where one's father "came from."[9] Since this "hometown" is associated with a language, we would expect a strong but not absolute (see note 9) relationship between these two criteria. The evidence is that the relationship does indeed exist and that although the Ga are not quite an absolute majority of the 1992 group, they are by far the largest single ethnic group in both surveys. However, people who claim Central Accra itself as their ethnic homeland are not a majority in either. The criterion giving the largest proportion of ethnic Ga is that of at least one Ga-speaking parent: 75% in 1989 and 65% in 1992 (table 3.5).

Table 3.3 displays the distribution of "hometowns" according to Region, and table 3.4 displays the distribution of parental languages in all cases (90% in 1989; 76% in 1992) in which it was claimed that both parents had the same language.[10] The traditionally Ga-speaking area is entirely contained within the Greater Accra

TABLE 3.4   The Language of Both Parents

Language	1989	(N = 153)	1992	(N = 152)
Ga	101	66.0%	70	46.1%
Dangme	2	1.3%	11	7.2%
Akan (Twi)	15	9.8%	6	3.9%
Akan (Fante)	2	1.3%	3	2.0%
Hill Guang	1	0.7%	3	2.0%
Ewe	14	9.2%	19	12.5%
Hausa	1	0.7%	1	0.7%
Other	2	1.3%	3	2.0%
Total Linguistically Matched Pairs of Parents				
	138	90.2%	116	76.3%

TABLE 3.5   Ethnic Ga, by Various Criteria

	1989		1992	
Origin from Greater Accra	103	67.3%	91	59.9%
2 Ga-speaking parents	101	66.0%	70	46.1%
1 Ga-speaking parent	114	74.5%	98	64.5%
Ga-speaking father	98	64.1%	86	56.6%

Region. The only other linguistic area included in this Region is the Dangme, except for the Krobo dialect of Dangme, which is spoken mainly in the Eastern Region. Table 3.5 displays the proportion of the sample that might be identified as Ga according to these various criteria. All figures are significantly lower in the 1992 group, indicating a more mixed population both in its geographical sources and in respondents' backgrounds, but only one figure, for those with two Ga-speaking parents in 1992 (tables 3.4 and 3.5) is below 50%. Significantly, in view of the Ga emphasis on patrilineal descent and inheritance (Robertson 1990: 48), the figure for Ga-speaking fathers in 1992 (57%) is closest to the 1960 census figure for Ga adults in Central Accra. That the 1992 group was generally more mixed is also suggested by the smaller number who gave the same language for both parents (table 3.4).

There seems to be no significant difference between the two groups in the proportion of people originating from the Akan-speaking Regions, namely, the Eastern Region (which also includes most Hill Guang speakers), the Central Region and the Ashanti Region but the 1992 group had slightly more people from the Volta Region and from outside Ghana. In 1989 all respondents from the Volta Region had two Ewe-speaking parents, but in 1992 one did not. Discrepancies between the region of ethnic origin (or allegiance) and the parents' language can be accounted for by the linguistic diversity of the parents, which was more prevalent in the 1992 group: in 1989, 91% of respondents reported the same language for both parents, but in 1992 only 76% did (table 3.4), which is still, of course, a considerable majority.

There appears to be no significant difference between the 1989 and 1992 surveys concerning the region of birthplace and place of current residence (table 3.6). In both cases, approximately 75% were born in the Greater Accra Region and almost 100% were living there at the time of the surveys, while 40% were born in Central Accra itself and virtually the same number lived there. Even fewer people were actually born in the Eastern, Central, and Volta Regions than claimed to come from there (tables 3.3 and 3.6), whereas the reverse is true for the Greater Accra Region, as is to be expected if many of the non-Ga are the descendants of recent migrants. In 1989, the numbers who claimed Central Accra as a homeland (table 3.3), birthplace, and place of residence were very close (respectively, sixty-two, sixty-one, and sixty-eight, all falling between 40% and 45%), indicating perhaps a static population; but the comparatively low claim of Central Accra as a homeland in 1992 (28%, compared to 40% for each of birthplace and place of residence) may indicate that in the past generation or two the original Ga population has been replaced by others to some extent (about 12%), especially by Ga from other parts of the Greater Accra Region.

TABLE 3.6   Regions of Birthplace and Residence

Region	Birthplace		Residence	
	1989 (N = 153)	1992 (N = 152)	1989 (N = 153)	1992 (N = 152)
Greater Accra*	116 75.8%	114 75.0%	153 100%	150 98.7%
Central Accra	61 39.9%	61 40.1%	68 44.4%	61 40.1%
Eastern	15 9.8%	14 9.2%	0	0
Central	3 2.0%	5 3.3%	0	0
Ashanti	4 2.6%	2 1.3%	0	0
Western	3 2.0%	1 0.7%	0	0
Volta	11 7.2%	1 8.6%	0	0

*Figures for Greater Accra include those for Central Accra.

To sum up, the market sellers are predominantly women, spread over a wide age range, about half of whom (but somewhat more of the few men) have been to school. The majority are ethnic Ga and reside in or near old downtown Accra, but they are by no means homogeneous.

If the Ga are the dominant ethnic-linguistic residential group in the market and its neighborhood, we might expect them to be less polyglot than other people, and this is partly the situation. Only people from the Greater Accra Region, who, as shown above, were almost all Ga, reported being wholly monoglot, that is, able to speak or understand only one language to any degree (table 3.7).[11] However, although such people accounted for a quarter of the 1989 group, there were no monoglots at all in the 1992 group. Even in 1989, most people had at least a little of two or three languages, and in 1992 a majority claimed three or four, while the average rose significantly, from 2.2 to 3.6.[12] In 1989, non-Ga claimed to speak significantly more languages than the Ga, averaging 3.0, with no monoglots, and a majority (54%) claimed some degree of ability in at least three languages; but there was no significant difference between Ga and non-Ga in 1992.

However, when we look at how many languages respondents felt they handled with some confidence (table 3.8), we find a more clear-cut opposition between Ga and non-Ga and little difference between the two survey years. Approximately two-thirds of the Ga claimed to speak only one language well, although in 1992 the number declined slightly and the number who claimed to speak two languages well went up. The average, however, actually decreased. Although the amount of decrease is tiny, from 1.5 to 1.4, it is the difference between a majority that speaks at least two languages and a majority that speaks only one. The average number of languages

TABLE 3.7   Number of Languages in Which Respondents Claim Competence of Any Kind

No. of Languages	Respondents from Greater Accra Region				Respondents from Other Regions			
	1989	(N = 103)	1992	(N = 91)	1989	(N = 50)	1992	(N = 61)
1	27	26.2%	0		0		0	
2	40	38.8%	8	8.8%	12	24.0%	5	8.2%
3	28	27.2%	40	44.4%	27	54.0%	26	42.6%
4	6	5.8%	28	30.8%	8	16.0%	20	32.8%
5	1	1.0%	13	14.3%	1	2.0%	10	16.4%
6	1	1.0%	2	2.2%	0		0	
7	0		0		1	2.0%	0	
Average	2.2		3.6		3.0		3.6	

the non-Ga thought they spoke well was significantly higher, 2.0 in 1989 and 1.9 in 1992. In both years, over 60% of the non-Ga thought they spoke two or more languages well.

Besides Ga, the main languages spoken were Akan, especially the varieties known as Twi, and English, with smaller numbers speaking Dangme, Ewe, and Hausa. These languages represent the major first languages of the population surveyed, plus the two major non-Ghanaian lingua francas of the country. A number of other languages, which vary widely in geographical provenance, genetic relationship, and international prominence, were spoken by a few individuals. In 1989 these included French and Yoruba, spoken by two people each, and Fulfulde, Krio, and Likpe, spoken by one each. In 1992 five people claimed to speak "Anago," probably indicating a Togolese dialect of Yoruba; four claimed to speak Hill Guang; and two each claimed Arabic, Dagbani, and French. Frafra (a Gur language related to Dagbani), Yoruba (which is, of course, a Nigerian language), and "Zugu" (the name of a town in the north of the

TABLE 3.8   Number of Languages Respondents Claimed to Know Well

No. of Languages	Respondents from Greater Accra Region				Respondents from Other Regions			
	1989	(N = 103)	1992	(N = 91)	1989	(N = 50)	1992	(N = 61)
1	69	67.0%	58	63.7%	19	38.0%	19	31.1%
2	23	22.3%	29	31.9%	14	28.0%	31	50.8%
3	7	6.8%	4	4.4%	12	24.0%	11	18.0%
4	2	1.9%	0		4	8.0%	0	
5	1	1.0%	0		0		0	
6	1	1.0%	0		0		0	
Average	1.5		1.4		2.0		1.9	

Republic of Benin, which denotes both a Bariba-speaking and a Dendi-speaking community)[13] had one speaker each.

The figures for speakers of the major languages, without attention to the degree or kind of competence claimed (table 3.9), indicate that all the more important languages had more speakers in 1992 than in 1989.[14] This is presumably a function of the generally higher rate of polyglotism noted above. Ga was claimed by well over 90% in 1989 but by 100% in 1992. Speakers of the varieties of Akan known as Twi were well over half the group in 1989 but over 80% in 1992.[15] When those few Fante speakers who did not also claim to speak Twi are added, Akan speakers totaled 68% in 1989 but 90% in 1992. Although the figures for Ewe, Dangme, and Hausa remained small in 1992, they more than doubled for Ewe and Dangme and almost doubled for Hausa.

The same pattern applies to English, with an overall rise in the number of speakers from about half the group in 1989 to almost 80% in 1992, rivaling Twi. However, there was an important difference between Akan and English, which we shall see repeated in other groups. Respondents were asked whether they thought they spoke each language well or a little or they only understood it. In effect, they were being asked whether they had a passive ("only understand") or an active competence in each language and, if active, to evaluate their competence according to whether they were confident of their ability to use it effectively whenever its use was in their experience appropriate (spoke it "well") or not (spoke it "a little"). Respondents usually thought they had an active competence in any language they claimed to know at all, and the numbers who claimed merely to understand were insignificant, except in the case of English (tables 3.9–3.12). English was also the only language for which the 1989 figures indicated a significant difference between market and shop sellers: 39% of the market sellers but 70% of the shop sellers were English speakers. The 1992 figure is not radically higher than the latter. English is also the only language for which, despite the small number of male respondents, especially in 1992, there seems to be a significant difference between the sexes, with more men claiming to speak it to some degree and less likely to claim passive knowledge (table 3.11).

TABLE 3.9   The Languages and Their Speakers:
All Degrees of Competence, Active and Passive

	1989		1992	
Ga	144	94.1%	152	100.0%
Akan: Total	104*	68.0%	140†	90.1%
Twi	86	56.2%	124	81.6%
Fante	19	12.4%	22	14.5%
English	76	49.7%	119	78.3%
Ewe	20	13.1%	42	27.6%
Dangme	8	5.2%	37	24.3%
Hausa	14	9.2%	26	17.1%

*One respondent spoke both Twi and Fante.

†Five respondents spoke both Twi and Fante.

TABLE 3.10   The Languages and Their Speakers: Confident Claims
to Active Competence

	1989 (N = 153)			1992 (N = 152)		
	M (n = 50)	F (n = 103)	Total	M (n = 20)	F (n = 132)	Total
Ga	42	91	133	14	118	132
	84.0%	88.3%	86.9%	70.0%	89.4%	86.8%
Akan						
Total	21	28	49	4	32	36
	42.0%	27.2%	32.0%	20.0%	24.2%	27.3%
Twi	18	24	42	4	23	27
	36.0%	23.3%	27.5%	20.0%	16.7%	17.8%
Fante	3	5	8	0	9	9
	6.0%	4.9%	5.2%	0.0%	6.8%	5.9%
English	23	13	36	4	10	14
	46.0%	12.6%	23.5%	20.0%	7.6%	9.2%
Ewe	6	12	18	1	20	21
	12.0%	11.7%	11.8%	5.0%	15.2%	13.8%
Dangme	1	6	7	2	16	18
	1.0%	5.8%	0.7%	10.0%	12.1%	11.8%
Hausa	3	6	9	4	5	9
	6.0%	5.8%	5.9%	20.0%	3.8%	5.9%

TABLE 3.11   Speakers of English, according to Sex and
Trading Domain

	Any Claim at All		Confident	
1989				
Market				
M (11)	6	54.5%	3	27.3%
F (89)	33	37.0%	10	11.2%
Total	39	39.0%	13	13.0%
Shops				
M (39)	29	74.4%	20	51.3%
F (14)	8	57.1%	3	21.4%
Total	37	71.2%	23	44.2%
Total				
M (50)	35	70.0%	23	46.0%
F (103)	41	39.8%	13	12.6%
Total	76	49.7%	36	23.5%
1992				
M (20)	20	100.0%	4	20.0%
F (132)	99	75.0%	10	7.6%
Total	119	78.3%	14	9.2%

TABLE 3.12   The Social Context of English Acquisition

	1989: 76 Speakers		1992: 119 Speakers	
School	69	90.8%	94	79.0%
Other	7	9.2%	23*	19.3%
Home	0	0.0%	2	1.7%
Friends	1†	1.3%	3	2.5%
Work	1†	1.3%	14††	11.8%
Friends + work	2	2.6%	4	3.4%
Home + work	3	4.0%	0	0.0%
Unknown	0	0.0%	2	1.7%

*Eleven claimed passive knowledge only.

†Claimed passive knowledge only.

††Included no confident speakers.

In view of the higher educational standard of men in these groups (table 3.2) and the association between English acquisition and schooling (table 3.12), this is not unexpected.

The picture provided by the figures for confident claims to active knowledge of various languages is somewhat different (table 3.10). The figures for 1992 are not significantly higher than in 1989 for any language (excluding Dangme, for which the numbers are very small), while the figures for Akan are somewhat lower and those for English very much lower. It is also true of both English and Akan, which emerge as the major second languages, that the difference between those who claim any competence at all and those who claim them with confidence is huge: well over 25% in 1989 and 60% or more in 1992. In 1989 these languages were spoken with confidence by significantly more men than women, especially English. In 1992, a higher proportion of men claimed to speak Hausa and English (but not Akan) with confidence and a lower proportion claimed to speak Ga well; however, the number of men included was far too small, and the absolute number of Hausa speakers was also too small, for these differences to be significant. In 1989 the percentages of both sexes (but especially men) who had had ten years or more of schooling was rather higher than the percentages confident of their English, but in 1992 they were lower by about the same amount. The significance of the differences is doubtful, and the numbers may in any case reflect differences in the perception of what constitutes adequate competence.

Despite the large numbers who claimed to speak Akan and English (table 3.9), Ga emerged as by far the strongest language in terms of confident speakers (Table 3.10). Even if the differences between the 1989 and 1992 surveys were to be interpreted chronologically, as reflecting change in the pattern of multilingualism in the market and surrounding area, then Central Accra would be seen as becoming more multilingual (in the sense of acquisition of low-level competence in more languages by more people), but no other language yet posed a serious threat to Ga as the main community and trade language of the area.

Another way of inspecting the strength of Ga is to examine the competence claimed in it more closely, both among natives of the Greater Accra Region (for most of whom we expect it to be the dominant language) and the rest of the population (which we expect to speak it as a second language). There was no significant difference between the groups of Greater Accra speakers: 98% were confident of their competence in 1989 and 97% in 1992. Among those regarded as non-Ga, not only was the proportion of active speakers larger in 1992 (at 97% compared to 78% in 1989) but also their opinion of their own competence was higher (at 72% confident speakers compared to 62% in 1989), a contrast with the apparent decrease in confidence regarding other language competencies. Again we find that the position of Ga is at least not deteriorating. In 1992, only 1% claimed merely passive control, compared to 8% in 1989.

Any incipient trend toward a shift ought to show up in the usage patterns of the main languages. In an urban environment (especially a linguistically mixed one such as Accra), nondomestic social domains of linguistic interaction like work, church, school, and leisure activities depend on networks of linguistic contacts that are not necessarily closely interlinked with the networks of kin and affines (which are important to domestic and certain kinds of ritual domains) or with one another, although they may in fact turn out to be so linked. We might therefore expect the use of particular languages to be distributed according to extradomestic fields of use, reflecting different networks of users. It turned out that extradomestic domains were not linguistically distinguished from one another. Except that a number of non-Akan respondents in 1989 used Akan only at school (table 3.13), whereas in 1992 a relatively large proportion claimed to use it only in selling (table 3.14), the great majority of speakers used these languages in several domains.

Neither Ga nor Akan was reported as being limited to use only among kin, or kin and friends, by any group. It is likely, of course, that the kin, friends, and work networks overlapped considerably, especially since women, who constituted large majorities in the survey groups, strongly tend to associate with their female relatives and friends in trading (Robertson 1990: 134). Furthermore, Ga domestic arrangements have never been spatially exclusive. Women frequently continue to live with their mothers and sisters after marriage and men with their brothers (Kilson 1974: 30; Robertson 1990: 57), a pattern that also occurs among the Akan (Oppong 1974: 32). On the one hand, a room in a house may be occupied by the heir of its original possessor, so that the occupants of a house are frequently only remotely related or not at all. Consequently, children may grow up in domestic situations that involve

TABLE 3.13   Contexts of Use of Akan in 1989 (86 Speakers)

	Ga* (*n* = 52)		Akan† (*n* = 35)		Others (*n* = 9)	
Kin + external	6	11.5%	18	72.0%	1	11.1%
External only	46	88.5%	7	28.0%	8	88.9%
School only††	7	13.5%	1	2.9%	2	22.2%

*Respondents who claim to originate from the Greater Accra Region.

†Respondents who claim to originate from the Eastern, Central, and Ashanti regions.

††Figures for respondents who report using Akan only in school are included in "External only."

TABLE 3.14   Contexts of Use of Akan in 1992 (124 Speakers)

	Ga* (n = 79)		Akan† (n = 24)		Others (n = 21)	
Kin + external	10	12.7%	15	62.5%	4	19.0%
External only	68	86.1%	9	37.5%	17	81.0%
Work/commercial ††	15	19.0%	1	4.2%	4	19.0%
Unknown	1	1.3%	0	0.0%	0	0.0%

*Respondents who claim to originate from the Greater Accra Region.

†Respondents who claim to originate from the Eastern, Central, and Ashanti regions.

††Figures for work/commercial domains are included in "External only."

numerous nonkin or very distant kin. Close kin, on the other hand, may be scattered among several domestic establishments. Thus the domestic domains are not likely to be limited to near kin, and the kinship networks are not necessarily domestically oriented. Even if it is true that many inhabitants of Accra have no "home life," and so do not participate in isolable domestic domains of language use, most of them certainly have kin, and it is the language of the kin networks that defines the community language. The crucial factor in community language maintenance is therefore not usage domain, what a language is used for, but network, the category of people who use it among themselves—specifically, kin.

In both years, not only the Ga but also a majority of others reported using Ga among kin, and in nondomestic contexts generally. Akan was reported as being used only in nondomestic domains by majorities of Ga and other non-Akan speakers, which probably meant that most did not use it with kin; as we would expect, the majority of speakers from the Akan regions, the Eastern, Central, and Ashanti, reported using it both among kin and nondomestically. However, in 1989 and again in 1992, about 12% of Ga and at least as many who were neither Ga nor Akan reported using Akan in both contexts. On the one hand, this might suggest the beginnings of a shift toward Akan in the kin networks. On the other hand, the proportion of Akan community speakers of Akan who did *not* report using the language with kin was significant in both years and slightly higher in 1992 (28% in 1989 and 38% in 1992: table 3.14). Although Akan is clearly an important language in the extradomestic life of those who speak it as a second language, there is more evidence of a shift toward the use of Ga in the kin networks by people of Akan origin than of shift toward the use of Akan with kin and friends by the Ga.

It has already been noted that a number of respondents were the offspring of linguistically mixed parents. There were also respondents whose dominant language, the language they thought they actually spoke best, was the language of neither parent, even if the parents had the same language and regardless of whether or not the respondent had learned the parent's language first.[16] Although such respondents were a small proportion of each survey group, they may be significant indicators of trends in linguistic assimilation, not in terms of language use within the kin groups of these respondents but in the behavior of the group as a whole. In 1989, fifteen, or 10% of the group, had linguistically different parents (compare table 3.4). In twelve of these cases, one parent was Ga-speaking. In the thirteen cases in which the respondent's dominant language was elicited, it was Ga in twelve, including a daughter of a Dangme and an Ewe who had actually learned Dangme first but believed she now spoke Ga better.

There were thirty-seven respondents (in 1989) whose parents spoke the same, non-Ga language. Six of them had learned Ga first in life, and seven (not including all of these six) regarded Ga as their dominant language. They included three children of Ewe speakers; two of Twi speakers; and one each of speakers of Dangme, Hill Guang, and another language. No language other than Ga appeared as the dominant language of anyone whose parents did not speak it, except for one dominant speaker of Hill Guang whose parents (and first language learned) were Ewe and two young men with secondary education who claimed to speak English best. One was the son of Ga-speaking parents, the other of Ewe.

In 1992, the situation was more complicated because more people (thirty-five, or 23%) claimed to be of linguistically mixed parentage. That is, they associated a different language with each parent. In twenty-eight of these cases one parent was associated with Ga, and in twenty-two (63% of respondents who claimed mixed parentage) the respondent's dominant language was Ga.

Fifty-two respondents had parents neither of whom was identified with Ga, whether they had the same language (forty-four) or different ones (eight). Ga was the respondent's dominant language in fourteen (27%) of these cases, including five of the eight with linguistically mixed non-Ga parents. The parents' language was maintained as the dominant language by thirty-two respondents (that is, all but six of nineteen children of Ewe speakers, two each of eight Dangme and three Fante, and one each of three Hill Guang and four "other").

A language other than Ga thus appeared as the target of shift only if it was associated with one parent or in a very small number of other cases that are no doubt related to atypical personal histories. Two respondents, one of Ewe-speaking parents and one of Hill Guang parents, gave Twi as the dominant language, while one with Ewe parents and one with a Twi father and Dangme mother gave Fante. One whose parents were both associated with Ga gave Dangme as the dominant language.

We must conclude that although linguistic assimilation into the community of Ga-dominant speakers is not the universal rule, the Ga language is nevertheless the most attractive target of shift and assimilation within these groups, certainly stronger than Akan.

Although Ga and Akan are clearly the most important languages for those who sell in and around the Salaga market, we need to consider the roles of English and Hausa if we are to situate Central Accra within the linguistic networks of the wider city and the country. We have already seen that although quite large numbers claim some acquaintance with English, very few speak it with any confidence. The Ga and the non-Ga did not significantly differ in this respect, in either year. As expected, most respondents claimed to use it only in nonkin contexts (table 3.15), and while very few claimed to use it among kin, it is perhaps surprising that any did at all. Rather few limited their use of English to school, which suggests that although its acquisition may be strongly associated with school (table 3.12), once they acquire it people find other uses for it. This is especially true of the 1992 group.

TABLE 3.15   Contexts of Use of English in 1989 and 1992

	1989 (n = 76)		1992 (n = 119)		Ga* (1992) (n = 74)		Non-Ga (1992) (n = 45)	
Kin/domestic only	0		4	3.4%	0		4	8.9%
Kin + external	16	21.1%	6	13.3%	6	8.1%	0	
Work/commercial only	10	13.2%	42	35.3%	28	37.8%	14	31.1%
School only	11	15.5%	3	2.5%	3	4.1%	0	
Various nondomestic	34	44.7%	53	44.5%	29	39.2%	24	53.3%
Unknown†	5	6.6%	11	9.2%	8	10.8%	3	6.7%

*Respondents who claim to originate in the Greater Accra Region.

†Includes mainly those who claim only passive competence.

Acquisition of Twi and Hausa for these groups was strongly associated with Accra. Relatively few reported learning Twi in any of the regions where it is the majority language, especially those who did not claim to have come from these areas (table 3.16). Although Hausa was spoken by very few respondents, most of those who did speak it had acquired it in Accra, contrary to the assumptions of most southern Ghanaians, who firmly believe that Hausa is spoken mainly in the north (table 3.17).

Multilingualism has been discussed so far from the point of view of face-to-face interaction: the repertoires available for *speaking*. But this is not, of course, the only medium available for verbal communication. Both graphic and audiovisual media are much in evidence in Accra and may be supposed to be significant in the lives of many people. They are also aspects, potential or actual, of the linguistic integration of Accra as a city and as the capital of a country. Since audiovisual media are perhaps more accessible than print to a wide educational and economic range of people in Accra, though not in the country as a whole, we shall consider them first.

There have been movie houses in Accra since the 1920s when the Palladium Cinema was built, the John Holt Bartholomew company began showing films on its premises, and mobile cinemas began to tour the nearby villages (Dadson 1989). The

TABLE 3.16   Where Major Second Languages Are Acquired: Twi

Region	1989 (n = 86*)		1992 (n = 123†)	
Accra-Tema	68	79.1%	80††	65.0%
Eastern/Central/Ashanti	7	8.1%	39	31.7%
Volta	10	11.6%	1	0.8%
Other	1	1.2%	3	2.4%

*Includes 52 who claim origin from the Greater Accra Region, 32 from the Eastern, Central, or Ashanti region.

†Includes 79 who claim origin from the Greater Accra Region, 29 from the Eastern, Central, or Ashanti region.

††Includes 55 who claim origin from the Greater Accra Region.

TABLE 3.17   Where Major Second Languages are Acquired: Hausa

Region	1989	(n = 14)	1992	(n = 26)
Accra-Tema	8	57.1%	21	80.8%
Central	0		1	3.8%
Western	4	28.6%	0	
Volta	1	7.1%	0	
Brong-Ahafo, Northern	1	7.1%	3	11.5%
Outside Ghana	0		1	3.8%

sources of their offerings have varied with the economic and political situation of the country and with the availability of foreign exchange to acquire them, but in general, publicly shown movies have been in English or in languages (such as Chinese or Hindi) that Ghanaian audiences do not expect to understand. Although such movies may be subtitled, their appeal is presumably based on music and spectacular action. A number of films have been made in Ghana for both local and foreign consumption, beginning in 1949 with the Gold Coast Film Unit, which became the Ghana Film Industry Corporation. These films were often made by British directors, and all, it seems, were in English.

The locally scripted and directed video dramas that began to be made in Accra in the late 1980s, and shown in public video theaters, are also mainly in English, not Ghanaian languages. Television programs produced and broadcast in Accra by the Ghana Broadcasting Corporation include weekly information and drama programs in one or more of four Ghanaian languages (Ga, Akan, Ewe, Dagbani) or Hausa, and there are also music programs that may present songs in one or more Ghanaian languages. However, the largest number of broadcast hours is in English, including foreign-produced programs in languages other than English, which are generally dubbed. It is only on radio that a variety of programs in Ghanaian languages, particularly the languages of southern Ghana, are available every day. Unlike television sets, which generally require electricity, are far more expensive, and never had government support comparable to the rural radio rediffusion boxes distributed in the 1950s and 1960s, radios are widespread throughout the country. Certainly in Accra there can be few who are not actually indigent who never hear radio.

It is a little surprising, then, that as many as 26% of the 1989 Salaga market group and 30% of the 1992 group claimed to listen to the radio seldom if at all. Of those who did listen, in both groups, considerably more listened to Ghanaian languages, mainly Ga and Akan (about 69%) than to English (about 40%). However, only about 30% did *not* listen to English; the majority of listeners in both years normally listened to both English and a Ghanaian language: 41% in 1989 and 37% in 1992 (percentages of the entire groups). Very few, indeed, in these predominantly Ga groups (16% in 1989 and only 7% in 1992) listened mainly or only to Ga, and the numbers listening only to one of Akan, Ewe, Hausa, or English were insignificant.

The practice of listening to English seems to bear little relation to claims of competence in the language or to education. Listeners who claimed to listen to English regularly were close to 40% of both groups (which means that 60% did not, including those who listened to no language at all). In the 1989 group, higher but still comparable proportions of respondents claimed more than six years of education (45%) and at least a little knowledge of English (50%). In the 1992 group, however, people in both of these categories were significantly more numerous than in 1989 (57% and 78%, respectively) and far more numerous than the radio listeners. At the same time, respondents confident of their ability in English were both far fewer in 1992 (a mere 9% compared to 24% in 1989) and in both years far fewer than the listeners to English.

English appears to be a major language in this area of communication, listened to by a majority of all listeners. It is possible that as a result of the predominance of English in the other audiovisual media, English is regarded by most people as the most salient media language. Nevertheless, it must be concluded, on the one hand, that either listeners' available competence in English was being underused or it was often unsuited to understanding the type of English spoken on the radio. The low figures for confident ability, particularly in 1992, are undoubtedly significant here. On the other hand, it cannot be assumed that the respondent was always in control of the choice of language. The politics of radio ownership must also be reckoned with, for it is probable that women, who formed large majorities of these groups, are less likely to possess or control radios than men or to find time to listen to them. Since men were included in the groups of nonlisteners, however, relative youth and affluence are also likely factors.[17]

Similar proportions in each year, around 45%, reported that they read and wrote from time to time. As expected, this was significantly less than the 70% or more who listened to the radio. As with radio listening, this figure is also lower than might be expected from the general level of education. In 1989, the proportion with more than six years of education matched the proportion that claimed to read and write at least occasionally, but in 1992 people with this degree of formal education were 10% more frequent than readers and 14% more frequent than writers.

Insignificant numbers reported using only a Ghanaian language for reading or writing. English was read by more people than any other language (reported by 36% in 1989 and 39% in 1992), but a significant number read Ga, and in 1992 more people claimed to read both Ga and English (22%) than English only (15%). The number who claimed to read Ga was about 10% larger in 1992 than in 1989. This was not paralleled in writing practice: in both years, the largest group (of writers) wrote only in English (23% in 1989 and 25% in 1992), and the only other significant group (13% each year) wrote in both Ga and English.

In other words, virtually everyone who reads and writes does so in English. A smaller but significant proportion also read and write in Ga, the only Ghanaian language taught in state-run schools in Accra. Since virtually everyone speaks Ga, the fact that the highest figure for its use amounted to about half (52%) of all readers in 1992 (compared to about 30% of all writers, and 30% of readers in 1989) must reflect radical differences in speakers' perceptions of its value in face-to-face as opposed to graphic functions. There seems little doubt that, overall, English is the major language of mediated communication in inner Accra and that it is actively controlled for this purpose by only about one-third of the market population.

Although it may be true that Central Accra has a core population of "Ga-speaking people who not only constitute the majority of the inhabitants of Central Accra, but are true townsmen in the sense that their social relations are fully encompassed in the urban centre" (Kilson 1974: 3), it is also true that an important segment of the population is closely related to the countryside and moves back and forth between urban and rural environments (Ewusi 1977: 11). Although every Accra lineage has a "family house" in Central Accra, most members live elsewhere and only gather at the family house on special occasions. For example, most of the permanent inhabitants of the house in Atukpai (Ussher Town) that belonged to Ajorkor Okai We—the lineage that is discussed in detail in Dakubu (1981)—were women traders, matrilaterally related to the lineage. Most women members of the patrilineage lived elsewhere in town and also engaged in trade, while the men of the lineage were either farmers living north of Accra or in various suburbs and were engaged in such occupations as mechanic, tailor, or driver. However, the farmers were mainly older men, who had lived in town and had urban occupations in the past. Some women also lived in the farming areas, but regularly spent time trading in Accra (Dakubu 1981: 43, 44). Although the people trading regularly in the Salaga market seemed for the most part to be living urban lives at the time of the surveys, that pattern is not necessarily lifelong or exclusive, and many of them must interact frequently with people who are based in the villages north of the city, even if they do not go there themselves.

To judge by the pattern in Ajorkor Okai We, such contacts must reinforce the pattern of multilingualism already described. The figures for knowledge (any degree) of Ga, Akan, English, Hausa, and Dangme were similar to those in the Salaga market 1989 survey, while the figures for Ewe were higher (Dakubu 1981: 73).[18] Since in the lineage survey all the Dangme, Ewe, and Hausa speakers and almost all the Akan speakers were second-language speakers, polyglotism in this group of Ga was actually higher. The men (56% of the group, in contrast to the female majority in the market surveys) spoke an average of 2.8 languages, the women 2.4 (2.2 in the 1989 survey but lower than the 3.6 of the 1992 survey). The difference was more marked in the languages reported as spoken with confidence, which averaged 2.2 among men and 1.9 among women in the lineage survey but only 1.5 and 1.4 in the 1989 and 1992 market surveys, respectively (table 3.8).

The relatively rural Ga group thus appears to be a little more polyglot than the urban, contradicting the usual stereotype. There are several reasons for this. One is the nature of the urban-rural relationship. While it may be true that many Central Accra Ga people are limited to strictly urban social networks, very few people in the lineage studied seemed to have led or to be leading purely urban or rural lives. More important, the Ga rural areas are far from homogeneous. The villages of this particular lineage are close to several Akan-speaking villages, where Akan-Ga bilingualism is common. Intermarriage is frequent. There are at least as many Ewe farmers as Ga in the Ga villages themselves, and Hausa speakers, though few, are not unknown.[19] Villagers, too, go to school and learn a little English. The multilingual environment observed in Central Accra is by no means a purely urban phenomenon.

Inner Suburbia

The multilingual atmosphere is rather different if one moves northward from old Accra, across Asafoatse Nettey Road (formerly Horse Road) into Riponsville and Korle Dudor. According to a recent study (Aminarh 1992) of language use in the primary schools of this area, few of the first settlers of this part of Accra were Ga. In the area known as Katamanto, they were Hausa and Togolese blacksmiths; Kwahu wood sellers; Togolese and Beninois washermen; Akan, Dangme, Ewe, Igbo, and Lebanese traders; and a few Ga. Korlewokong (Kɔɔle wɔŋ kooŋ "at Korle's sacred grove") was first built on by Europeans. After initially avoiding the place, Ga eventually acquired properties there, which they rented to Togolese, Hausa, and Akan. People of Sierra Leonean origin settled Fearon Road.[20] The Timber Market area began with Dagomba, Hausa, Togolese, and a few Ga. In the 1950s, Rouch (1956) identified it as a center of Zabarima settlement. In 1992 it had Dagomba, Nanumba, and Konkomba yam sellers; Ga, Ewe, Akan, Yoruba, and Igbo sellers of ironmongery and traditional medicines; and Akuapem (Twi) and Ewe chopbar keepers. Aminarh reports that throughout the area, Akan is the major trade language, followed by English, with Ga and Hausa also in common use according to the area and the object of trade.

There are local and institutional variations. At the railway station and the banks within the area, English is official and normal. Carpenters' workshops tend to be run by Ewe. In one workshop visited by Esther Aminarh, the master was Ewe, while the fourteen apprentices included Ewe, Akan, Dangme, and Gonja, all of whom spoke (at least) Ewe, Ga, Akan, and English. Carriers in the market, who come mainly from Togo and the Republic of Benin and represent a variety of languages and ethnicities, use Ga, Akan, and Ewe.

Most people live in large dwellings shared by several families that are often linguistically diverse. A linguistic heirarchy was observed, in which Akan occupied the apex: the general rule seemed to be that in a house that included Akan, Ewe, Dangme, and Ga, the Ewe and Dangme learned Akan and Ga, the Ga learned only Akan, and the Akan learned nothing. But this applied only to the adults: children acquired at least a little of all four (Aminarh 1992: 57).

It might be expected that such a situation would pose problems for the local schools, and indeed it does. Outside the school itself, in the yard, English, Ga, and Akan were observed to be dominant, but Ewe, Dangme, Gonja, Dagbani, Kasem, Hausa, and several others were also to be heard. As might be expected, this seems to reflect the distribution of the children's home languages (table 3.18). Inside, the teach-

TABLE 3.18   The Home Languages of Children in the First Three Primary Years, in Three Schools of Central Ashiedu Keteke

Akan	44.1%	Kasem	0.8%
Ga	36.0%	Zabarima	0.7%
Ewe	10.1%	Hill Guang	0.5%
Dangme	3.0%	Sisaala	0.2%
Hausa	2.3%	Gonja	0.2%
Dagbani	1.8%	"Mali" (Bambara?)	0.2%

Total 405 children: class 1 = 137; class 2 = 129; class 3 = 139.

Data from Esther Akusika Aminarh, The Multilingual Situation in the Central Ashiedu Keteke Area, and Its Effects on Primary Class 1–3, Diploma Long Essay, Language Centre, University of Ghana, 1992.

TABLE 3.19   Speakers of Major Ethnic Languages of an
Adabraka Neighborhood (100% = 423)

	Total	Percent
Akan*	167	39.5
Akim	4	
Asante	19	
Kwahu	109	
Fante	25	
Brong	5	
Wasa	5	
Ga	74	20.3
Ewe	68	18.7
Dangme	20	5.5
Yoruba	18	4.9
Hausa	10	2.7
Songhai	6	1.6
Dagaare†	1	0.3

*Akuapem dialect speakers are not mentioned.

†Numerous other languages had one speaker each. None were languages of
northern Ghana.

Data from Roger Sanjek, Cognitive maps of the ethnic domain in urban
Ghana: Reflections on variability and change, *American Ethnologist* 4(4):
603–22.

ing language is officially Ga, the local language, for the first three primary years.[21]
In the 1950s and 1960s, many of the teachers in the area's schools were Ga; but since
1970, non-Ga teachers have been in the majority, and it is not surprising if they tend
to use other languages in these circumstances, especially since some do not speak
Ga at all. In several instances, teachers had pupils translate from Akan or English
into Ga for the benefit of those who did not understand those languages and needed
interpreters to talk to some of their pupils. Aminarh's (1992) figures indicate that by
the time they reach the third primary year, there are still a number of Ga and Akan
monoglots, but most speak at least Ga, Akan, and English.[22] Even in the first year,
many are already bilingual.

Farther north, in the less crowded suburb of Adabraka, Sanjek (1977) studied
multilingualism as a key to ethnic identity, in the early 1970s, about the same time as
our survey of Ajorkor Okai We. Unlike the studies discussed so far, Sanjek's was
residentially based on data collected from 423 residents of eleven buildings on a single
street. Educationally this population was not very different from our 1992 Salaga
market group.[23] Comparable percentages had never been to school (9% of males and
37% of females; compare table 3.2), although more men and fewer women had had
at least ten years of school (80% and 41%, respectively). Sanjek found that among
these people, fourteen languages were languages of individuals' ethnic identification (table 3.19). He does not state whether they were also dominant in individuals'
repertoires, but this seems to have been assumed. Of the fourteen glossonyms listed,

however, seven are interintelligible dialects of Akan. If they are combined, Akan was definitely the language spoken by the most people (at just under 40%) but still not that of a majority. It was followed by Ga and Ewe, spoken by similar numbers (20.3% and 18.7%, respectively), and others spoken by smaller numbers, including Dangme (5.5%), Yoruba (4.9%), Hausa (2.7%), and Songhay (1.6%). Others were the language of single individuals. They included Dagaare, but no other language from northern Ghana, and no other Sahelian West African language such as Fulfulde.

Sanjek (1977: 604) found that 19% of individual households in his study were ethnically mixed and that 37% of adults who had ever married had been in ethnically mixed marriages. This is higher than the proportion of linguistically mixed parents in either of the Salaga market groups (compare table 3.4), but since various ethnolinguistic subtypes of Akan were distinguished, it is likely that the proportion was actually much lower for marriages between people who spoke mutually nonintelligible languages. He also found that adults spoke at least two languages, usually more than that, and that most spoke at least two languages every day (p. 605). Language diaries kept for four days by twenty people indicate that the languages in which encounters took place were most often Akan (all varieties), Ga, and Ewe, in that order, with three times as many encounters in Akan as in either of the others (613). Not surprisingly, these languages also proved to be most salient in the perceptions of the group, followed most closely by Hausa, even though this was the community language of a tiny minority (p. 610).[24]

To conclude, it can be stated that Ga Mashi is still very Ga, although none of our surveys showed it to be truly homogeneous and it is by no means unilingual. Except that it is much larger, it is not linguistically very different from a Ga rural village. Ga-speaking households are proportionally fewer as one moves northward into Riponsville and Korle Dudor and fewer still in Adabraka, but the other large linguistic community, the Akan, does not include an absolute majority in any of these places. This is not a new situation, for the Ga were not usually the original settlers of the areas north of Asafoatse Nettey Road, and as will be shown in chapter 5, even Ga Mashi was multilingual in its origins.

It is clear that Akan is the dominant second language throughout this inner city. However, there is also evidence that any linguistic assimilation that takes place in Ga Mashi is targeted at Ga, not Akan. The lagoon does indeed break through to the sea. We have no data on this subject for the areas to the north, but as a second language Ga is clearly very strong in Riponsville, where most non-Ga migrants, as well as local schoolchildren, seem to learn both Ga and Akan. It is not clear from Sanjek's account how many of his group actually spoke Ga, but since most people spoke at least two of the languages listed and since Akan, Ewe, and Ga had the highest salience and were most often encountered in practice, it must have had a considerable number of second-language speakers in Adabraka. Although Ewe speakers are present in significant numbers, the language has relatively fewer second-language speakers, except perhaps in Adabraka. Hausa does not appear as a second language in general use, although it is certainly relatively important in specific locations in connection with specialized kinds of trade, such as yams in the Timber market. English is plainly of major importance as a second language, despite the small numbers of speakers that might be considered competent from the point of view of the educated speaker of standard English.

4

Modern Multilingual Accra II

Accra, north of the Ring Road and between the Nsawam Road and the Kanda Estate, looks different from Ga Mashi: it sprawls over a wide area and, except on its fringes (where one sees private bungalows, often of two stories or more), consists of numerous large compounds of long, rectangular, single-storied blocks of rows of rooms, of the kind typical of *zongo* sections of towns anywhere in Ghana. It is almost as crowded as the old Ga core and much more cosmopolitan.

Although many Ga and other southern Ghanaians live in outer areas like Nima and Accra New Town, they seem to be in a minority. The population mainly consists of people from northern Ghana and neighboring West African countries, especially from northern parts of Togo, Republic of Benin, and Nigeria and from Burkina Faso, Niger, and Mali. Many southern Ghanaians assume that all these people are both Hausa and Muslim, and the Hausa language and Islam go together in the minds of most. It is believed that "all northerners" speak Hausa and, consequently, that Hausa is the main language of northern Ghana. An early motive for collecting the data discussed in this chapter was finally to refute these assumptions.

Another motive was a desire to consider more fully the proposition that Hausa, which is undoubtedly a lingua franca in this part of Accra and several other suburbs, especially among people of northern origin, is or is becoming the marker of an emerging northern ethnicity. There are two questions here: whether a northern ethnicity exists or is in process of formation, and if it is, whether the Hausa language marks it. These questions were raised and dismissed by Enid Schildkrout (1978: 86, 112), with reference to the Kumasi Zongo, where Hausa is similarly widely used. She was right to decide in the negative, but the problem still remains: what special function does this language have for its speakers since the other languages of wider currency in Accra—Ga, Akan, and English—are also available to these people and in fact, as will be shown, are widely known and used? Further, if the language does not mark ethnicity, what does it mark? For it is clear that it is a cultural index, to southerners and northerners alike. A psychosociolinguistics that accounts for the linguistic behavior of migrants by accommodation to the behavior of members of the host group (Giles 1985, 1977) does not seem to provide a complete answer.

Hausa does not appear on lists of languages indigenous to Ghana, mainly because there is no place in Ghana that can be designated the homeland of a Hausa-speaking community. People who identify themselves as Hausa trace their origins to Hausa-speaking regions of Nigeria, usually not more than three or four generations back. Unlike Hausa in Lagos (Scotton 1975), the language is not a marker of politically salient Ghanaian group membership. This is not at all to say that it is "neutral," for as I have already suggested, Hausa does index northern otherness in the eyes of south-ern Ghanaians. Consequently, if choices among the four major second languages (Akan, Ga, Hausa, and English) are to be accounted for by a cost-benefit strategy, whether conscious or unconscious, as proposed by Scotton or by Laitin (1991), it must be a complex strategy with complex, multileveled goals.

More generally, we need to examine the extent to which Accra operates as an urban linguistic community. Do the available routes for communication, the languages used, suggest that Nima and Ga Mashi, or even Nima and Adabraka, can and prob-ably do speak to one another to any significant extent, or do they merely coexist? It is certainly beyond the scope of this study to examine social integration in detail, but a study of patterns of multilingualism may indicate the character and extent of potential speech networks, within and between areas of the city, on which social interaction depends. They may also suggest the nature of linguistic interaction between the city, or sections of it, and the rest of the country. Concerning the migrant communities of outer Accra, we are particularly interested in whether patterns of language repertoire and use distinguish them from their source areas, and so reflect adaptation to a spe-cifically urban environment; whether they import and adapt home-area usages; or whether some other process is at work.

Nima and the adjoining suburbs of Accra New Town and Maamobi are not the only areas of northern migrant settlement in the city. We have seen that parts of the downtown area outside Ga Mashi once had this character but that some now have a larger proportion of southern migrants and Ga. West of the Korle lagoon, Sabon Zongo and Abossey Okai have always had a strong northern component since they were first settled in the 1930s. There are also significant numbers of northerners in areas farther to the north, such as Achimota, North Kaneshie, and Madina.

The fact that most of these settlements hardly existed before the 1930s and were very small until the 1950s does not mean that there were no northerners in and around Accra before then. Meredith (1812: 218), remarking on how cosmopolitan Accra had been in slave trade times, mentions the presence of "a remote inland people who went under the appellation of Duncoes." He and Cruickshank (1853) agreed that the appellation (Ga odɔŋkɔ "northerner," now also the proper name Donkor) was de-rogatory.[1] In the nineteenth century there were considerable numbers of slaves and later ex-slaves of northern origin, especially in the farming villages immediately north of the town (Christaller 1889: 107; Rouch 1956: 23). Such people were not in a position to form autonomous communities, and when domestic slaves were emanci-pated in 1874, they either were integrated into the lineages that had owned them or went back home. Although slave origins are not an approved subject of discussion in present-day Ga society, traces of such origin and even of a slave ancestor's place of origin can sometimes be found by inspecting genealogies and traditions associated with a lineage's ritual practices. Slaves assimilated into Ga lineages are often recognizable by the names given to them, which were characteristically appellations in Akan (Dakubu 1981: 144). Another relic of their presence may be a shrine—such as the one belonging to Ajorkor Okai We in Mayera Okai Mang, which is said to have been brought by an ancestor from Mosi (p. 50)—or even places remembered in prayers. An elder of Ajorkor Okai We at Manchie (near Mayera) regularly invoked a deity called Sankana that was apparently connected with a place (p. 232). He did not seem to know where it was and there is no place of this name in the Accra area, but there is such a place in the Upper West Region, a few miles north of Wa, famous for successfully resisting Babatu in the 1880s (Wilks 1989: 116). The village of Sankana is under Kaleo, whose chieftaincy is said to have been founded by a Mosi group. It thus seems very likely that at least one of the adopted sons of the founder of Ajorkor Okai We came from there.

Return from servitude in the Accra area may explain the occurrence of "Accra" and the names of a few other nearby places, such as Achimota (Akimata) and Katamanso (Tantamasso), in traditions of migration from the Upper West Region of Ghana (apparently during the later nineteenth century) that are preserved by several groups of Dagara in Burkina Faso, as recorded in Hébert et al. (1975: 37–40). Numbers of northerners, especially from what is now the Upper East Region, were recruited into the armed forces created by the British on the Gold Coast after 1840, but they also failed to establish permanent local communities (presumably because they lived in barracks) and returned north upon completion of service: several of Rattray's (1932) informants on northern culture were returned ex-servicemen. At any rate, there seems to be almost no continuity between nineteenth-century migrants and the present communities, which represent voluntary movements of individuals on a much larger scale than before in response to the superior prospects for gainful employment offered by the metropolis.

The following descriptions of the groups surveyed are intended to characterize them for the purpose of evaluating the language data they provided. There is no way of knowing how closely they matched the migrant populations from which they were drawn in such dimensions as sex and age ratios and education levels, although we may sometimes hazard a guess. There is also every likelihood that the populations have changed since the survey period, 1982–1986. The economic situation in Ghana was particularly bad at that time. Although it is not likely to have improved very much since then for most of the people interviewed, migration patterns may well have altered. Since Accra became even more crowded after that time and the northern suburbs have greatly expanded, it is likely that communities have grown.

Three Migrant Communities

The Dagaaba, the Bulsa, and the Kusaasi occupy discrete homelands distributed from west to east across Ghana's northern savannah tier. Their languages, respectively Dagaare, Buli, and Kusaal, all belong to the Oti-Volta group of Central Gur languages and are closely related but not mutually intelligible (Naden 1988). Their homelands—respectively, Dagao, in the Upper West Region, and Buluk and Kusaug, in the Upper East—are not far apart in terms of motor travel, but they are not contiguous and are socially and historically quite distinct. Even today there is little direct interaction among them. Each is represented in Accra by a sizable migrant population, although in the migrant community as a whole they are apparently tiny minorities.[2]

My surveys of polyglotism, language use, and language acquisition patterns were carried out in the Accra communities between 1982 and 1986. Migrant neighborhoods and the compounds within them are extremely mixed, and there are current data on neither the numbers of migrants from particular areas nor their geographic distribution in Accra. Since linguistic communities were to be considered in relation to their places of origin, a random sample seemed out of the question. Survey populations were constructed through personal contacts and by visits to community leaders, such as chiefs,[3] and places of group activity, such as churches, where members of a particular language community congregate. The aim was to collect a sample that was reasonably representative of the migrant population in demographic terms and also large enough to capture the range of variation within it. This means, for example, that more people who did not have formal education were interviewed than people who did because it was clear that the former were a major part of the population; also, the proportion of respondents over the age of fifty is untypically large because a range of age groups for both sexes and all degrees of education, as far as possible, was desired.[4]

The Dagaaba

Dagaaba is the name used for themselves by people who speak the Dagaare language and whose land, Dagao, covers most of the Upper West Region. The language, which varies considerably from place to place, belongs to a dialect continuum that has four major divisions: Dagaare, or the central dialects, on which the present written language is based; the Dagara, or northern dialects, whose speakers also call themselves Dagara, which extend into Burkina Faso to the north and west; the Birifor, or western dialects, spoken in Burkina Faso south of Dagara, in Ghana south of Wa extending into the Northern Region, and in the adjoining northwest corner of the Ivory Coast; and Waale, the language of the town of Wa and surrounding villages, whose speakers call themselves Waala (Bodomo 1988). The ethnonym "Dagaaba" is used in this chapter in an extended sense to refer to a survey population that included speakers of both central dialects (Dagaare) and northern (Dagara) dialects whose hometowns were in Ghana. At the 1984 census, the areas from which these speakers came had a combined population of 237,896 (Oti-Boateng et al. 1989: *Upper West Region*). It may be assumed that virtually all spoke the language.

With the exception of Wa, which has long been a state on the pattern of Dagbon (Levtzion 1968; Wilks 1989), and of Kaleo, which has a chiefship founded by Mosi (Hébert et al. 1975: 24), the peoples of the Upper West Region were historically noncentralized, or "acephalous," in their political organization (J. Goody 1967). The institution of chieftaincy in this area was mainly a colonial introduction. At the time our surveys were conducted in 1985–86, Dagaaba migrants in various parts of outer

Accra were very informally organized. There was no single chief for the entire community, although one was elected several years later.[5] Groups of people settled in different areas maintained relations mainly by attendance at funerals.

Three areas were investigated: besides the Central Nima–New Town–Mataheko area, where 252 people were interviewed, 100 people were interviewed in Achimota, a village to the north of Accra that is now a suburb of the city, and 150 in a rather diffused settlement area to the west of the city that includes such suburbs as Odorkor, Mataheko, and Russia. The Achimota community is considerably older than the others (or any of the Bulsa or Kusaasi communities interviewed).[6] It was founded by Dagaaba, who came before the railroad was finished, that is, before 1923 (Dickson 1969: 233), and at least two of their descendants still lived there. Nevertheless, over 80% of the group had been born in Dagao. This relatively small group had a chief and a Dagaaba Union, concerned with mutual aid and organizing funerals.

The Dagaaba community in Nima is very much larger and contains many societies and groupings, none of which include the entire language community. The chief at the time of the survey (Jato from Fian, now deceased) had arrived in 1943. He knew of two men still living in the area who had arrived before him, but it is unlikely that the community had existed continuously for much longer. At the time of the survey, Nima had a number of town citizens' organizations, such as the Gwo Citizens' Association and the Nandom Youth and Development Association, as well as an Upper West Citizens' Association. St. Kizito's Roman Catholic church was also a major arena of Dagaaba activity. An estimated five thousand Dagaaba above the age of fifteen lived in the Nima–Maamobi–New Town area.

Parts of the western settlement area, on land belonging to Sempe, still had a semirural aspect in 1986. The Dagaaba who had been there longest had arrived in the 1950s. There was a Dagaaba Union, whose monthly meetings were attended by about eighty men, and there were Dagaaba groups in both the Mataheko Catholic church and the local Jehovah's Witnesses. There were probably not more than three or four hundred Dagaaba adults in the area.

In all three residential subsections, the average age was thirty to thirty-four years. Ten percent more men than women were interviewed in the northern (Achimota) and western sections, but in the central (Nima) section the sexes were about equally represented. On average, people had lived in Accra for about ten years.[7]

Forty-five percent of the survey respondents had never been to school, but among those who had, most had completed at least a few years of secondary school (table 4.1). About 5% had attended adult literacy classes, and the percentage who had had a formal Islamic education was negligible. As might be expected, the economic level was not high. Most people were low-wage service workers, petty traders, or unemployed. The last category includes women who reported being housewives with no other occupation. Many women brewed or sold pito, a beer made from guinea corn, and are included in the 25.5% who were petty traders. Variations across the three settlement areas seem insignificant.[8]

The group as a whole maintained strong ties with the home area. All respondents were able to name their hometown in Dagao and their patriclan (*dɔgróŋ*). Figures for length of residence in Accra seem to reflect a steady influx of migrants, with 53.6% having lived there not longer than twelve years and 11% for less than a year.

TABLE 4.1   Formal Education in the Dagaaba Community Group

	North $n = 100$	Central $n = 252$	West $n = 150$	Total $n = 502$
None	51.0%	44.0%	43.3%	45.2%
Primary				
to class 3	4.0%	5.2%	4.0%	4.6%
to class 7	6.0%	6.0%	8.7%	6.8%
Secondary				
to form 2	17.0%	21.4%	22.0%	20.7%
to form 5	10.0%	11.5%	12.7%	11.6%
Form 6 or more	7.0%	6.7%	3.3%	5.8%
3 yrs. Koranic school	2.0%	0.4%	0.7%	0.8%
Night school	3.0%	4.8%	5.3%	4.6%

About 80% had been born in their hometown or somewhere else in Dagao, so that this is mainly a community of first-generation migrants, but it also has a considerable experience of other parts of the country. Of the approximately 20% who had been born outside Dagao, 10% of the whole group and 16% of the Nima subgroup had been born in the Accra-Tema area and most of the rest in Akan-speaking areas. Although more than a third of those born outside Accra had moved there directly, a larger proportion, about 40%, had previously lived in an Akan-speaking region (far more than were born there), and a number had lived in several regions. Since only 3% of respondents had never lived outside Accra, compared to the 7% who were born there, it appears that contact with the Upper East, Northern and Volta Regions had been insignificant for this group but that residence in the home Upper West Region and/or an Akan-speaking region, as well as in Accra, was part of most respondents' backgrounds. Achimota had a higher proportion than the other sections of respondents who had also lived in the Upper West but not elsewhere.

The Bulsa

The land of the Bulsa people, called Buluk in the Buli language, is in the Upper East Region, in the center of the country's northern tier, separated from Dagao to the west by the Sisaala-speaking area. The Kasem-speaking area lies to the north between Buluk and the Burkina Faso border, and the Gurune-speaking area lies to the east. The country to the south of Buluk is very sparsely populated, although in western Mamprusi to the southeast there is a historically important market (Yagaba). To the southwest is the Konni-speaking area. Konni, with only a few thousand speakers, is closely related to Buli. In 1984, the Sandema Local Council area, which essentially coincided with Buluk, had an enumerated population of only 66,357.

Like the Dagaaba, the Bulsa were historically relatively isolated. They were even farther removed from major trade routes, did not form a centralized state, and suffered considerably from Mande and Zabarima raiders toward the end of the nineteenth century. In both Dagao and Buluk, the traditional settlement pattern is highly dispersed, and nucleated towns are a twentieth-century development. Nevertheless, it has been suggested that in precolonial times the Buluk towns (or settlement areas) of Sandema and Kanjaga had begun to develop as local capitals in response to influence from the neighboring Mamprusi state, on the one hand, and from Zabarima and Mande raiders, on the other (Schott 1970: 89). In colonial times, when Bulsa migrated to the Gold Coast, they were usually known as Kanjargas; Koelle's ([1854] 1963) *Polyglotta Africana* includes a word list of Buli under this name (Köhler 1964). Sandema is now the largest center.[9]

As in the Dagaaba survey, the Bulsa were surveyed in three sections (in 1983). Of a total of 419 respondents, 53.9% were resident in Nima, including a few in the adjoining Accra New Town and Maamobi. This is the longest established Bulsa residential area in or near Accra. Unlike the Dagaaba, the Bulsa had a chief for the whole Accra community, who lived in Nima. About a quarter (125) of the group lived west of the Korle lagoon, although not as far west as the western Dagaaba but mainly in Abossey Okai and Mamprobi. A northern (and eastern) section of 68 respondents was scattered through Achimota, Legon, Madina, Burma and Michel Camps.

Women constituted only about 36% of the total of each subsection. The great majority of respondents of both sexes were under forty, and well over 50% were between the ages of twenty-five and thirty-nine. Only 38.5% of the men and 26.5% of the women had any formal education, but this varied according to age. Formal education was universal among the group under the age of twenty but dropped off sharply thereafter, especially among women (table 4.2). Only 11% of the men and a

TABLE 4.2   Formal Education in the Bulsa Community Group, by Percentage of Age Group

| Age Group | | Years at School | | |
		1–3	4–7	7 or More
15–19	M (21)	18.5	33.3	42.9
	F (13)	30.8	30.8	38.5
20–24	M (28)	21.4	21.4	35.7
	F (12)	8.3	58.3	8.3
25–29	M (37)	27.0	18.9	18.9
	F (30)	16.7	20.0	0.0
30–34	M (62)	6.5	9.7	3.2
	F (42)	7.1	2.4	4.8
35–39	M (77)	0.8	9.1	6.5
	F (34)	2.9	0.0	0.0
40 and over	M (39)	5.1	2.6	2.6
	F (13)	0.0	0.0	0.0
Unknown	M (4)	25.0	25.0	0.0
	F (7)	0.0	0.0	0.0
Total	M (268)	12.7	13.1	12.7
	F (151)	9.3	11.9	5.3

mere 5% of the women had gone beyond middle school (upper primary). No one had attended a traditional Koranic school (*makaranta*), and no woman had attended adult literacy classes, although 17% of all men had done so. Most of the latter were thirty-five years old or more, and many were or had been soldiers or policemen. The occupation range is accordingly at the lower end of the economic scale, rather more so than for the Dagaaba, with more laborers but fewer unemployed. The Bulsa women were less economically engaged, with more than 75% claiming to be housewives only. Bulsa women do not have a characteristic occupation comparable to pito brewing and selling among Dagaaba women or petty trading among Ga and Akan women.

Like the Dagaaba, all the Bulsa were able to name a town of origin in Buluk, and most could name their clan (*dok*). Sandema, Wiaga, and Fumbisi were the most strongly represented home localities, with Sandema contributing 42% of all respondents. Almost 70% of them lived in Nima. People from Fumbisi, constituting 10% of the whole, were concentrated in the West, while Wiaga people, a little over a quarter of the whole, were evenly distributed.

The great majority of the responding group, 87.4% of the total, were born in the places they "came from." However, 57% of those under twenty and 35% of those under twenty-five were born in Accra. Everyone born in Accra was under thirty, all but two under twenty-five. Over all, slightly more than a third of the group under the age of twenty-five were born in Accra, and a little over half of those under twenty were born in the south. People born in the south seemed to be particularly concentrated in Nima.

Among people not born there, the average length of residence in Accra was about nine years, although a number of the older people had been there much longer. A majority of those not born in Accra claimed to visit Buluk at least once in two years. On the whole, the Bulsa respondents seemed to have traveled less than the Dagaaba and to have had less formal education.

The Kusaasi

Far fewer Kusaasi were interviewed than Dagaaba or Bulsa, both absolutely and relative to the size of the homeland source population of a little over a quarter of a million. Two, not three, residential subsections were discerned: a western section, made up of people residing in or near Abossey Okai and Sabon Zongo, and a central section of people residing mainly in Nima and Accra New Town. No northern residential community of any size was found. In this case it was the western that was the larger and better established community, not the central, and the chief of the Kusaasi in Accra lived in Abossey Okai. He was from eastern Kusaug, called Agole (rather than the western portion, Toende) as were almost all the people interviewed. Although the Accra Kusaasi community may indeed be smaller than the Dagaaba or the Bulsa, it is sufficiently large that the Assemblies of God in Adabraka and in Abossey Okai hold services in Kusaal and have Kusaasi pastors. It is estimated that in the western and central areas together there were about 2,000 adult Kusaasi at the time the survey was taken in 1983. The size of the community relative to the migrant population as a whole may be indicated by the fact that Kusaasi did not appear at all among the 1,010 people belonging to forty-four ethnic groups in Sabon Zongo listed by Moser (1979).[10]

The Kusaasi survey population also differed from the other two in presenting a complicated ethnic picture that had no parallel in the generally homogeneous Bulsa and Dagaaba and is largely explained by the historical demography of its homeland. Unlike Dagao and Buluk, which had little or no tradition of nucleated settlement before this century, eastern Kusaug includes an old indigenous town, Bawku. In the nineteenth century the Mamprusi state established a chieftaincy there, to protect caravans coming south from Hausaland through Tenkodogo in Burkina Faso to Gambaga and Salaga (Benneh 1974; Hilton 1962; Syme 1932). Besides the Gurune-speaking people to the west[11] and the Mamprusi to the south, whose language is called Ŋmampurli (*anglice* Mampruli), Kusaug is bordered by the territories of the Busansi (speaking Bisaa) and Mosi (speaking Moore) to the north and Bimoba to the east.[12]

In 1909, when it became a colonial government station and an official caravan assembly point, Bawku had Fulani, Mosi, and Hausa quarters, as well as the Mamprusi chief's section. In 1935, 60% of its taxable males were Mosi and Hausa, while only twenty were Kusaasi (Hilton 1962: 84, 86). Three or four years earlier, Syme had found that Kusaasi were about two-thirds of the population of the Kusaasi district as a whole, but that there were none in some parts of it. An exploratory survey indicated that in the mid-1980s, Hausa and especially Moore (the language of the Mosi) were more widely spoken in the center of Bawku than was Kusaal. According to the census of 1984, the Bawku Urban Council area had a population of 110,797, and Agole as a whole (Bawku, Pusiga-Pulimakum, and Tempane-Garu) had a population of 251,221. This is slightly larger than the Dagao population and much larger than the Buluk, but it cannot be assumed that all spoke the community language, although a majority probably did.

Busansi and Bimoba have migrated into the area, from Burkina Faso and Togo, respectively, during the twentieth century. The Mamprusi royal clan has intermarried for political reasons, not only with the Kusaasi but also with most of these other peoples, who have also intermarried with each other to some extent. This is not an isolated case of such a policy, for in Nalerigu (the capital of Mamprusi itself) there has also been a tendency for Mamprusi men to marry women of neighboring groups, resulting in a situation in which "language is rarely the single outward indication of 'ethnic' identity," and most Mamprusi commoners trace descent from another ethnic group (Susan Brown 1975: 25, 28).[13] As a result, in eastern Kusaasi, boundaries between linguistic and ethnic reference groups are politically very porous. The community interviewed in Accra reflects this situation: of the 227 respondents, only 136 regarded themselves as Kusaasi in the sense of recognized membership in a Kusaasi patriclan. Others regarded Bawku as their ethnic home, and at least in some contexts regarded themselves and were regarded by others as part of the Accra Kusaasi community, with which they had kinship connections; they also regarded themselves as Mosi, Mamprusi, or Busansi (table 4.3). Such people are referred to here as nonethnic Kusaasi. The Hausa community of Bawku is apparently not included in this web of kin ties or in the eastern Kusaasi community in Accra.[14]

At 40.5%, the proportion of women in this survey group was somewhat higher than in the Bulsa community and lower than in the Dagaaba. Nonethnic Kusaasi were very unevenly represented by age and sex (table 4.4). There were more Busansi and Mosi women (sixteen) than men (thirteen) but far more Mamprusi men (twenty-two) than women (seven). As in the other communities, the overall majority were under

TABLE 4.3 Kusaasi Community and Ethnicity:
Ethnic Composition, Entire Group

	Central (n = 106)	West (n = 121)	Total (n = 227)
Kusaasi	63.2%	57.0%	60.0%
Mamprusi	9.4%	15.7%	12.8%
Busansi	16.0%	9.9%	12.8%
Mosi	5.7%	14.9%	10.6%
Other*	5.7%	2.5%	4.0%

*"Other" includes 6 Bimoba, 2 Fulani, and 1 Frafra.

forty years of age, but the women were considerably younger than the men in all the nonethnic Kusaasi subgroups. Half or more of Mamprusi, Busansi, and Mosi men were aged thirty or over, but more than half the women in each of these groups were under that age.

As in the other groups, formal education depended on age and sex, with younger men having the most education, although the difference between the sexes was less than in the other groups (table 4.5). The overall level of education was somewhat higher than in the Bulsa group.

Unlike the other groups, the Kusaasi showed significant utilization of nonstate types of education. About 15% of each sex had attended Koranic schools, and almost 15% of the men (but only one woman) had attended adult literacy classes (night school). Most of those under forty who had been to a Koranic school had had state schooling as well. Everyone under twenty, as well as most of those under twenty-

TABLE 4.4 Kusaasi Community and Ethnicity. Nonethnic Kusaasi: Percentages in Age and Sex Categories, According to Ethnic Label

Age	Mamprusi M (n = 22)	Mamprusi F (n = 7)	Busansi M (n = 13)	Busansi F (n = 16)	Mosi M (n = 11)	Mosi F (n = 13)	Other M (n = 5)	Other F (n = 4)
15–19	9.1	42.9	7.7	12.5	9.1	30.8	0.0	0.0
20–24	9.1	14.3	0.0	0.0	18.2	15.4	40.0	0.0
25–29	13.6	28.6	30.8	43.8	18.2	15.4	20.0	0.0
30–34	22.7	0.0	0.0	18.8	9.1	7.7	40.0	75.0
35–39	13.6	0.0	30.8	6.3	9.1	15.4	0.0	0.0
40–44	13.6	14.3	7.7	0.0	9.1	0.0	0.0	0.0
45–49	9.1	0.0	7.7	18.8	18.2	7.7	0.0	0.0
50–54	0.0	0.0	0.0	0.0	0.0	0.0	0.0	25.0
55–59	4.5	0.0	15.4	0.0	9.1	0.0	0.0	0.0
60 and up	4.5	0.0	0.0	0.0	0.0	7.7	0.0	0.0

TABLE 4.5   Formal Education in the Kusaasi Community
Group, by Percentage of Age Group

		Years at School		
Age group		1–3	4–7	More
15–19	M (13)	38.5%	30.8%	15.4%
	F (25)	40.0%	28.0%	20.0%
20–24	M (15)	20.0%	26.7%	40.0%
	F (9)	0.0	22.2%	55.6%
25–29	M (18)	16.7%	11.1%	44.4%
	F (21)	4.8%	19.0%	19.0%
30–34	M (26)	15.4%	19.2%	19.2%
	F (14)	28.6%	7.1%	0.0
35–39	M (19)	10.5%	5.3%	31.6%
	F (10)	0.0	0.0	10.0%
40–44	M (14)	0.0	14.3%	21.4%
	F (5)	0.0	0.0	20.0%
45 and up	M (30)	3.3%	0.0	3.3%
	F (8)	0.0	0.0	0.0
Total	M (135)	13.3%	13.3%	23.0%
	F (92)	16.3%	13.0%	17.4%

five, who had had any state education were still at school. There was a relatively high rate of Koranic schooling but a low rate of state schooling in the Busansi subgroup, while the opposite was the case among the Mamprusi.

On the one hand, the Kusaasi group reported a higher rate of economic engagement than the Bulsa or the Dagaaba, with only 8% of all respondents reporting themselves as unemployed, including the retired, and only 20% of the women (compared to 92% of the Bulsa women) regarding themselves as housewives with no other economic activity. On the other hand, the largest single occupation claimed, by about a quarter of the whole, was "student." This is no doubt related to the fact that a relatively high proportion, 22.7.%, was aged under twenty-five. Thirteen percent of the women were housewives engaged in petty trade. The most frequent occupation among the men, almost a third, was manual laborer or watchman, more than among the Dagaaba but less than for the Bulsa. There were a few domestic workers but no policemen or soldiers. About a dozen individuals were tailors, seamstresses, butchers, electricians, and mechanics. Members of various professions that require training past the primary level, such as teachers, nurses, a secretary, and a veterinary officer, accounted for 7.5% of the people surveyed. Although there is a very wide range within each community, the Kusaasi interviewed seem to be on average a little better educated and slightly better off economically than the others.

The survey group represented "hometowns" from all over Kusaug, but the vast majority were from the Agole district: 85% of the entire survey group and 95% of the nonethnic Kusaasi. Almost half claimed to come from Bawku itself, and most others were from villages not far away.

Almost everyone claiming Kusaasi ethnicity could name his or her patrilineage (*duu*). As in Dagao, but unlike the more localized Bulsa clans, these lineages seem to be scattered in villages throughout the whole area. Apart from the fact that the majority of members of *all* subgroups claimed to come from "Bawku," members of the nonethnic Kusaasi subcommunities tended not to claim the same hometowns. The Mamprusi typically referred to the Mamprusi-founded chiefs' towns, such as Bawkuzua, Binduri, Natinga, and Sinebaga, while the Busansi came from Bado, Kulungungu, Pusiga, Widana (in the extreme north), Kugri, and Bulugu. Mosi also come from Widana, but others were from Mogonori, on the Burkina Faso border; Manga, near Bawku; and Tempani, farther to the south and east. Bimoba come from the southeastern extremity of the area, from Kpikpira and Worikambo.

Where people were actually born presented a significantly different picture. Almost the same number that claimed to "come from" Bawku claimed to have been born there (close to 50%), but 28.6%, more than in either of the other community groups, were born outside the ethnic homeland (Kusaug). The rest, including members of non-Kusaasi ethnicities, were almost all born in Agole. (Thus, for example, Busansi who mentioned "hometowns" on the northern border of Kusaug had not been born there.) A variety of birthplaces in the south were named, but Accra was by far the most frequent (being the birthplace of 16.3%), which again is appreciably more than in either of the other groups.

Not only were more of this group born in Accra or elsewhere in the south, but also the average length of stay in Accra of persons not born there was slightly longer: almost twelve years rather than about eleven years among the Dagaaba and about nine years among the Bulsa. However, the men of this group claimed to travel home rather more often than the Bulsa did, especially in the central (Nima) area, where more than half the men claimed to go at least once a year. An overall majority of both sexes claimed to go at least once in two years, but of the women among them, only a rather small minority claimed to go as often as once a year. Thus, while this group may represent a slightly more settled migrant community than the others, it appears to have maintained equally strong ties with the homeland.

Polyglotism and the Multilingual Dynamic

It was expected that each group would have its community language (Dagaare, Buli, or Kusaal) in common and that this language would be an obvious bounding feature. This expectation was not entirely realized, for only in the Bulsa group did everyone actually claim to be able to speak it (table 4.6); and as we have already seen, Kusaal does not have the same indexical function for the Kusaasi community that Dagaare and Buli do for their respective groups. The numbers who did not speak the community language were very small, to be sure, but several more were not confident of their ability to speak it well—about 5% of Bulsa and Dagaaba and 14% of the Kusaasi (table 4.7). The latter figure is no doubt related to the more diverse composition of that community. Nevertheless, the proportions who spoke Kusaal at all (96%) or even confidently (85.6%) were significantly larger than the proportion that claimed Kusaasi ethnicity, measured as membership in a Kusaasi patriclan (60%).

The total inventory of languages spoken by members of these survey groups is truly impressive, and there is no reason to think that it is not typical of the commu-

TABLE 4.6   Migrant Communities: Total Language Inventory, All Degrees of Competence

	Numbers of Speakers in Group:		
	Dagaaba (n = 502)	Bulsa (n = 419)	Kusaasi (n = 227)
A: Major Community Languages			
Dagaare	99.0%	0.2%	3.1%
Buli	0.2%	100.0%	0.0%
Kusaal	0.6%	0.2%	96.0%
B: Major Second Languages			
Akan	89.9%	95.0%	81.1%
English	62.8%	62.5%	83.2%
Hausa	56.2%	98.3%	96.5%
Ga	47.2%	17.9%	79.7%
C: Secondary Community Languages			
Moore	2.0%	0.0%	33.9%
Bisaa	0.2%	0.0%	17.2%
Mampruli	0.0%	0.9%	9.7%
Bimoba	0.0%	0.0%	3.1%
Sisaala	3.4%	0.0%	0.4%
Kasem	0.4%	5.2%	0.0%
D: Minor Second Languages			
Ewe	4.4%	0.5%	7.9%
French	4.2%	9.0%	7.5%
Dagbani	3.0%	2.4%	16.3%
Gurune	2.6%	0.7%	16.3%
Jula	2.2%	0.0%	0.9%
Anyi-Sehwi	1.0%	0.0%	0.0%
Yoruba, Zabarima (each)	0.4%	0.0%	0.9%
Losso*	0.4%	0.0%	0.0%
Dangme	0.0%	0.0%	3.1%
Tem (Kotokoli)	0.2%	0.0%	3.1%
German	0.0%	0.2%	0.4%
Nzema or Ahanta	0.2%	0.0%	1.7%
Basari	0.0%	0.0%	2.6%
Fulfulde	0.0%	0.0%	1.3%
Gurma	0.0%	0.0%	0.9%
Nchumburu, Krachi, Larteh (each)	0.2%	0.0%	0.0%
Gonja, Konkomba, Dogon (each)	0.0%	0.0%	0.4%

*"Losso" is a geographical term, used as an ethnonym by speakers of various languages along the middle portion of the Ghana-Togo border, including Nawdem, Tem, and Kabiye (Naden 1988: 44).

nities or that enlarging the surveys might not add more languages to the list of thirty-five (table 4.6). Four categories of languages may be distinguished, according to whether or not a language occurred as a first or a second language and the proportions of each set of respondents that claimed to speak it. Category A consists of the three languages historically identified with each community. Category B includes the major second languages, which are essentially those we have seen in chapter 3: Ga, Akan, English, and Hausa. Quite unlike the situation in inner Accra, none of these are the first languages of significant numbers. Category C includes languages of

TABLE 4.7   Migrant Communities: Total Inventory, Languages Spoken
with Confidence

	Numbers of Speakers in Group:		
	Dagaaba	Bulsa	Kusaasi
A: Major Community Languages			
Dagaare	95.8%	0.2%	0.4%
Buli	0.2%	95.2%	0.0%
Kusaal	0.2%	0.0%	85.6%
B: Major Second Languages			
Akan	69.1%	52.3%	54.2%
English	34.1%	21.9%	45.4%
Hausa	42.8%	75.6%	84.6%
Ga	30.7%	9.3%	39.2%
C: Secondary Community Languages			
Moore	1.0%	0.0%	23.8%
Bisaa	0.0%	0.0%	13.2%
Mampruli	0.0%	0.2%	8.8%
Bimoba	0.0%	0.0%	3.1%
Sisaala	2.6%	0.0%	0.0%
Kasem	0.0%	3.1%	0.0%
D: Minor Second Languages			
Ewe	1.6%	0.0%	2.2%
French	1.4%	0.0%	2.2%
Dagbani	1.0%	1.9%	4.8%
Gurune	1.0%	0.2%	9.2%
Jula	1.0%	0.0%	0.0%
Anyi-Sehwi	0.6%	0.0%	0.0%
Losso	0.5%	0.0%	0.0%
German	0.0%	0.2%	0.4%
Tem (Kotokoli)	0.0%	0.0%	0.9%
Dangme, Basari, Gurma, Gonja (each)	0.0%	0.0%	0.4%

peoples closely associated with the three major communities, which we might expect to find spoken by significant numbers as either first or second languages. These
include Moore, Bisaa, Mampruli, and Bimoba, that is, the languages of people most
closely associated with the Kusaasi and included as being "from Bawku"; Sisaala, a
South-West Grusi language of the Upper West Region whose speakers are closely
associated with the Dagaaba in some areas; and Kasem, a North Grusi language spoken by the Kasena, northern neighbors of the Bulsa, with whom some sections of
Sandema frequently intermarry. Most of the languages in category D are spoken by
insignificant numbers, but they are included because they pattern differently among
the three groups. Although the list of languages spoken with confidence by at least
one respondent is somewhat shorter (down to twenty-seven) and the numbers of
speakers of each are also smaller (table 4.7), clearly all groups are very multilingual
and there must be a large proportion of polyglot individuals. Indeed, the average
person speaks four languages at least a little (except members of the Kusaasi community, who average six) and speaks three of them with confidence (or four in the

case of the Kusaasi). Very few indeed, about 1% of the Dagaaba and none at all of the others, did not claim some knowledge of at least one second language. In the Kusaasi group only one individual, a young man, did not claim to know at least one second language well (table 4.8).

The Kusaasi community inventory is the largest, at twenty-eight languages, although the survey group was much the smallest. The Dagaaba inventory, of twenty-five languages, is comparable, but the Bulsa list of thirteen is significantly smaller. All these inventories are reduced when limited to languages people speak with confidence, but the differences among groups remain. Despite the insignificant numbers of speakers of many languages in category D, it is remarkable that the Kusaasi inventory of languages is still by far the largest, with twenty-one in this category, compared to sixteen for the Dagaaba and eleven for the Bulsa.

Although the home areas of these communities are not adjacent to one another, they are not separated by great distances, and the languages are closely related. It is therefore striking that they do not speak one another's languages (category A). Only the Kusaasi speak neighboring languages to any extent, with small but significant percentages speaking Moore, Bisaa, and Mampruli (category C), as expected, but also Gurune and Dagbani (category D). Knowledge of Sisaala among Dagaaba and of Kasem among Bulsa was by contrast very low, especially as languages spoken with confidence (table 4.7). Percentages of speakers of category D languages are generally insignificant, except in the Kusaasi community.

According to both inventories, as many Kusaasi spoke Hausa as spoke Kusaal, and this community also had the highest proportion of speakers for all the languages in category B except Akan. The Dagaaba had proportionally the fewest speakers of Hausa but the largest proportion who spoke Akan with confidence. Akan was in fact the only B language spoken with confidence by more than half the Dagaaba, whereas both Akan and Hausa were spoken confidently by more than half the Bulsa and the Kusaasi. Ga was the least spoken of the four, especially among the Bulsa.

The position of English is again peculiar. Although it had more speakers than Ga on both counts, if all three communities are averaged, it showed the largest discrepancy between users of any kind and confident speakers: a difference of 35.7%, compared to 30.1% for Akan, 25.2% for Ga, and only 16.0% for Hausa. That is, a majority of the people who claimed to speak any of these languages claimed to speak them with confidence, but the majority is greatest for Hausa and smallest for English.

Despite the general underrepresentation of women in the surveys, it is clear that there were gender differences in repertoires both within and between groups, espe-

TABLE 4.8   Individual Repertoires: Average Number of Languages Spoken

	Dagaaba	Bulsa	Kusaasi
Any competence	3.8	3.9	5.7
Highest number	9	6	9
Lowest number	1	2	2
With confidence	2.7	2.6	3.8

cially in claims to Ga and English, that is, the major second languages that on the average are the less widely known of the four (table 4.9). Among the Bulsa in particular there was a significant difference: more than 80% of the men spoke some amount of English, but relatively few women spoke English of any sort. In contrast, a higher proportion of women than men spoke Ga. This was also true among the Kusaasi, although all the figures are higher, and the difference with respect to English is less dramatic. More generally, if all claims to speak category B languages are considered, higher proportions of Bulsa men spoke all these languages than Bulsa women, except Ga, whereas among the Kusaasi, higher proportions of women than men spoke all languages except English. In terms of claims to speak these languages well, however, these two groups differed only with respect to English; all the other languages were spoken by higher proportions of women. In the Kusaasi group the gender difference with respect to English is not significant, but in the Bulsa group it probably is. The intragroup gender difference can be accounted for by differentials in formal education, which is the main avenue for acquisition of English for most people, and by the fact that the economic activities of most women (especially the Bulsa) are more limited to the residential neighborhood than men's, and so they are more likely to require other African languages than English. The difference that appeared between Kusaasi women and Bulsa women is probably attributable to age and education since the Bulsa were on average older and had had less formal education. Although the intragroup gender differences are likely to be characteristic of the communities at large, the intergroup differences probably are not.

All three of these groups thus operated a system of five languages: the community language, Hausa, Akan, English, and Ga. This does not mean that every individual among them must have had all five in his or her repertoire; most people obviously did not or did not speak them all equally well. They probably did not constitute a language repertoire according to Laitin's definition, a "set of languages that a citizen must know in order to take advantage of a wide range of mobility opportunities in his or her own country" (1991: 5). Having observed that people *do* speak these languages, we may assume that they find some advantage in each of them but that it

TABLE 4.9   Claims to Category B Languages, by Gender

	Bulsa		Kusaasi	
	M (n = 268)	F (n = 151)	M (n = 133)	F (n = 94)
Any competence				
Akan	94.0%	95.4%	77.4%	86.2%
Hausa	99.6%	96.1%	94.0%	100.0%
English	82.1%	27.4%	88.7%	75.5%
Ga	25.0%	32.7%	75.9%	85.1%
Confident claim				
Akan	50.0%	56.3%	51.8%	57.6%
Hausa	75.0%	76.8%	81.5%	89.1%
English	26.9%	13.2%	45.9%	44.6%
Ga	8.2%	13.2%	33.3%	47.8%

is not normally necessary for an individual to speak all of them. The question is, why do so many people find it useful to speak several, and why these particular languages and not others? On some levels the answers may be obvious, but on others they are not. Insight into why people speak the languages they do should help to establish whether or not this is a stable configuration and, ultimately, what the repertoire in Laitin's normative sense might be.

It is evident that these three survey groups—which, although not constructed as random samples, were nevertheless drawn from them according to uniform principles—are not sociolinguistically the same, despite the general similarities of their situations in Accra. They did not all use the same languages to the same degree and in the same numbers. This might be the product of differences in their relations with Accra, which might in turn encourage different patterns of accommodation to the urban situation. If this is so, we must ask the sociological question, to whom are the groups accommodating themselves to produce such different results? After all, most members of these groups lived and worked in the same place, Nima and Accra New Town. That Ga was the least widespread of the B languages in all groups, while Hausa was very widely known, suggests that accommodation to the established local population as presented in the preceding chapter was not the primary concern. Another possibility is that the differences were imported, rooted in conditions in the home areas. Examination of the roles of the various languages in the different groups leads necessarily to a historical question: how and where were the languages acquired in the first place?

It is almost a sociolinguistic cliché that among urban migrants whose community languages have relatively few speakers, community languages are reserved for domestic life and intragroup affairs, while languages of wider currency are used in intergroup affairs and in most extragroup contexts. In practice, the boundaries between the domains of the various languages cannot be so sharply drawn. In the case of the Dagaaba, although the community language was dominant in interactions with kin and friends and Akan was dominant in all external domains except school, other languages were reported in all these contexts (particularly English among kin other than the respondent's parents), and all languages other than Dagaare were reported in external domains (except at work and in drinking places, where Dagaare was also used by significant numbers) (table 4.10). The drinking places in question are very often pito bars, frequently run by Dagaaba women. For all languages, the most frequent single reported context of use was among friends. Except with members of the most immediate family (parents, spouse, offspring), it is clear that most people used more than one language in all contexts.

The pattern among the Bulsa was comparatively simple, Buli being clearly dominant for use among kin and Hausa with everyone else (table 4.11). Hausa was also used with kin, however, to the extent that unlike the Dagaaba, many Bulsa obviously used two languages with all categories of kin. On the one hand, younger people were particularly likely to use Hausa with their parents and siblings: 60.8% of those under twenty-five claimed to speak Buli to their parents, compared to 41.9% who claimed to use Hausa; the numbers in higher age groups who claimed to speak Hausa to their parents were negligible. On the other hand, older people were more likely to use Hausa with spouses and especially with their own children: for example, over 90% of those

TABLE 4.10   Contexts of Language Use in the Dagaaba Community (100% = Total Group, 502)

	Dagaare	Akan	Ga	Hausa	English
Kin network					
Parents	85.1%	2.2%	1.4%	2.2%	3.0%
Spouse	65.5%	4.6%	2.5%	2.8%	12.0%
Offspring	66.7%	3.4%	3.2%	3.0%	8.6%
Siblings	91.0%	7.6%	6.2%	5.2%	23.5%
Others	95.4%	16.7%	6.2%	15.3%	30.7%
Friends	95.8%	88.1%	44.8%	54.2%	59.4%
Networks in Nondomestic Domains					
Work	39.8%	62.2%	26.1%	33.1%	46.6%
Hospital	2.8%	64.1%	24.7%	26.1%	43.4%
Transport	4.0%	77.9%	29.5%	36.3%	41.0%
Shops	1.6%	79.3%	31.1%	33.9%	42.4%
Market	4.8%	85.1%	37.6%	39.6%	42.6%
Drinking	38.4%	60.4%	20.3%	33.5%	36.1%
Eating	5.6%	52.8%	17.3%	20.3%	29.1%
Cinema etc.	1.8%	41.4%	12.4%	19.7%	29.3%
School	0.8%	4.6%	3.8%	2.2%	8.6%

in the twenty-five to twenty-nine age group who had any children spoke Buli with them, compared to 47% who spoke Hausa; but in all age categories over thirty, while more than 90% used Buli with their children, more than 60% also used Hausa. Presumably this means that parents were more likely to use Hausa with their older children than with very young ones. Both languages were much used in interactions with friends, with Hausa dominating in the youngest age group.

TABLE 4.11   Bulsa Community Group: Contexts of Use of Buli and Hausa

	Buli	Hausa
Kin network		
Parents	17.9%	8.8%
Spouse	66.3%	40.3%
Offspring*	93.3%	59.7%
Other	61.8%	12.6%
Friends	78.0%	81.4%
Networks in nondomestic domains		
Work†	0.9%	52.3%
Public services	0.7%	89.5%

*Percentage of those who report the use of any language at all with their own children, that is, the likely total of actual parents. Other figures are percentages of the total group (n = 419).

†The great majority of respondents are men. The generally low figures are related to the rate of unemployment, 11.6% among the men and a reported 92.1% among the women.

TABLE 4.12   Contexts of Language Use in the Kusaasi Community Group

	Kusaal	Hausa	Other Language(s)
Kin network			
Parents	89.4%	32.6%	56.8%
Spouse*	56.3%	50.2%	48.5%
Offspring†	52.4%	46.3%	41.0%
Siblings and others	90.5%	69.0%	70.2%
Friends	94.3%	95.6%	97.8%
Networks in nondomestic domains			
Work	18.1%	49.9%	56.4%
Public services	82.4%	92.1%	56.4%

*No one under 25 claimed to speak any language to a spouse.

†A total of 131 persons claimed to speak at least one language to their own children.

In the Kusaasi group, there seemed to be more overlap in the situations of use of Hausa, Kusaal, and the other ethnic languages; but Kusaal was nevertheless the dominant language for use with kin, although not by such a large margin as Dagaare for the Dagaaba or Buli for the Bulsa (table 4.12). Apart from Kusaal, other languages, particularly Akan and Ga, were spoken more than Hausa with parents, although among members of the same generation, Hausa and the other languages (taken together) were used about equally.

The pattern of languages that the Kusaasi group used with its own children is particularly complex (table 4.13). The languages of the various non-Kusaasi ethnicities, or subcommunities, were used by far fewer than the numbers claiming to belong to them. The most used was Moore, by 9% of the parents. Bisaa, Mampruli, Bimoba, Gurune, Dagbani, and Ewe were each used by less than 5% of the parents. In contrast, Kusaal, Akan, Ga, Hausa, and even English were used by large propor-

TABLE 4.13   Kusaasi Community Group, Languages Used with Own Offspring (100% = 131 parents)

Age Group*	Kusaal	Akan	Ga	Hausa	English
25–29	75.0%	83.3%	33.3%	91.7%	41.7%
30–34	94.4%	30.5%	19.4%	63.9%	16.7%
35–39	84.0%	56.0%	44.0%	76.0%	20.0%
40–44	89.5%	31.6%	26.3%	94.7%	26.3%
45–49	100.0%	50.0%	28.6%	85.7%	7.1%
50–54	100.0%	66.7%	66.7%	88.9%.	0.0%
55 and over	93.3%	40.0%	26.7%	93.3%	0.0%
Total parents	90.8%	45.8%	32.1%	80.1%	16.8%
Total group	52.4%	26.3%	18.5%	46.3%	9.7%

*Only one individual below 25, woman in the 20–24 age group, claimed to speak any language to her own children, namely, Kusaal and Ga.

tions of parents of all ages. The youngest group of parents showed a decline in the use of Kusaal, accompanied by a marked rise in the use of Akan. Use of Hausa was very high at all ages. Very few parents over forty-five used English, which overall was used at a rate comparable to that which was found in the Dagaaba group. Since the total percentages of parents add up to 288.6, it appears that parents in this group on the average spoke three languages with their own children, or at least one more than parents in the other groups.

The Kusaasi, unlike the Bulsa but like the Dagaaba, used the community language externally to a significant extent. Although Hausa was reported to be spoken more than Kusaal in public areas, it was not so clearly dominant in these areas as it was among the Bulsa, partly because of the greater use of Kusaal but also because of the more extensive use of other languages. As in the other two groups, all languages were reported to be used with friends more often than with kin or in economic contexts external to the community. There is no doubt a considerable degree of overlap between friends and people met at work and elsewhere.

Clearly, a large proportion of the latest generation of the Accra-born Kusaasi was acquiring both Kusaal and Hausa, and well over half of Bulsa children must also have been acquiring Hausa in addition to their community language; but the children of the Dagaaba were in general acquiring only Dagaare, at least from their parents. If these communities were accommodating their linguistic behavior to that of others, they had not gone so far as to give up their community languages, although assimilation of this kind appears to have happened internally within the Kusaasi and Bawku community since few who belonged to the non-Kusaasi ethnicities included in that community seemed to be teaching the associated languages to their children. To determine whether the use of category B languages with kin and other community contexts constitutes accommodation, we need to know how and especially where their speakers acquired them.

Generally, the community languages had been learned at home and in the region of origin, but most people had learned the major second languages in the south. All who had learned their community language in the south had been born in the south, but since the proportions are smaller, it appears that some community language speakers born in Accra had not learned it until they visited the home area. This is particularly true of speakers of the subcommunity languages (category C) associated with the Kusaasi. No significant proportion of the Dagaaba had learned any language other than Dagaare in northern Ghana, except English, at school (tables 4.14 and 4.15). However, a majority of Akan speakers in this group (48%) had learned

TABLE 4.14   Dagaaba Community Group, Places of Language Acquisition

	Dagaare	Akan	Ga	Hausa	English
Dagao	85.9%	2.2%	0.0%	1.4%	30.9%
Elsewhere in Northern Ghana	0.0%	1.2%	0.0%	4.2%	0.8%
Akan regions	6.2%	48.4%	0.0%	7.8%	6.5%
Accra-Tema	8.2%	37.8%	47.2%	42.4%	19.3%

TABLE 4.15   Dagaaba Community Group, Social Contexts of Language Acquisition

	Dagaare	Akan	Ga	Hausa	English
Home	97.8%	1.8%	0.8%	0.8%	0.2%
Friends	0.2%	49.0%	28.3%	35.5%	6.8%
Work	0.0%	3.8%	0.8%	1.4%	3.6%
School	0.0%	0.6%	0.2%	0.0%	45.2%
Market	0.0%	0.0%	0.0%	0.0%	0.4%
Combinations	1.2%	33.1%	15.9%	17.9%	5.4%
Unknown	0.4%	1.6%	1.2%	0.4%	0.8%

the language in Akan-speaking regions of southern Ghana, a pattern not found in the other groups. Since the 1920s, significant numbers of Dagaaba, but not Bulsa or Kusaasi, have made seasonal trips south to work as farm laborers or in the gold mines of south-central Ghana. Although the proportion of Dagaaba born in Akan-speaking regions was not large (7.4%), it was larger than for the Bulsa (2.4%) or Kusaasi. More significantly, 40% of Dagaaba respondents had previously lived in Akan-speaking regions, almost as many as had learned the language there.

Although most of the Bulsa had learned Hausa in the south, at work or among friends, a significant number had learned it in the north, among friends (table 4.16). Whereas the majority of both ethnic Kusaasi and others in that community had learned Hausa in Accra, it appears that members of the other ethnicities were more likely than the ethnic Kusaasi to have learned it in Kusaug, especially in Bawku (table 4.17). There is no doubt that as far as these groups are concerned, acquisition of all category B languages, including Hausa, was normally a function of living in southern Ghana, especially Accra.

The community languages of these people were not in general available for use in mediated communication. By 1986, Buli, Dagaare, and Kusaal (as well as Kasem, Sisaala, and Gurune) were all being broadcast from Bolgatanga on URA-Radio (a component of the Upper Regional Agricultural Development Project), but this was not yet true in 1982–83, and in any case, URA-Radio cannot be received in Accra.[15] People from the Upper regions residing in Accra therefore depended on the four major

TABLE 4.16   Bulsa Community Group, Places and Contexts of Acquisition of Hausa

	Contexts*			
	Home	Friends	Work	School
Buluk	1.2%	13.2%	1.2%	7.7%
Elsewhere in northern Ghana	1.7%	14.7%	7.7%	4.1%
Accra	7.5%	37.0%	15.9%	6.5%
Elsewhere in southern Ghana	1.4%	16.8%	11.8%	1.9%

*The total for whom there was adequate data was 416 individuals. Several speakers indicated more than one context of acquisition, so that the table totals well over 100%.

TABLE 4.17　Kusaasi Group, Places of Acquisition of Community Languages and Hausa

	Kusaug	Elsewhere in North	Accra	Elsewhere in South
Kusaal				
Ethnic Kusaasi	80.1%	1.5%	11.0%	7.3%
Others	75.8%	0.0%	11.0%	4.4%
Hausa				
Ethnic Kusaasi	13.2%	3.7%	75.0%	4.4%
Others	27.5%	3.3%	56.0%	8.8%
Other community languages*				
All speakers	58.2%	4.4%	6.6%	5.5%

*Moore, Mampruli, Bisaa, and Bimoba.

second languages—English, Hausa, Akan, and Ga—if they wished to listen to the radio.

About 70% of the Bulsa and the Kusaasi reported that they listened to the radio at least occasionally. This proportion is comparable to that for radio listeners in the inner Accra market groups, but the languages favored were different. English and Hausa were the most commonly reported listening languages for both groups, while Ga was reported least (by less than 20% in each group). There seemed to be major gender differences, reflecting variation in education and mastery of English and also perhaps of worldview. Most men who listened at all (over 80%) listened to English and about the same proportion listened to Hausa, with a somewhat lower proportion (64%) who listened to Akan. Among the women, however, nearly all listeners listened to Hausa and three-quarters listened to Akan, but less than half listened to English. Akan was listened to by almost 10% more women listeners than men, and Ga, which had surprisingly few listeners compared to the numbers of speakers, was listened to (as well as spoken) by higher proportions of women than men. In other words, the importance of English in this domain is mainly its importance among men. Bulsa and Kusaasi women depended on southern Ghanaian languages, especially Akan, and even more on Hausa. Hausa thus appeared to be the single most important radio language for these two communities. Unfortunately, insufficient data were obtained on the listening practices of the Dagaaba. However, it seems that, as expected, very few in that community listened to Hausa, while far more people listened to Ga than in the other groups.

Print materials in the community languages were only marginally more available than radio broadcasts. Since the 1970s, Dagaare (but not Buli or Kusaal) has been one of the languages in which "mother tongue education" is officially available at the early primary level; it is therefore a language in which the Bureau of Ghana Languages, a publisher for the Ministry of Education, is expected to publish materials for school use. Very little has actually appeared, however, and in all three languages the available reading matter consists mostly of religious materials produced by Christian missions. The Roman Catholic church has been particularly active in Dagao, including in religious translation, and it is probable that more was available in Dagaare (but only in the Central dialect) than in the other languages. At any rate, 23.7% of the Dagaaba claimed to read the community language at least occasionally, compared to less than 20% of the Bulsa or Kusaasi, but in no group did a significant number claim to read it on a daily or even weekly basis. Almost everyone who read at all, a slightly lower proportion than those who had ever been to school (about 50%), read in English, and about half of those also read occasionally in the community language.[16] Less than 10% of any group reported reading Akan or Ga (French, a language limited to those with a secondary education, was reported by as many), and less than 1% claimed to read Hausa. The low incidence of Islam in these groups is indicated by the fact that Arabic was reported only by 7.4% of the Kusaasi group. The pattern for writing was similar, except that slightly fewer people claimed ever to write at all, and the dominance of English was even more pronounced.

Continuities and Trends

That the major second languages were most often learned in Accra does not mean that the home areas are linguistically homogeneous. For example, in parts of the Dagaare-speaking area, particularly near Lambussie, Sisaala speakers and Dagaare speakers are geographically interspersed. Dagaare evidently dominates since only Sisaalas are likely to be bilingual in these languages. Also, towns like Nandom and Babile have many "stranger" residents, including southerners (J. Goody 1967: 4). Scattered through the Upper East and West Regions are resident groups known variously as the Kantosi, Yarse, or Dagaare-Jula, believed to be the descendents of immigrants of Mande origin who entered the Wa area as early as the sixteenth century (Wilks 1989: 54). They now speak Yaare (in Dagaare, or Ya'an in Kusaal), a language very closely related to Moore and Dagaare.

A survey of three Buluk localities—Sandema, Wiaga, and Fumbisi—carried out shortly after the Accra Bulsa survey, indicate that although the proportions of monoglots seemed to be relatively higher (totaling 9.7% of the men and 15.4% of the women interviewed), polyglotism was also probably at least as high as among the Accra Bulsa, with an average of two languages spoken with confidence by both sexes in all three localities (Dakubu 1983). Although knowledge of Hausa, Akan, or English was by no means as widespread as in Accra, it was not negligible. Few claimed to know Ga, but in Sandema Kasem had more speakers (52%, any competence) than Hausa or Akan (both 47%, any competence).

The multilingual character of Bawku, which has existed since its foundation, has been alluded to already. Syme (1932) found that he was able to communicate everywhere in Hausa, including with a brother of the Mamprusi chief of Bawku. Multilingualism is also prevalent in the domestic context, for the policy of interethnic marriage—in a society where marriage is both polygynous and virilocal and households normally encompass several generations—means that the women in a compound are likely to represent several different language groups. Women who are working together sing in all available languages, look after one another's children, receive visits from relatives, and generally provide a situation in which many children grow up in several languages. Although the actual languages that Accra parents claimed to use with their children are not the languages most used in the households they came from in Bawku, it seems that the practice of raising children in several languages almost simultaneously is in some sense a continuation of Bawku practice.

Since Bawku and Sandema are administrative and market centers, it seems likely that members of the Accra communities who had learned category B languages in the north had done so mainly through association with economic activities typical of such centers. That is, their move to Accra was not simply rural to urban but also proceeded via a small urban or quasi-urban center to a big one. The majority, who had not learned languages in the north, must have come south directly, and the small numbers who reported having lived anywhere in the north apart from their hometowns bear this out. Most people apparently migrated in their early twenties, at the beginning of the most active periods of their lives. The situation also implies that most first-generation migrants learned category B languages other than English in early adulthood, not sooner, as an aspect of urban life, whether in the north or the south.

The multiple overlaps in usage areas of category A and B languages suggest that the situation may not be stable. Although all three groups were teaching the community language to the next generation, there is some evidence that the youngest, Accra-born group of parents may not have been doing a thorough job of it and that those who were not yet parents often preferred to speak one of the category B languages, even to their parents. One not infrequently hears complaints that young people born and raised in Accra do not speak their community language well. The question arises whether significant shifts away from the community languages are in progress that may have implications for the future of multilingualism and intergroup communication.

The homogeneity of the Dagaaba in the generations preceding the respondents' is indicated by the fact that only 0.6% reported their father's language as anything other than Dagaare (Sisaala 0.4%; English 0.2%) and 1.8% their mother's (Sisaala 0.8%; Ga 0.4%; Akan 0.2%; and Waale, which is mutually intelligible with Dagaare, 0.4%.). The situation was similar with the Bulsa: 1.3% had fathers and 5.0% had mothers whose languages were Kasem, Nankani (a western dialect of Gurune), Mampruli, or Akan. In all cases, at least one parent spoke the community language. There seems therefore to have been very little ethnic-linguistic intermarriage or assimilation among the parents of these groups.

In the Bulsa group, everyone had learned Buli first in life, so that initially there was no intergenerational shift away from that language. The Dagaaba were slightly more complex: only 91% had learned Dagaare as their language of initial socialization. Akan had been learned first by 4.0%, Ga by 3.0%, Hausa by 1.2%, and Sisaala by 0.6%. Since these figures, though very small, are higher than those for non-Dagaare parents, it is likely that they are a function of the slightly larger proportion of Dagaaba born outside the home area (28.7%).

As might be expected, the Kusaasi group was very much more complicated. The father's language of nine respondents, 4.0% of the total, was different from the expected one, given the patrilineal bias of all the ethnic groups involved: of four Mamprusi and two Mosi, the father of one Mosi was a Bisaa speaker, and the fathers of the rest were Kusaal speakers. There had therefore been a certain amount of shifting toward Kusaal, which had taken place in Kusaug itself. In addition, 23% spoke a language that was the language of one parent only, compared to 10% of the Dagaaba and 6% of the Bulsa, which must reflect a much higher incidence of linguistically mixed parentage.

Fully 40% of the Kusaasi group had begun life in a language that was not that of one or both parents. The father's language was slightly more likely than the mother's to be the language first learned, which I take to be a reflection of virilocal marriage patterns and patrilocal residence in early life. Since 60% of those whose initial language was also that of one parent, but not both, were over the age of thirty (that is, thirty-two of fifty-two individuals)—even higher than the proportion of the total group members who were over thirty (56%)—this phenomenon was not a simple function of the move to Accra. However, in the group whose first language was that of *neither* parent (thirty-one, or 14% of the total)—which included people whose parents had the same language, as well as others whose parents had different languages—more than three-quarters (twenty-four individuals) were under the age of thirty, and in fact a third of the entire group under thirty had not learned to speak either parent's language first. This kind of total shift between generations was therefore a relatively recent development and took place at least partly outside Kusaug.

Languages that appeared to be the language of one parent only and were not learned first include Mampruli, Kusaal, Bisaa, Moore, Bimoba, Gurune, and Kotokoli (the last two occurred only as the language of a respondent's mother).[17] The first language learned had been any of these same languages (other than Gurune and Kotokoli) or Akan or Ga. When the first language was the language of neither parent, the parents' language(s) could have been any of the foregoing, with Dangme and Ahanta also occurring as the language of one parent. In such cases, the first language learned had been Kusaal, Moore, Mampruli, Akan, Ga, or Hausa, that is, the main community language, one of the two more widely diffused associated community languages, or a category B language other than English. Hausa was thus the only language to appear solely as a target of shift. When the numbers who spoke each language as the language of initial socialization are compared with the numbers of parents who spoke each language, it is clear that across generations Akan, Ga, and of course Hausa had gained speakers and that Kusaal had barely held its own, while the other languages had all lost speakers (table 4.18).

The language in which a child first participates in social life does not invariably remain the adult's language of primary competence. A change of linguistic environment at an early age often results in a language that was acquired later becoming psychologically dominant, and it is not unknown for a change of this kind to occur later in life. It is not necessarily the case, therefore, that the kind of intergenerational shift represented by the initial language acquisition pattern of a portion of the Kusaasi group indicates a permanent shift or a trend, for it could conceivably have been reversed as these people grew up.

In fact, responses to the question "What language do you think you now speak best?" indicate that a shift in the language of primary competence had been a frequent occurrence in the Kusaasi group and was not unknown in the others (tables 4.19– 4.21). In all groups, the community language had lost speakers; that is, fewer people regarded it as the language they spoke best than had learned it first in life. The trend was most pronounced in the Kusaasi group, where only 35% thought they

TABLE 4.18   Shift away from Parent's Language in the Kusaasi Community

	At Least One Parent Speaker	Respondent's Initial Language
Kusaal*	17.6%	17.2%
Hausa	0.0%	9.3%
Akan	0.4%	8.4%
Ga	0.4%	4.8%
Moore	6.2%	3.1%
Bisaa	8.8%	1.8%
Mampruli	9.3%	1.8%
Bimoba	1.3%	0.4%
Guruni	1.8%	0.0%
Kotokoli, Ahanta, Dangme (each)	0.4%	0.0%

*Includes only cases in which *only* one parent spoke Kusaal.

now had a better command of Kusaal than of any other language, compared to 63% who learned it first; but 39% thought they spoke Hausa best, a gain for that language of 35% (table 4.21). There had also been a slight shift toward Hausa among Bulsa born in Accra. There was no trend toward Hausa nor Akan among the Dagaaba, but as many as 11%—and an even more surprising 18% of the Kusaasi—believed they had a better command of English than of any other language.

There was thus a trend toward those languages of intergroup communication that do not signify any local ethnic identity and away from the language that indexes the community. The trend was very small in the Dagaaba and Bulsa groups, favored different languages, and appeared to be a function of migrant status. In the Kusaasi group the trend was much stronger and seems to have been present in previous generations. It is therefore possible that it is a variation on a process of linguistic assimilation into the Kusaal-speaking community that took place in Bawku, even though Kusaal has lost speakers among ethnic Kusaasi, as well as others.

Studying Zabarima immigrants in Accra in 1954, Rouch came to the conclusion that migrants from what were then the Northern Territories of the Gold Coast were

TABLE 4.19   Shift in the Language of Primary Competence in the Dagaaba Community

	First Language Learned	Language Spoken Best	Difference
Dagaare	91.0%	79.7%	−11.3%
Ga	3.0%	5.2%	+2.2%
Akan	4.0%	3.2%	−0.8%
Hausa	1.2%	1.2%	0.0%
English	0.0%	10.8%	+10.8%

TABLE 4.20   Shift in the Language of Primary Competence in the
Bulsa Community

	First Language Learned	Language Spoken Best	Difference
Buli	100.0%	95.3%	−4.7%
Hausa	0.0%	4.7%	+4.7%

fundamentally part of the same cultural grouping as other immigrants from the north, whether from other British territories or from French; behaved in similar ways; and could not be meaningfully studied separately. Southerners, in contrast, were clearly different (Rouch 1956: 10). In other words, Rouch found "traditional" cultural, political, and linguistic groupings to be more powerful predictors of migrant behavior than "modern" political boundaries. There was no doubt a good deal of truth in this at the time. Present residence patterns, for example, seem to reflect it. However, it is to be expected that thirty years of political change, particularly the hardening of international boundaries and the enforcement of immigration laws that followed independence, have made a difference. Surveys of communities that originated from well outside the borders of modern Ghana in fact indicate somewhat different patterns of linguistic adaptation.

The most important difference concerns the role of Hausa. It has been shown that Hausa appears to be a target of shift in the three communities from northern Ghana but that, except in the Kusaasi community—where there seems to be a history of language shift and assimilation, including assimilation of peoples historically originating from outside present-day Ghana—only a tiny minority appears to be affected. Even where Hausa seems to be taking over some of the domains associated with the

TABLE 4.21   Shift in the Language of Primary Competence in the Kusaasi
Community

	First Language Learned	Language Spoken Best	Difference*
Kusaal	63.0%	35.2%	−27.8%
Ga	9.7%	11.9%	+2.2%
Akan	8.4%	12.8%	+4.4%
Hausa	9.3%	38.8%	+35.2%
English	0.0%	17.6%	+17.6%
Moore	0.0%	2.6%	+2.6%
Mampruli	0.0%	0.9%	+0.9%
Bisaa	0.0%	0.9%	+0.9%
Bimoba	0.0%	0.9%	+0.9%
Gurune	0.0%	0.4%	+0.4%

*Several people claimed equal competence in two or three languages as the language they spoke best, and a few claimed to have learned more than one language first at the same time.

community language, as among the Accra-born Bulsa and Kusaasi, almost everyone learns the community language. In contrast, the Dogon community, originating from Mali, seems to be losing the Dogon language and replacing it with Hausa. In a survey group that comprised the members over the age of fifteen of two households in Nima (fifty-one persons, of whom twenty-two were female), only about half the people interviewed, and hardly any of the Accra-born, claimed to speak Dogon well (Dakubu 1991). In contrast, everyone spoke Hausa, and only one person (male) did not claim to speak it well. Ga and Akan were also widely known, especially the former, which in this community was spoken as well by men as by women and claimed to be spoken well by more of both sexes than Dogon. People born in Accra had not learned Dogon as their initial language, and this pattern seemed to be persisting.

Reduced contact with the Dogon homeland is undoubtedly a factor. Immigration has evidently ceased, for all respondents born in Mali were more than thirty years old, with a mean age of over forty. Intermarriage in the Accra situation had been frequent since of those born in Accra, 60% (thirteen) had non-Dogon mothers. This may be the result of the cessation of immigration but also the failure of male immigrants to return home. Another factor may be linguistic diversity within the Dogon community itself. Besides non-Dogon women, the households surveyed included speakers of at least two dialects (Jamsay and Pinyay) that were not mutually intelligible, so that knowledge of a variety of Dogon does not in itself necessarily facilitate communication with the rest of the group. In a context where no variety of Dogon is usable beyond that small community, an externally useful lingua franca (Hausa) might seem a more efficient solution to internal communication needs than a second Dogon dialect. It is nevertheless a striking departure from the pattern in the homeland where, it seems, community dialects are carefully maintained, and although knowledge of other languages is highly valued, very few speak Hausa or Akan (Calame-Griaule 1986: 302–6).

The life-style of this group was thoroughly urban, and unlike any of the groups previously considered, its members were Muslims.[18] It may be contrasted with a Fulani group, also Muslim, that has strong contacts with Accra but is otherwise very different. Some Fulani live in the city, working as watchmen and in other jobs, but many families maintain cattle kraals on the Accra plains, practicing a rural and historically Fulani way of life. Their relations with Ghanaians have sometimes been hostile, but usually southern Ghanaians seem hardly to notice their presence. Rouch (1956: 133) thought they were isolated from other migrant groups; at any rate they generally maintain a low profile.

In July 1993 I interviewed thirty people who resided in one large compound near the Ga village Maajor (from Ga *maŋ lɛjɔ* [mãã´ã` jɔ] "the town is peaceful") at Ashale Botswe, about eight miles north of Accra, a mile or so beyond Madina. The group consisted of two widows, twelve sons, seven daughters, six daughters-in-law, one son-in-law, and a granddaughter and a grandson of one man, Alhaji Belko—recently deceased but originally from Namuno in Gurmaland in eastern Burkina Faso—who had established himself there in 1941. The sons were from sixteen to forty-six years old, the daughters from fourteen to forty-eight; the youngest person interviewed was the fourteen-year-old daughter. The oldest was the son-in-law, aged sixty-two, who is the imam for Ashale Botswe. He lived with his wife, the eldest daughter, in his own compound adjacent to the Belko compound and the family mosque. The widows were in their fifties, the daughters-in-law were in their twenties, and the two grandchildren were both eighteen.

The founder of the family had been very prosperous, and all his wives and several of the older sons and daughters had been on a pilgrimage to Mecca. Eleven members of the group had been to a Koranic school for widely varying periods, but among those over twenty-five years old, only one daughter-in-law had been to any other kind of school. If the patriarch was not interested in modern education, the present attitude is different, for everyone under twenty-five and unmarried was going to school. The Arabic-English School in Madina was particularly popular.

All the daughters-in-law were Fulani, but several, as well as both widows, said their own mothers were not. They had married into the family from other places—a few from Namuno but more from southern Ghana: Juapong near Akosombo, Winneba in the Central Region, Ho in the Volta Region, and the suburbs of Accra. Married daughters were visiting from Sogakope in the Volta Region and Abidjan. There seemed to be a strong tendency to learn the languages generally used in whatever place they happened to be living, so that although the men traveled more and were slightly more polyglot, the inventory of languages spoken by the women was slightly larger.

The rate of polyglotism was high, rivaled only by the Kusaasi rate. The average number of languages the men claimed to speak was 5.7, so the average man actually spoke six, and the average for women was 5.1 (effectively five). There were no monoglots at all because all without exception spoke both Fulfulde and Hausa; most were at least trilingual, for the only people who did not also speak Ga were two daughters-in-law, one from Ada and the other from Winneba (who spoke Dangme and Fante, respectively). The respondents attributed knowledge of Ga to their close relations with the adjacent Ga village.

Fifty-seven percent claimed to speak some variety of Akan, comparable to the proportions claiming to speak it with confidence in the Kusaasi and Bulsa groups. Fulani are not expected to be strongly associated with Akan-speaking country since cattle do not survive in most of it, so that this figure is, if anything, surprisingly high. Fifty-three percent claimed to speak English, which is higher than might be expected from the distribution of education but from observation not implausible. It may even be a little low, for virtually all the men could manage in broken English (if not better) when necessary, and they listened to Ghana FM radio and to the BBC (British Broadcasting Corporation) in English, as well as to the Hausa service.[19]

Other languages spoken were Arabic—which 30% claimed to know for religious reasons but could probably only read—and several languages learned through family connections and residence, including Ewe (27%), Ada (17%), Gurma (17%), and Zabarima-Dendi (17%). The imam, who came from Benin, knew Bariba, and one woman, who lived in Abidjan, claimed to know Jula, Bete, Moore, and French. These two people claimed to know eight and eleven languages, respectively. Two people claimed to know seven languages and eight to know six.

For the present, despite universal acquisition of Hausa, it does not seem that a major shift toward that language as a language of initial socialization and/or of primary competence is in progress. Few children under five can speak it. Most parents claim to speak Fulfulde to their children, but there were a few significant exceptions: one young man said that his son, who was living and attending school in Nima, spoke no Fulfulde, and a couple whose (only) child was living with its grandmother in Winneba also spoke to the child only in Hausa. These can probably be regarded as instances of linguistic assimilation under urban conditions.

In the rural compound, it was observed that casual conversation was often in Hausa, especially between men and women and especially, but not only, when visitors were present. Major oral art forms in Fulfulde were reportedly maintained: storytelling in Fulfulde was practiced, and songs were sung at traditional celebrations, particularly weddings and the celebration of a woman's first-born. However, it was also said that a few women tell stories in Hausa, and Hausa wedding songs were also sung. It seems clear that maintenance of the Fulfulde language depends fundamentally on the traditional occupation of cattle ranching, which is mainly the business of the men. The kraal was adjacent to the compound, and all the conversation that goes on there—its entire vocabulary and culture—is in Fulfulde.[20]

If maintenance of the cattle culture accounts for the strength of the Fulfulde language and for the distinctiveness of the Fulani people, it does not account for the universal acquisition of both Hausa and Ga. A remark made by a visitor to the compound may provide a clue. A young Wangara woman—married to a Wangara man, living in Madina, and claiming to speak Wangara, Hausa, Ga, Twi, and broken Arabic—emphatically asserted that she spoke Hausa to her children, not Wangara. Hausa, she said, is Ghana; Wangara is not.[21] On the one hand, this attitude must sound strange to linguists and social scientists and also politicians, who are used to defining Hausa as non-Ghanaian on (not necessarily the same) historical grounds. On the other hand, it seems to confirm the popular southern opinion that Hausa is the language of Ghanaian "northerners." What the young woman meant was that Hausa is the language of the contemporary world. Adoption of Hausa represents identification with a particular segment of modern Ghanaian society, for which "Ghanaian" means "modern, up-to-date, urban, nonethnic." To its speakers the language may index a kind of northern identity but precisely *not* northern ethnicity, if "ethnicity" implies conservative acceptance of a bundle of inherited attributes that include political status, symbolic culture, and language. In the case of the Fulani, it permits them to live in two worlds at once in spite of their very limited means of access to one of them. It allows the Dogon a solution to their linguistic dilemma that permits selective identification with Ghanaian groups with which they are in close contact in the urban environment, but it does not obviously compromise their cultural integrity. Northern Ghanaians, we may suppose, find Hausa attractive for the same reasons, but since their position as undoubted nationals makes them relatively secure compared to the Fulani and since, unlike the Dogon, they can maintain contact with the homeland with relative ease, it is not absolutely essential and so not universally acquired. It will probably not appear in a repertoire as defined by Laitin. Yet it is also probably no coincidence that among the three northern Ghanaian communities examined, the only significant shift to Hausa was taking place in the most ethnically fluid and the least unambiguously "Ghanaian."

Neither Akan nor Ga could accomplish this dual task for either Ghanaians or non-Ghanaians because, in Accra, neither of these languages can be divorced from the local culture it expresses. Akan for the Dogon and the Fulani groups seems to be specifically associated with public and workplace situations and is used less than by the Ghanaian northern groups, who in turn are much less likely to know Ga than are the Dogon or Fulani or to use it in personal situations. Ga is a language of strictly local accommodation, learned by people whose traditional livelihood depends on access to Ga lands, just as they learn Ewe in Ho or Dangme in Ada to ingratiate themselves. They are aware that the relationship is unequal and contingent—hence the need for a lingua franca through which they can identify with people in situations comparable to their own, that is, other "strangers." As far as the Fulani are concerned, this function of Hausa may be specific to conditions around Accra. Another visitor to the Belko compound, who had grown up in the Fulani community in Tamale, remarked that in Tamale the Fulani all speak Dagbani but not Hausa.

Finally, we may examine a group occupationally comparable to the inner-town market traders of chapter 3, except that they work in kiosks and stalls attached to supermarkets, not in the market, selling European vegetables and relatively expensive types of imported commodities in the economically elite areas beyond Nima— Roman Ridge, the Airport Residential Area, and near Danquah Circle in Osu—to a clientele that consists mainly of relatively wealthy Ghanaians and foreigners. Forty such sellers were surveyed in 1989.[22] They included nine men and thirty-one women, and more than half (of both sexes) were under the age of thirty. Not all were full-time sellers: a few also worked as hairdressers or apprentice mechanics. Several were selling to help out a relative who owned the stall. They could be divided by geographical origin into three groups: southern Ghanaians (63%); northern Ghanaians (23%); and Hausa from Kano, Nigeria (15%). The southerners could be further divided into Ga-Dangme (13%); Akan, including speakers of Guang languages and Nzema (38%); and Ewe (13%). The northern Ghanaians included one or two each of Nankanse, Bulsa, Kasena, Kusaasi, and Dagomba. Although the people from Kano were comparatively few, they included two stall owners, the only respondents identified as such. Only 60%, including five Ga, had been born in their linguistic homeland, compared to 31% (excluding the Ga) who had been born in the Accra Region. Consistent with the relative youth of the group, six of the nine from northern Ghana had been born in Accra. Most of the Akan and Ewe, however, had been born in their homelands. Three of the six from Kano had been born in Accra.

Our interest here is in whether Ghanaian southerners, Ghanaian northerners, and northern strangers, all engaged in an economic activity that forces them to interact with customers who are not members of their own or even related communities, maintain different or convergent patterns of multilingualism. Despite the small numbers, it appears that they remain different, in ways consistent with the patterns examined already but with very slight indications of convergence that might be accounted for by the shared economic activity. The four category B languages, and no others, appeared as significant second languages. All but English were also community languages. The six "strangers" from Kano all spoke both Hausa (which, of course, was their community language) and, significantly, Ga. Eighty-three percent (that is, five of the six) spoke Akan (mainly Twi), which is higher than in the Dogon or Fulani groups but consistent with an urban trading life. The nine northern Ghanaians also all spoke Hausa, but only two spoke Ga, while five, just over half, spoke Akan, a pattern generally in accord with the northern survey groups. Seventy-two percent of the twenty-five southerners spoke Akan, 52% spoke Ga, but only 28% spoke Hausa, which is, however, higher than in the market survey groups. Seventy-two percent of the southerners also claimed to speak English, as did about half of the northerners and the Hausas. As in the survey groups, English patterned differently from other languages in terms of perceived competence: most people who claimed to know an African language at all were confident of their ability, but most people who claimed to know any English were not.

Nevertheless, in the 45% of the whole group that claimed to read and the 38% that claimed to write, English was by far the language most used for these purposes, and most of the few who read or wrote an African language read or wrote English as well. (Exceptions were two in the Kano group, one of whom read Hausa and another who read and wrote Arabic.) It was also the dominant language of radio listening, although by a much smaller margin: of the 75% who claimed to listen to the radio at least occasionally, 60% said they listened to English (as did only about 40% of the Salaga market groups), 57% to Akan, 43% to Hausa, 40% to Ga, and 20% to Ewe. These figures are roughly proportional to those claiming to speak the languages but slightly lower.

There is no reason to believe that the community languages of either northern or southern migrants or the local Ga are being eliminated from domains where they were once employed. By virtue of being used in new surroundings, it can be assumed that they have added domains and have developed the appropriate registers. Whenever they are used to discuss new experiences with an interlocutor of a type that may hardly have existed in the homeland—for example, in a discussion of housing difficulties in Nima or a community organization between members of the same community who are neither kin nor from the same village—both the range of (sub)domains and the overall network density have been increased. However, the prevalence of polyglotism implies that when individuals have access to certain networks of speakers, as part of participation in new subdomains of discourse, new languages are usually added to their repertoires.

To the extent that outer Accra functions as an internally cohering network of northern migrants, it does so by means of Hausa. However, this clearly does not unite members of all communities equally, for it has been shown that communities differ considerably in the distribution of control of the language. Hausa alone is not enough; for some communities (at least, the Dagaaba), Akan is an essential tool of external communication.

Akan seems to be the main potential vehicle for communication with inner Accra, since Ga, while by no means unknown, was far less widespread in most groups. This is the most likely source of any claim Akan may have to function as an urban lingua franca since there is no reason to believe that within inner Accra, Akan is widely used in situations in which it is not the community language of at least one party. The same is true of the functions of Ga in outer Accra. Since a little more than half the outer Accra respondents reported that they spoke Akan well, we may conclude that, although the two parts of the city constitute separate network systems characterized by the use or non-use of Hausa, they are by no means completely cut off from each other.

The main importance of English is not in direct contact between communities within Accra or any part of it but in mediated contact between communities and the rest of the country, including, through letter writing, the community homeland. Use of English in the "official" domains of government departments, where forms must be filled out and documented transactions negotiated, is an aspect of such contact. English is at the same time the only language taught and used throughout Ghana, its only universally recognized lingua franca, and the least spoken (in the communities investigated) of its languages of wider communication, lingua franca or not. It is a language in which a fairly large proportion of the people receive messages but far fewer send them. And the quality of the reception is debatable.

The hows and the whys of the situation are by no means obvious. In the outer city, a system of four languages of wider use (category B) has been observed. Can it be reconciled with the trilingual configuration outlined earlier? How long has it existed, and why are these particular languages salient? Hausa is popularly associated with Islam, and yet Islam was hardly present in the Hausa-using Bulsa and Kusaasi communities: what is the source of the association? On the one hand, why is Akan (and not, say, Ewe, also the language of a large migrant community) a major second language in inner Accra, and what, on the other hand, explains the persistence of Ga? English, of course, is the language of the former colonial power and is taught in the schools, but is the observed pattern of appropriation of the language a colonial or a postcolonial phenomenon, or does it go back even further?

It has been seen that to some degree, differences in the behavior of migrant communities can be explained historically. Different community histories, and different histories of individuals within the contexts of their communities, result in different patterns of accommodation, affecting both second-language use and language shift. There is a tendency to assume that Accra's population explosion of the past half century has created a linguistic situation without historic parallel. In the next chapters, it is argued that while the linguistic situation has indeed become more complex, multilingualism in Accra is the product of a long and evolving tradition. Not all the questions posed can be answered with certainty, but it can be shown that the present situation is neither historically inevitable nor accidental.

5

To the Sea: The Formation of the Ga Language Community

In this chapter we unravel the origins of the association between Accra and the Ga language. More generally, we trace the spread of Ga and its close relative Dangme on the Accra plain. But Ga-Dangme has never had the territory to itself, and so the account of how and in what sense Ga acquired and maintained linguistic hegemony in its present territory leads to investigation of a series of relationships with other language communities.

The external history of the emergence of the Ga language also requires attention to the history of contacts with speakers of other languages before arrival on the plain. There is no doubt that such contacts occurred, but they are difficult to place in a chronological sequence, let alone date. The available migration traditions do not seem to reflect events before the fourteenth century. Painter's (1966) lexicostatistical figures for the onset of the Ga-Dangme split point to an earlier date, about the ninth century. However, if the theory to be proposed is correct—that Ga originated as Dangme in the mouths of a grouping of mostly Guang-speaking populations—ease of intelligibility between Ga and Dangme probably declined rather abruptly, and the glottochronological figure, based as it is on the hypothesis of a constant rate of replacement of culturally non-specific vocabulary, is thus misleading. The Ga-Dangme migration traditions have been published and discussed by numerous authors, including me, but for our present purposes they must be examined once again.

The Accra area has been inhabited for a very long time, since the fourth millenium B.C.E. at the latest. The Iron Age begins at the outset of the current era, with radiocarbon dated sites at Kpone (C.E. 150 ± 75) and Tema (C.E. 100 ± 90), at the eastern end of the present Ga-speaking coast (Anquandah 1982: 142). From about C.E. 500, the period of the middle and late Iron Age saw considerable expansion of village settlements, as well as alterations in pottery styles. The in-migration of Ga-Dangme–speaking people, as well as Guang groups, was probably complete by C.E. 1400, but as we shall see, the present linguistic and political configuration was attained gradually in a process of consolidation and assimilation lasting into the twentieth century. Continuity in the archaeological record suggests either that another population has been entirely assimilated into the immigrants or that Guang-speaking people were already present several centuries before the migrations of the tradition. In either case, the language of the earlier group has vanished. The southern Guang languages of today are very closely related, and all appear to be directly descended from the language(s) of immigrants (Dakubu 1988b: 79–80).

The evidence that the Ga-Dangme–speaking people arrived from the north and east comes mainly from oral tradition, as written down by several authors. According to one of the major sources, the Krobo (a Dangme-speaking group who now live on the northeastern fringe of the Accra plain) came from Sameh, an island to the southwest of the "River Ogum adjoining Ladah and Dahome" (Azu 1926: 242).[1] This no doubt refers to the river Ogun, which flows directly south into the Lagos lagoon, to the east of Alada and Dahomey. I have suggested elsewhere that the "island of Sameh" might be identified with the Yoruba kingdom of Shabeh (Dakubu 1972: 95). The Krobo tradition has the people moving north of Dahomey to Zugu ("Djougou" on maps of the Republic of Benin), then southwestward to "Tsamla," which may be identified with the Chala [tšālā] people.

This contact probably took place in north-central Togo, in the neighborhood of Sokodé. The Chala today speak an Eastern Grusi (Gur) language, closely related to Delo (Naden 1988: 17), and are situated just north of the Adele and the Achode on the Ghana-Togo border; their capital is at Odomi, where most have shifted to the Gichode language.[2] They, too, have a tradition of migration from the east, from the Niger River through Nikki (which, like Zugu, is in the northern Republic of Benin) and Tchaudjo (in Togo somewhat north of their present location), where they first acquired the name ("Challa" in Kondor 1990). The name Tchaudjo refers to a state in the area of Sokodé, formed by a Kotokoli (Tem-speaking) group from the north, which incorporated local Kabre elements, and its people (Cornevin 1963: 72; Westermann 1932: 5).[3] It is therefore a possibility that the Sokodé area was the scene of contact before the Chala had reached their present home and probably before they spoke their present language.

Later, the Krobo moved farther south to Kpesi or Kpeshi, which may be identified with Kpessi (often spelled "Pessi") on the Mono River north of Atakpame. According to this tradition, the Krobo together with some of the Kpesi people then continued south to Atakpame, Agome, and Tagologo in today's southern Togo, then westward to Akrade.[4] Old Akrade was on the east bank of the Volta, just above present-day Kpong.[5] At this point some of the group, presumably Guang-speaking, crossed the river to found what became the Guang-speaking state of Kyerepong (Ɔkere Kpɔŋkpɔ "Great Okere"), presumably at the ancient location west of the present Akuapem hill towns (Kwamena-Poh 1973: 125). The Krobo (among whom Azu includes most of the Dangme) crossed lower down, at a place called "Humer," and settled for a time at Biam in the Ada district at Kunyenya.[6] The name Biam or Biambi (Dangme *bia mi* "at Bia") appears in the vicinity of the Volta River on some of the earliest maps of the Gold Coast, for example Blaeu's of 1665, but disappears after the seventeenth century.[7]

An Ada tradition also mentions the Zugu connection (Dakubu 1972). Reindorf ([1889] 1966: 21, 48) refers to a strictly Dangme tradition of migration from Tetetutu or Same "in the East between two large rivers," the Efa and the Kporla, in the course of which they traveled north of the kingdom of Dahomey.[8] The Efa and Kporla rivers might be identified with the northern course of the Weme, which flows into the lagoon at Cotonou, and its major tributary, the Okpara. Henrici's map of 1890 labels them the Ofe and the Okpara. Alternatively, the Kporla might be identified with the Kwara, or Niger, shifting the possible area of origin farther east, into the far north of Yorubaland.

The very sketchy Ga traditions available say little about a journey south through Togo. Reindorf ([1889] 1966: 19) pays more attention to a tradition that the original Accra people (the Akras) arrived from the sea, which may incorporate recognition of an ancient population that preceded both the Ga and the Guang. Field also mentions Tetetutu as being somewhere to the east, probably on the Mono (Dakubu 1972).

These traditions are not exclusively Ga-Dangme. Ewe traditions also mention a place of origin that may be identified with Sameh, and there is a group of lineages by this name in the Abutia traditional area, southwest of Ho (Verdon 1983: 64). Some western Ewe also have a tradition of former residence farther north, in Adele country, to which they still had ritual ties early in this century (Westermann 1932: 4). Ancestors of the Ga and Dangme evidently were associated with some of the Ewe in their travels south and west. Several writers have suggested that later connections of the Ga with the Anecho area, in the lagoons at the Togo-Benin border, reflect an old, migration-period association; but it is significant that these connections go no farther east than the Mono River, for there is no history of early movement across the southern part of the modern Republic of Benin. It seems likely that the migrations moved north and west from somewhere between the Weme and the Niger—as it bends westward north of the Republic of Benin—and then moved south, assimilating en route other groups with other places of origin and speaking languages other than the precursor of Ga and Dangme. Below Atakpame, most of the group moved southwestward toward the Volta above Kpong, but a few must have continued down the Mono beyond the Tado area before going west to cross the Volta above Ada.

Following attacks by another group, the Dangme, or the ancestors of what became their ruling clans, left Biam for Lolovor (a place famous in Dangme lore but not now inhabited by them), in the northern corner of the plain between the Osu and Krobo hills. From there they dispersed into approximately the present divisions, probably during the fourteenth century. The Krobo and the Osu did not move very far, at least initially. The Shai went a few miles southwestward, while the Ada went southeast, back to the vicinity of Biam. As political entities, Ningo and Gbugbla (Prampram) on the coast were established later by groups of Krobo, Osu, and Akan and other immigrants (Azu 1927: 81). Both towns appear on Dudley's map of 1646–47, as Miongo and Pempena. These immigrants did not settle uninhabited spaces. The dispersal from Lolovor, which resulted in a political configuration that is reflected in dialect geography (Dakubu 1987b), projects a political realignment, with linguistic ramifications, that was completed relatively late in the establishment of the present population, perhaps early in the seventeenth century (Wilson 1991: 15).

The piecemeal nature of the migrations and the political nature of the accounts of them are particularly noticeable in connection with Accra. According to Azu, the

Ga were originally a division of the Krobo, who had crossed the Volta with them and later sent Krobo two bullocks every year "as a token of gratification" for having been "led to the coast." Not surprisingly, this emblem of subordinate status does not appear in the published Ga traditions. The people who founded Gbese, one of the major quarters (*akútsèi*, sing. *akutso*) of Accra, left Krobo a little later than the other Ga. Some remained behind and are known as the Kplelii, "Kpele people" (Azu 1926: 262–63).

According to Reindorf's most detailed version, on the other hand, the Gbese, on whose Guang origins Reindorf and Azu agree, were the first to arrive on the coast. Then, "King Ayi Kushi and his tribe of Tungmawes with Obutus and Ningowas followed." Tungma We (according to Reindorf) was the origin of the quarter now called Abora (or Abola). The ancestors of the Asere arrived third, from where we are not told. According to Field (1940: 142–3), the first to inhabit the site above the beach were the ancestors of the Sempe and of some of the Asere. Both accounts may be read politically, as Ga claims to the lands between Osu and the Densu.

It was only after this that the Ga capital was established on Okai Koi Hill near Ayawaso, when Ayi Kushi's son Ayite led a mixed group up the Densu to the Nsaki river valley (Bredwa-Mensah 1990: 49; Reindorf 1966: 19, 25). By Field's account, Ayi Kushi's group, who later formed the nucleus of Abola, went inland almost immediately to found the Ga capital, where they met, or according to Reindorf were joined by, the Obutu. The idea that they were preceded at the site of Great Accra by Obutu or other Guang speakers is supported by the tradition that there they found the suggestively named Nii Gua [gùa], god of thunder and blacksmithing, residing in a brass basin (Bredwa-Mensah 1990: 41).[9]

The Ga capital, known to Europeans as Great Accra, became an important center of the gold trade (Anquandah 1982: 117; Ozanne 1964). It was also the cradle of the modern Ga language. The traders' town on the plain, which is probably the Accra capital referred to by Tilleman ([1697] 1994: 28), consisted of three ethnically distinguished quarters plus a market quarter, strung out at the base of the long Kpla hill (Bredwa-Mensah 1990: 90, 239). They were separate from the king's town on the hill, which came to be known as Okai Koi Hill and brings to mind the defensible hilltop settlements of the Krobo, Shai, Osu, and Hill Guang. Great Accra was overrun during the third quarter of the seventeenth century by Akwamu (a growing Akan power based in southwestern Akuapem), upon which King Okai Koi, the sixth remembered king in the line beginning with Ayi Kushi, committed suicide on 20 June 1660 (Field 1940: 144; Reindorf [1889] 1966: 34) or was killed (Wilks 1957).[10] Some of the Ga ruling group fled to Anecho and founded a state at Glidji in 1663 (Bole-Richard 1983: 6). The Ga continued to fight the Akwamu for the next twenty years, but by 1678 the Ga capital had been moved to Little Accra near the Dutch Fort Crèvecoeur (now Ussher Fort), which had been built in 1649 on the site of an earlier lodge (Van Dantzig 1980: xi); Okai Koi's son Ashangmɔ also fled to Anecho (Reindorf [1889] 1966: 28).[11]

The modern political structure of the Ga-speaking coast began to take shape with the establishment of Ga Mashi at Little Accra as the Ga capital, and from this time we can be confident that Ga, in contrast to other dialects of Dangme, was spoken at the shore.[12] The traditions more or less agree that the present-day Asere quarter was established first, and Asere and Abola were both founded by people from Great Accra

(Field 1940; Kilson 1971: 13, 1974: 6). A relic of Tungma We was part of Abola (Field 1940: 147), but the remnant of the royal line fled to the Anecho area in 1682, and Accra ceased to be a monarchy (Wilks 1957: 111). Gbese became independent of Abola almost immediately (Field 1940: 182). According to the former leader (Nií `Akwaashɔ́ŋ Màntsɛ) of the Ga Mashi State Council (akwaashɔ́ŋ), the lineages at the beach responsible for the major deities were incorporated into Asere (Sakumo, Dantu) and Gbese (Nai, Korle). This departs from Field (1961: 86), who placed the responsibility for Korle in Sempe and for Sakumo in Gbese, but the location of the shrines and residences of their priests is in accord with Nii Akwashong's statement. He also stated that the post of the Korle Wúlɔ̀mɔ (priest) moved from Asere to Gbese. At one time Abola, Gbese, Asere, and their war captains (asafoatsɛmɛi) presented firewood to Sakumo annually, in a traditional act of homage (Field 1961: 89–90), but according to Nii Akwaashong this is no longer done, at least by the Asere war captains. These facts seem to reflect a period of political tension and realignment. According to Field, the other previous inhabitants of Little Accra formed the Sempe quarter, but as late as Tilleman's time (1682–1697) they lived at Chorkor, west of the Korle lagoon.

In line with his tendency to emphasize the seniority of the Krobo over the Ga and the position of its royal family within Krobo, Azu (1926: 263) is at pains to point out that Kɔɔle is identical with Dangme Kɔle, the deity of the Krobo royal family (Jebiam-Nam-Odumase).[13] If Kɔɔle was indeed introduced from Krobo, perhaps by the "Kplelii" of Great Accra now represented by Gbese, then she literally went to the sea when the capital moved.

The Guang Factor

It is not clear to what extent the coast between the Tsemu lagoon at Tema and the Sakumo Fio ("Lesser Sakumo") lagoon west of Chorkor was Ga-speaking before 1660. In 1601, De Marees (1987: 85–86) found that the language of "Chincke," seven kilometers beyond Tema (that is, near Kpone), was similar to but not mutually intelligible with the Accra language, which in turn was different from the (presumably Guang) language of Bereku to the west. Since his "Chincke" numbers were in a Ga-Dangme dialect, this suggests that the dominant language at Little Accra, or of the Accras trading there, was already a form of Ga. However, he had nothing to say about the language at Labadi, Nungua, or Tema.

Traditions imply that Ayi Kushi and Tungma We were different from other people, and Ga, or the ancestors of the Ga, thus were the nucleus of the future Ga-speaking community. According to Field (1962b) the first Ga to arrive were actually the Ga Wɔɔ, who eventually founded Nungua. These people, who seem to have had little further to do with the people of Great Accra, probably spoke a Ga-Dangme dialect but not the one that became modern Ga.[14] Reindorf ([1889] 1966: 21, 23) thought that the aboriginals of the coast spoke the "Ahanta, Obutu, Kyerepong, Late and Kpeshi languages" but that the Le people, who at one time were spread over the entire Ga-Dangme coast and perhaps beyond, spoke Dangme at least at the eastern end. (Ahanta, which is mutually intelligible with Nzema, is spoken west of Takoradi.) He states (p. 40) that before the Osu people arrived at Osu, the area was settled by two brothers and a sister, whose deity's name indicates that they were Le (La), and also that besides these earlier Osu inhabitants, the Gbese, as well as the Larteh, Lakple, and Kpone people, were all La.

In modern Ga, the ethnonym and glossonym "Obutu" refers to Accra's Guang-speaking neighbors across the Densu to the west—the Awutu. The Awutu language is very closely related to the Afutu of Winneba and Senya Bereku and to Kyerepong (in the language, Ɔkere) and Larteh (Ga Latɛ; Larteh Lɛtɛ), spoken in the Akuapem hills northeast of Accra. There is no doubt that Guang-speaking people on the western Accra plain were closely associated with the Ga. Reindorf's account of the appearance of Ayi Kushi with his Tungma We people (Ga) and Obutus (Guang), immediately followed by the king of Obutu, states as much. According to the same writer, when the Ga led by Ayi Kushi's son Ayite established themselves at "Okaikoi" they acted in concert with the Obutus and a "Twi prince" ([1889] 1966: 19). One of the quarters of ruined Great Accra is by tradition the Obutu quarter (Bredwa-Mensah 1990: 90), and we have seen that it may have pre-dated the Ga arrival.

The gold trade at Great Accra gave rise to friction among these groups, resulting in the Obutu being driven westward (Field 1940: 143). Nevertheless, the fourth remembered Ga king, Mankpong Okai, married Dode Akaibi (Dɔde Akaíbi, or Akaî), granddaughter of the Obutu king who had been associated with Ayi Kushi. Dode is the name of the present Awutu royal lineage (Field 1962a). Reindorf ([1889] 1966) remarks that their son was named Okai Koi (Okai's son Koi) because Koi was an Obutu royal name, but already the king preceding Mankpong Okai (according to Reindorf) had been called Nikoi (Nii Koi) Malai. Today, Ga patrilineages give names according to a system in which two related sets of names are given to alternate generations (Dakubu 1981). "Okai" is particularly associated with lineages belonging to the Asere and Gbese akutsei, of which the latter is said to be Guang in origin.[15] The implication is that the Ga ruling family of Great Accra was thoroughly mixed with Guang stock. The group remembered as Obutu was still Guang-speaking, but the politically successful Ga must have assimilated proportionally large numbers of the Obutu community, who shifted to (proto-)Ga, or whose children did. The Great Accra community as a whole was undoubtedly bi- or multilingual. The story of the destruction of the tyrannical Dode Akaibi after Mankpong Okai's death may be read as a step in the assertion of the Ga's political and, coincidentally, linguistic hegemony over the Obutu.[16] According to Field, the Akanmaje quarter of Accra was founded by the Obutu who remained with Accra after Dode Akaibi's death.[17]

Ga was therefore in all likelihood the dominant language in daily life of the community that moved down to the sea. However, the major cult practices that it is believed to have brought from Great Accra were long performed at least partly in a Guang language, which the practitioners call Obutu. Field ([1937] 1961: 107) states that although most Kpele songs were sung in Ga, they had originally been in a Guang dialect and in some cases still were, though garbled because the singers did not understand them. Although she originally called the Guang language of these songs Obutu, in conformity with current Ga idiom, she later decided that it was not Obutu but Kpeshi, another Guang dialect (Field 1940: 82).[18] All of the cult songs presented by Kilson (1971: 45), who worked only in Accra, are in either Ga or Akan, but she also noted that the texts of some were distorted to the extent that she could not use them

because the singers did not understand them. It is known that when a song in a language Ga singers do not understand well becomes incomprehensible to them, they
may reshape it so that it does make sense, in language they understand better (Dakubu
1981: 285). In this way it is likely that the Guang language (whether Obutu or Kpeshi)
has been gradually eliminated from Kpele songs, usually by being recast in Akan, to
which it is much more closely related than Ga. This has surely happened with the
well-known Ga hymn that begins *"Awo Awo! Agbaa ee Bleku tsɔɔ!"*, which many
Ga believe to be in Twi. Most versions of the song do not quite make sense in Twi,
and Bereku (Blekú in Ga) is a major Guang deity (Field 1940: 82). (For texts see
Field 1961: 13 and Kilson 1971: 117.)

Obutu is thus not the only name that signifies the Guang language and people
among the Ga. Reindorf mentioned Kpeshi, together with Kyerepong and Larteh, as
another Guang language, and Field accepted it as such without question. This is the
name (pronounced [kpeéʃí]) of the lagoon just east of Labadi and of people thought
to have been present at the sites of several Ga towns before their foundation, forming quarters or subquarters within them, such as Awudung in Tema, Lɛɛshi in Teshie,
and in Labadi. It is also said that Kpeshi people, as well as Obutu, were present at
Great Accra (Field 1940: 143). Kpeshi origins are implied by the name of Tete Kpeshi,
who, together with his brother Odote (Adote?), gave the English the land for James
Fort, built in 1673 (Reindorf [1889] 1966: 38; Van Dantzig 1980: xi). Sempe was
founded when these people moved from the western side of the Korle lagoon to settle
by the fort. Their earlier settlement was Chorkor, mentioned (as Sioco) by Tilleman
([1697] 1994) as the African town associated with James Fort.

It has been noted that in the tradition according to Azu, the Krobo (or Dangme)
left Kpessi in central Togo accompanied by some of the Kpessi people. The town of
Kpessi is Ewe-speaking today, but apparently it was not always so (Cornevin 1963:
76). The place figures in numerous migration traditions, including those of the Akposo
and of an Akan group, Cornevin's "Achanti-Kpessi." Although the only Guang language presently spoken in the area is Ginyanga (a dialect of Gichode, the language
of the Achode, a little to the north), it is likely that the Kpesi group that joined the
Dangme was Guang-speaking, and as Field (1940) indicates, represents a different
Guang tradition from the Obutu.[19]

Azu does not explain why the Gbese who remained among the Krobo are known
as "Kple people," but the name is surely that of the body of Ga religious practice,
lore, text, and music called Kpele (Kilson 1971).[20] The name also occurs as an
ethnonym in "Lakple," mentioned as people who left Prampram for Anlo in southern Eweland (Reindorf [1899] 1966: 36). The possibility therefore arises that Kpele
was the contribution of one element in the pre-Ga association of Dangme- and Guang-
speaking groups and that since Kpele texts preserved Guang language material, that
element was originally Guang-speaking.

The migration accounts available do not mention Kpele, but a place by that name
exists southwest of Kpessi in the direction of Palime, which is in some way connected
with the Ga-speaking area. Kpele (or possibly another place close by) is called Kpele-
Ele, which is the same combination of names as La-Kple, in reversed order.[21] Like
Kpessi, Kpele is now Ewe-speaking, but Cornevin (1963: 44, 63) mentions it as
the ancestral land of Akposo tradition and also states that it was at one time Twi-

speaking.[22] His list of chiefs of Kpele-Ele includes some Akan names—Kotia, Ansa, and Amou (Amu)—and some Ewe elements, particularly the suffix *-vi* "junior, the younger"; but Aklo (in Aklovi) means "Krobo" in the Dangme language, where it also occurs as a name. The male name Tete (in the name of a chief called Tetevi) and the related suffix *-te* are typical of both Ga and Dangme, and they also occur frequently in historical names with a Guang connection, such as Tete Kpeshi. Perhaps these names are evidence of a connection between Kpele-Ele and the group that went back to Kpessi from Podoku near Tema, about the time of the founding of the latter (Field 1940: 85). At any rate, the name Kpele in Ga and Dangme probably records a Guang-speaking group that joined the group that spoke proto–Ga-Dangme in this area. It may have been identical with the Kpesi (Kpessi) people mentioned by Azu, or it may have been another, closely related group. Amoah (1964: 9) identified Kpesi with Gbese, the "Kpele people."

Relations between Ga-Dangme and Guang seem to have become critical at the point or points where the groups crossed to the west side of the Volta River. In Azu's (1926, 1927) version, the Kyerepong and the Krobo separated at Akrade Island below Akosombo, that is, where the Volta emerges from its gorge and bends eastward. A Basel mission map of 1885 shows Akrade Island opposite Senchi. "Pesse," a little to the north opposite Anum in Zahn's (1867) map, probably represents a new Kpessi, established after a northward movement by some of the Guang. However, if the Kpele people, and thus the Gbese, were also Guang, then the Dangme who eventually dispersed from Lolovor must either have still included Guang groups—who may well have become Dangme-speaking in the course of these events—or rejoined them soon after the dispersal.

The ethnonym "La" also denotes historically Guang people, although, like the Gbese, many must have shifted to the Dangme language or been systematically bilingual very early. Reindorf was of the opinion that the Gbese, the Late, the Lakple, the Poni (Kpone), and the earlier inhabitants of Osu were all La people, and even that "the Le [La] people reached from Mount Langma [at the Sakumo Fio lagoon west of Chorkor] to the Volta," although the Le near the Volta spoke Dangme ([1889] 1966: 21, 23). According to Azu (1926, 1927), the La were the last of the Dangme to cross the Volta, not at Humer but at Lasibi (Dangme *la sī bihi* "people under La"), just below Akrade opposite Kpong and not far from where the Kyerepong had gone their separate way. Reindorf (p. 48) recounts a tradition according to which a sister of the founder of Manya Krobo settled at Lasibi, but her husband the king of La left for the coast. The import of this separation is that the La moved to the coast independently of the Dangme, maintained control along the lower Volta, and founded a kingdom that controlled the coast from the Songaw lagoon to Nungua (at least) until it was conquered by the Akwamu in 1679, about the same time as the defeat of Accra (Wilks 1957: 109).

Field mentions that some of the Kpã songs associated with La Kpã, a deity peculiar to Labadi, were in Obutu or "a gibberish said to be the Bonni language" brought from that place. Neither language was understood by the singers (Field 1961: 4, 41). Unfortunately she presents no texts. A comprehensive examination of the Kpã tradition also found unintelligible portions of texts that were said to be in either Obutu or the "Boni (Nigerian) language,' which the author attempted to identify as either Awutu or Yoruba, but without success (Akuffo-Badoo 1967: 108, 132). Formally, the few "unintelligible expressions" cited seem suggestive of an archaic Guang variety and possibly of an archaic variety of Dangme.

La relations with the Dangme of Azu's tradition were hostile; perhaps it was the La who drove the Dangme from Biam. Old Labadi, near Lekponguno ("La on the hill") toward the eastern end of La territory, was attacked and defeated by a Dangme alliance of Osu (that is, Osudoku), Krobo, and Shai. This "Old Labadi" is the "Labadde" of Dudley's seventeenth-century map, which seems to have been out of date long before it was published. Isert ([1788] 1992: 35) referred to its ruins, halfway between Ningo and Ada, as "Lai." The La state seems at that time to have been allied with Akwamu, for Akwamu is said to have given the refugees land at Ajangote, a hill at the northwestern edge of the Accra plain (Azu 1926: 267). Others settled in Shai at Ladoku ("deserted La"), a town that was established by the thirteenth century, throve in the sixteenth century, and was finally defeated by Akwamu at the end of the seventeenth (Ozanne 1965: 7; Wilks 1957: 109). As relations with Akwamu deteriorated, the La at Ajangote moved to the site of present-day Labadi. The land in which today's La state claims allodial rights stretches from the shore at Labadi northwestward to Ajangote (Michael Johnson 1989). It is not clear exactly where the "Labida" that sent a trade embassy to Elmina Castle in 1517 was located (Vogt 1979: 86), but the Labadi visited by De Marees ([1602] 1987) in 1601 seems to have been in its modern location. Some of the La of Ladoku fled to the hills, where they were reintegrated into a Guang-speaking community as Larteh Ahenease (Kwamena-Poh 1973: 127). The dispersal of the La after these defeats, first by the Dangme and later more completely by Akwamu, partly accounts for the wide cross-language distribution in southeastern Ghana of personal and place names based on the element *La-* or *Da-*.[23]

Azu (1926: 266) quotes Dangme verses about the war against La, in which the La are given the sobriquet Bɔne, after the place they came from. Since the name is also associated with the present town, we can assume that one is the heir to the other. According to Reindorf ([1889] 1966: 43), La requested the new land from the Nungua people but eventually consolidated possession of it by force. This is consistent with Field's (1940: 123) account of the early history of Nungua, which may be interpreted as Nungua resistance to the La attempt to maintain hegemony on that part of the coast.[24] According to Azu (1926), however, Labadi got its land from the (Dangme) Osu, who themselves had only arrived on the coast after La had fled to the protection of Akwamu and after the appearance on the coast of Europeans, that is, toward the middle of the sixteenth century. The name of the lagoon at Osu, Korlete (Kɔɔleté), signifying "Korle's eldest son," suggests that Osu's land was controlled from Accra.

There is a persistent legend that the Ga, and also the founders of Larteh Kubease, came from the Nigerian kingdom of Benin (Kwamena-Poh 1973: 127). If the current notion is derived from Reindorf ([1889] 1966: 18), Reindorf himself largely attributed it to Rømer. It may be significant that Rømer (1760) was best acquainted with eighteenth century Labadi. In his time (the 1740s), about 150 years after their destruction, there must have been considerably more knowledge about the former sites and their traditions. Old Labadi is said to have been noted for weaving (Azu 1926: 265). It is generally agreed that there was considerable trade between the Gold

Coast and Benin long before European times and that cloth was a major article of this trade (Fage 1962). The Kotokoli country, where the La may have sojourned with the Ga-Dangme, was also known for cloth before Europeans arrived (Cornevin 1963: 86). There seems to be an assumption that the Benin–Gold Coast trade route was seaborne or ran immediately inland parallel to the shore, presumably because of the known historical relations between Benin and sixteenth-century Lagos and between Lagos and the Porto Novo area (Agiri and Barnes 1987), because the lagoon system is thought to have been open between Lagos and the Volta until early in the nine-teenth century (Kea 1969: 39) and because the seagoing Portuguese are believed to have taken over this trade as middlemen (Fage 1962: 344; Feinberg 1989: 9) How-ever, Ryder (1969: 23) insists that at the time the Portuguese arrived, Benin's trad-ing interests lay inland, and it is also the case that the migration tradition south from Zugu traces an old trade route. Therefore, Old Labadi may have been on a trade route between Benin and the Gold Coast that followed that shoreline, but it may also, or alternatively, have represented a terminus of Benin-connected activity along a route that ran north of Dahomey. Such activity would have been related to almost certain contact with Yoruba. Kpessi and Kpele are just north of Atakpame, which also fig-ures in the Dangme migration route, and has an old Yoruba-speaking population known as Ana, dating from no later than the eighteenth century (Debrunner 1965: 12), which was preceded by an earlier one (Cornevin 1963: 57).

North-central Togo may also provide a location for Bɔne. A little to the north-west of Kpessi is Agbande, similarly the scene of movements by many peoples and probably originally Guang (Cornevin 1963: 63). Gichode-Ginyanga and some of the other most northern Guang languages have the consonant [gb], but in Krachi and the Guang languages that are presently spoken farther south it is rare, occurring mainly in loanwords if it occurs at all. It is thus possible, but of course highly speculative, that the *bɔ* of **bɔdē* corresponds to the *gban* of "Agbande."[25]

Extant tradition seems to point to a preponderance of Guang speakers on the plain before 1660, with Ga and Dangme speakers inland and the La a linguistic ques-tion mark, perhaps speaking both Guang and Dangme. De Marees's ([1602] 1987) list of numbers is clearly Ga-Dangme, not Guang, and constitutes evidence that the language was spoken on the La coast. Chincke, the place these numbers came from, has usually been identified with a place called Kinka, "Cinka" on Tilleman's ([1697] 1994) map, near present Kpone and thus Ladoku (Dakubu 1972). Dudley's map puts "Cincho" between Accra and Prampram, but also "C(abo) Chican" between "Labadde" (that is, Old Labadi, Lai), and the Volta River. In the unstandardized spellings of the time, "Chincke" could represent either of these or Sɛga, a place be-tween Tema and Kpone, or the still extant settlement Sɛge, at the western end of the Ada district. We shall take the list as evidence that a Dangme dialect was spoken on the La coast between Tema and Ada and had been at least since the "divorce" at Lasibi, but whether it was the dominant language on all of this coast or only part of it is not known.

The Nungua people were early allies of the Accra (Reindorf [1889] 1966: 21), and a sector of Nungua's founders (the Ga Wɔɔ) is the only group on today's Ga coast (apart from Great Accra's Tungma We) that was probably Ga-Dangme in ori-gin, but they must have spoken a Dangme dialect not directly antecedent to modern

Ga. There is a hint of this in the second name of the early leader of what became the Amafa section of Nungua. "Bɔkɛte Lawei" (Field's spelling) seems to carry the Dangme name Lawɛɛ, used for a male twin. The Ga today use a different name.

I conclude that the Ga language, as distinct from Dangme, first appeared on the coast at Accra as the variety of Dangme used in Great Accra, probably not much before the seventeenth century. It then spread eastward to the Guang- and Dangme-speaking populations of Osu, Labadi, and Teshi, which last was founded by a faction from Labadi on a piece of land inhabited at the time by Fante fishermen (Reindorf [1889] 1966: 46). This spread, which coincided with an increase in the political and economic importance of Accra, was accomplished by a combination of political domination and colonization. The former ensured that the Guang, and perhaps the Dangme as well, were at least bilingual in Ga.[26] The latter occurred as members of the politically dominant group settled outside the center; for example, Asere people were among the founders of important sections of both Labadi and Teshi (Field 1940). Expanding contacts, especially by marriage, among Ga, Dangme, and Guang speakers resulted in the general adoption of the politically and economically dominant language as the language of initial socialization of children and of most public occasions. The name of its leader suggests that in Nungua, the Akwamu section of the founders of the town may have been responsible for the shift from Dangme to Ga, for "Odai Koto" is both Akwamu (Akoto) and La or Ga (Odai). The latter appears to be the given name, the former a patronymic. The relationships among the Akwamu, the La, and the Ga of Great Accra are discussed later in this chapter.

In the nineteenth century, Tema was sometimes referred to as Dangme by Zimmermann (1858: 385), who explicitly claimed it was Dangme-speaking, as well as by Azu (1926: 261), but Meredith (1812: 217, 222) had recognized it much earlier as the eastern limit of the Ga domain, linguistically different from "Pony" (Kpone). In Field's (1940) account of the formation of Tema, there were Kpeshi, La, and Akwamu elements, of which the La are the most likely to have been Dangme-speaking.

It may be that Tema was not a single-language community during the nineteenth century but shifted to Ga in sections, as happened in Kpone. Kpone (Ga *kpoŋ*, *kpo-ni; Dangme *kpō-m*, *kpō mi* "at the hill") did not complete the shift from Dangme to Ga until early in the twentieth century, and Dangme is still used there in ritual contexts. The town has two clearly defined quarters, Jɔ Shi, the originally Dangme-speaking (La) town that still provides the chief, and Alata, settled by immigrants originally associated with the small lodge built there by the Dutch in 1701 (Van Dantzig 1980). The Alata section spoke Ga from the beginning and eventually became much larger than the older section. People from the two sections also intermarried considerably.[27] Zimmermann (1858) based his description of Dangme on the language of Kpone; but by 1936, Field (1961: 10) recognized that although Dangme had been generally spoken there until quite recently, Kpone was Ga-speaking in daily life.

Prampram, or Gbugbla, the next town down the coast to the east, is Dangme-speaking, but a short word list collected by Bowdich indicates that a Guang language was still spoken in the area as late as the early nineteenth century (Dakubu 1969a). Although its Dangme shows signs of Ga influence (for instance, palatalization of *s* to *sh* [ʃ] before *i*, a feature typical of Ga but otherwise unknown in Dangme, and a few vocabulary items), I am not aware of any signs of incipient replacement of the community language.

To sum up, early in the seventeenth century, if not before, more than one dialect of Ga-Dangme and of Guang were spoken inland on the Accra plain, especially around its periphery, and at the shore between the Volta and the Sakumo Fio lagoon. Ga, which we may think of as initially a second-language speakers' variety of Dangme, perhaps began to diverge from Dangme east of or at the Volta, took definitive form inland in the western end of the territory during the sixteenth and seventeenth centuries, became established on the shore in the seventeenth, and in the course of the next two hundred years spread as the dominant community language west to the Sakumo Fio (at the expense of any remaining Guang varieties) and eastward as far as Kpone (at the expense of both Dangme and Guang). The Kpeshi were assimilated by the eighteenth century, and the Obutu were assimilated (as at Sempe) or driven out.[28] Field (1962a) reported an Awutu tradition of departure from earlier residence near Ningo, presumably reflecting flight from the final destruction of Ladoku in the seventeenth century. In the middle of the eighteenth century, Protten (1764) was aware of the Obutu language but apparently did not associate it with Ga-Dangme territory.

The development of the present political map of Dangmeland seems to have been accompanied by linguistic rationalization, in the sense that not only Guang but also varieties other than the main streams of development from the proto-Dangme that divided at Lolovor largely disappeared. This seems to be the best explanation of the fact that wherever they may have been used, De Marees's ([1602] 1987) numbers are the direct ancestor of neither the Ga nor the Dangme system.[29] It seems instead to have been a third, though extremely similar, system, which has disappeared.[30] If this list reflects the dialect of the La, the dispersal of the La and their subsequent shift to Ga (and Awutu and Larteh) may account for the disappearance; but there may have been more such cases, for example, the dialect of the Wɔɔ of Nungua. The irregular distribution in both Ga and Dangme territory of versions of the name La, Lai, and Lɛ, in place-names might also be accounted for in this manner, as relics of Ga-Dangme dialects that have disappeared (Dakubu 1969b).

It is still not possible to say where the exclusive linguistic ancestor of Ga and Dangme was first spoken and where its first speakers lived, nor will it be possible until we have a more solidly based genetic classification than the present one and a much more detailed, complete, and chronologically organized account of migration within north-central Togo and the Republic of Benin (which seems unlikely to appear soon). The route south from Zugu through Kpessi and Atakpame to southern Togo and Ada traces the old commercial salt and slave route (Cornevin 1963: 138). North-central Togo seems to have been the scene of much movement by people speaking very many diverse languages, and it seems fairly clear that it was the scene of the common development and the earliest stages of diversification of the Ga-Dangme people and of their language. It is probably during this period, for example, that the counting system shifted from a six-base to a decimal system and the week changed from a three- or four-day to a seven-day cycle.[31]

The historical situation suggests that during a period of more than a hundred years before 1660, the Ga language took shape at the Ga capital in the northwestern

part of the Accra plain as the dialect of people who had been linguistically assimilated to the Dangme-speaking ruling group but were almost entirely Guang in origin, as was much of their culture. The structure of the language itself supports this
view. Both Ga and Dangme include a few words, some shared and some not, that are
probably borrowings from Guang (Dakubu 1972: 108). For example, the verb *flìkì*
"fly" occurs in Ga, in the Ada dialect of Dangme, and in Northern Guang languages.
The Ga nouns *māmá* "cloth" and *hīī* "men" (replacing singular *nuu*) are probably
from Awutu (Southern Guang) *-bamá* "cloth," *-hī* "man," or similar forms in a closely
related language. But the most striking feature that distinguishes Ga from Dangme,
the verb system, aligns it typologically with southern Guang and not Dangme. The
Ga paradigm is systematically almost identical with the Awutu as described by
Frajzyngier (1968) and very similar to other southern Guang systems, while the
Dangme is much more similar to the Ewe. In the progressive construction, for instance, Ga and the Guang languages (except Nkonya, Dakubu 1988: 85) use a verbal
prefix and normal SVO word order, but Dangme and Ewe use an auxiliary verb plus
a verbal suffix, and SOV order, which in these languages is marked. The following
sentences mean "Kofi is drinking water" in all languages:

	Kofi	progr-drink	water
Afutu[32]	Kofi	lee-nu	onutɔ
Ga	Kofi	miŋ-nu	nu

	Kofi	progr.	water	drink-suff.
Dangme	Kofi	ŋɛ	nyu	nu -e
Ewe	Kofi	le	tsi	nu -m.

In other aspects, Dangme tends to string particles before the verb, where Ga uses
prefixes and suffixes (Dakubu 1988: 108). Comparison of the morphemes involved,
which in the main are not borrowed, in relation to the typology of the area suggests
that Dangme is on the whole more conservative than Ga.

　　Another change that distinguishes Ga from Dangme is the reduction of a system
of three tones to two through the loss of contrast between mid and low tones. The
mid-low tone contrast plays a role in the negative and aspectual systems of the Dangme
verb, so that the restructuring of the verb system in Ga was at least partly triggered
by the loss of contrast in the tone system. All southern (and most northern) Guang
languages have two-tone systems. It is true that Akan also has a two-tone system and
has been in close and prolonged contact with both the Guang languages and Ga.
However, Dangme, particularly the Krobo and Shai dialects, has had equally long
and intense contact with Akan without undergoing tone reduction (Wilson 1991: 16).
These radical changes are best explained as innovated in the course of an emerging
community's creation of a proto-Ga variety during a shift away from a language that
had a two-tone system and a verb paradigm of the Guang type. It is clear that formerly Guang-speaking groups were indeed a major component of the early Ga-
speaking population, while Akan-speaking groups seem not to have been assimilated
until a little later. The essential differences between Ga and Dangme therefore represent a Guang rather than an Akan substratum, although the assimilation of Akan
speakers undoubtedly reinforced them. One undoubted effect of contact with Akan,

the acquisition of the [p] sound, is entirely absent from Protten's (1764) Ga and so cannot have occurred until late in the eighteenth century.

The name Ga [gã`] is actually a version of the name Akan, one of a few words in which [g] in Ga corresponds to [k] in Akan, including "ring" (Ga *gà*; Akan -*kaa*) and a type of ant (Ga *gāgā*; Akan *ŋkraŋ*).[33] We do not know what bounded the use of this ethnonym in the past. It might have been applied to a Guang group or to a previously Akan-speaking group (in the modern sense) that had shifted to Guang and hence to Dangme as spoken by these people. As the language names demonstrate, initial *k* has been voiced (to *g*) in Gichode-Ginyanga, the Guang language with which the Dangme are most likely to have been in contact north of Kpessi. It is tempting to think that Accra [akra] was the same name in another Guang language, possibly related to Akrade, but southern Guang languages today all use the Akan name, Nkran. The popular theory, that *akra* was a European mispronunciation of the Akan name, is unsatisfactory since no vestige of the initial nasal *ŋ* appears in the earliest citations.[34]

The Akan Contribution

Ga speakers were, of course, in contact with Akan from the outset. If Akan speakers play no direct role in the earliest migrations and settlement of the plain, they were certainly present in the Great Accra area during the critical formative period of the Ga language. Reindorf's ([1889] 1966) story that the ancient capital was founded by the Akras, the Obutus, and a "Twi prince" implies this, as does the story that Akwamu was founded by a Twi prince brought up by Mankpong Okai (Reindorf [1889] 1966: 20, 25). The Abola quarter of Accra included an Akan section at its foundation (Field 1940: 147). We have seen that in the sixteenth century the La were allied with (and dominated by) Akan-speaking Akwamu and that this alliance, as much as connections with the Ga, probably accounts for their access to land near Accra.

In discussing the influence of Akan speakers in Accra, the process whereby large numbers of Akan speakers (and others) were assimilated into the Ga polity—among other ways by adopting Ga as the language of initial socialization of children, of primary competence in adult life, and of public use within the community—must be distinguished from the development of Akan as a major second language, if only because many descendants of the assimilated Akan do not speak the language. Yet the obvious starting point for both phenomena is the same: the military supremacy of Akan-speaking states. As a result of this supremacy, the city and the entire Accra plain were dominated by Akan speakers from 1660 until the end of the nineteenth century, first by Akwamu, at least until 1730 (Kea 1969: 33), then by Fante (Feinberg 1989: 10) and Akyem, until about 1742, when Ashanti invaded Akyem, Accra, and the coastal towns to the east (Wilks 1975: 21). The 20,000 Ashanti troops that Wilks says occupied Accra are not much less than the estimated population at the time (Marion Johnson 1977). Ashanti retained its dominant position until the end of the nineteenth century, although it was weakened after the first Anglo-Ashanti war and the battle of Katamanso in 1826 (Crooks [1923] 1973: viii; Reindorf [1889] 1966). Fante also remained a threat until the nineteenth century (Meredith 1812: 196). The Fante together with the Obutu invaded Accra in 1809 (Reindorf [1889] 1966: 142).

Although wars may have helped to spread the Akan language, a more immediate effect was to create refugees, many of whom eventually swelled the ranks of speakers of other languages. Thus Ningo is said to have been populated partly by Denkyira refugees, who had joined the Krobo (Azu 1927: 81). Adoption of the Dangme language was one of the conditions under which Akan- and Ewe-speaking refugees were accepted into the Krobo community (Huber 1963: 19). Depending on their numbers and political clout, such groups established either a new quarter of the host town or lineages within an existing quarter. Nungua and Tema included at their foundation quarters of Akwamu origin, which have always provided the chief of the town (Field 1940: 85, 121).[35]

The best known of the Akan quarters is Otublohum in Accra. Wholly integrated into the Ga-speaking community, it nevertheless betrays its Akan origins by such cultural practices as its yam and puberty festivals (although it also celebrates Homowo, the Ga national festival) and by its personal names, which although given in conformity with the Ga system of alternating generations are entirely Akan in origin (Amartey 1969; Dakubu 1981). There is disagreement about whether its founders were originally from Denkyira or Akwamu and whether they joined the Ga before or after the final move of the capital to the coast (Reindorf [1889] 1966: 39; Wilks 1959: 392), but there is no doubt that Otublohum's founders were Akan-speaking, that Akwamu people joined it, and that it was already in place very early in the eighteenth century.

Labadi also incorporated formerly Akan groups. The quarter called Abese Fantebii ("Abese Fante people") provides the chief fisherman (*woleiatse*) for the town (Michael Johnson 1989), and there is a clan (*we*) called Akɔnnɔ, an Akwamu royal name. The closeness of the Labadi-Akwamu relationship is indicated by Tilleman's ([1697] 1994) statement at the end of the seventeenth century that the Akwamu commonly traded with European ships through merchants who lived in Labadi. According to Reindorf ([1889] 1966: 42) the Labadi were so strongly influenced by the Akwamu that "it was said the Labades are Twis." Such a situation suggests intermarriage, if not the assimilation of whole groups, and lends historical depth to the accepting if slightly ambivalent attitude of the La toward the Akan language that was noted in chapter 1. Kle Musuŋ We of Teshi is said to have been founded by Fante, but since they are said to be Fante from Sekondi, perhaps the founders were actually Ahanta (Field 1940: 207).

From Eweland and Beyond

Not only Akan speakers shifted to Ga in the process of being integrated into Ga society. After the seventeenth century there seems to have been a large number of Ewe-speaking immigrants as well. The Ga participated in a number of wars against Dahomey in 1758, the Anlo Ewe in 1769–70 (Kea 1969: 37) and in 1784 (Debrunner 1965: 29; Isert [1788] 1992), and the northern Ewe in 1829 (Reindorf [1889] 1966: 246). The last two are particularly well remembered in Ga songs and traditions (Dakubu 1981: 29), partly because large numbers of prisoners were brought back and settled on Ga lands (Dakubu 1981: 31; Reindorf [1889] 1966: 249). In addition, as late as 1875, refugees from Ewe-speaking Peki, fleeing the Ashanti, settled on Ga land near Mayera (Marion Johnson 1965: 48). Some may eventually have gone back, but others were integrated into the lineages that held the land.

Accra and Osu each have a major quarter called Alata, which grew up around the local European establishment in the seventeenth or early eighteenth century. Nleshi ("English") Alata in Accra is said to have been founded with the building of James Fort in 1673. The name seems to be derived from either Alada or (less likely) Ardra, early states of the Dahomey coast. Reindorf ([1889] 1966: 40) considered it the Fante name for the Yoruba. Slaves had been imported to the Mina coast from farther east since the fifteenth century, and it was probably women slaves from the Ardra area who introduced the making of millet beer; at any rate, in the seventeenth century they were well known for it (Müller [1676] 1968: 167).[36] In Ga towns, the name Alata was given to settlements established by slaves and, later, free people who were brought in as labor for European forts and lodges from anywhere east of the Gold Coast. In a sense, the Alatas were the *zongos*, the strangers' quarters, of a different age. The Gbugbla quarter of Teshi had a comparable origin (Field 1940: 209). The fact that Kpone Alata remained Ga-speaking suggests that the Dutch may have brought workers there from Accra and also that such people preferred to identify with the metropolis rather than attempt to assimilate to "provincial" Dangme-speaking society, thus spatially extending networks for the spread of Ga.

Major nineteenth-century additions to the Ga-speaking community were freed slaves and their descendants. After slavery was abolished by the colonial government in 1874, slaves belonging to the Ga themselves either departed or were absorbed into the lineages of their owners and must eventually have increased their numbers considerably, judging by the 1841 report of a special commission on local slavery (Crooks [1923] 1973: 275). As discussed in chapter 4, such people were probably a large proportion of the ancestors of the Ga now farming in Accra villages. However, integration was not necessarily immediate. In 1882, the Basel missionary Bohner found that most people in these villages still spoke their own, northern languages. Few understood Ga, although more understood Akan because they had previously been slaves in Akan lands (Christaller 1889: 107). It may be partly for this reason that so many of the place-names in the immediate hinterland of Accra are in Akan.

Preceding the abolition of domestic slavery, there were two major influxes of freed slaves from other countries, most of whom were integrated into Accra's Nleshi Alata and Otublohum. When British ships began actively suppressing the Atlantic slave trade in 1807, they sent confiscated slaves to Freetown. A rather large proportion were from Nigeria, and some made their way back home—to Badagry, Lagos, and Abeokuta, where Freeman met them in 1842 (Freeman 1844: 229)—but others settled in Accra. After Brazil freed its foreign-born slaves in 1831, many left in 1836 (Debrunner 1965: 37). Again, most had come from Nigeria, whither many returned, but many also came to Accra, where they became known as the "Tabon people."

Observations

As far as the Ga as a speech community were concerned, after the initial critical input of the Guang, the impact of the Akan was by far the greatest. Although they became Ga-speaking for everyday purposes, under Akwamu rule the Akan language was institutionalized in all Ga and Dangme towns in the form of court ceremonial established by the Akwamu (often at the very foundation of the town) and reinforced by later conquerors. The music of the drums and horns of Ga chiefs is based on Akan texts, never Ga, and large numbers of songs (especially those associated with war and royal ceremonial and also with cults), are in Akan. Some of these verbal-musical forms may well have already been practiced in Great Accra. Today, many of the texts are poorly understood by even the most expert performers. They are pronounced in a peculiar style of archaic Akan that is unlike the Akan ordinarily spoken as a second language by Ga, including by performers of the texts, making it most likely that the conventions for performing Akan texts (if not in all cases the texts themselves) were established before the nineteenth century (Dakubu 1981: 77–81). This archaic pronunciation resembles that found in Ga appellations and place-names of Akan origin. For example, velar stops are not affricated, as in the name of the River Nsaki (modern Akan [n̩sátçì]), and *n* between nasal vowels is often lateralized, the result of a strictly Ga sound shift, as in the appellation *Oshiahēlē* "Kingmaker" (compare Akan [-hĩnĩ]). Although much of the large Akan component of the Ga vocabulary is attributable to loanwords acquired through widespread bilingualism, some of it— for example, the substitution of the Akan word *mpáé* (Ga *ŋmkpáí*) for the Dangme *tɛlímī* "libation, invocation"; some Akan-derived greetings; certainly the large Fante-derived vocabulary related to fish and fishing; and many personal names and probably some place-names—is more likely to be substratum borrowings, relics of the previous language maintained after the shift to Ga and then acquired by other Ga speakers.

The ethnic origins of Accra, and therefore aspects of its linguistic history, are partly reflected in its political constitution into quarters (*akutsei*). Abola and Asere were the principal carriers of the emergent Ga language, but the Dangme and Guang strands seem to have become so thoroughly mixed within them during the Great Accra period that they cannot now be sorted out in any meaningful way. If it is true that Akanmaje was originally Obutu,[37] it may have maintained that language for a time, while Otublohum perhaps maintained a higher than usual rate of Akan-Ga bilingualism. A common theme unites this spatial constitution in terms of origins, the developments of the Alatas and later of *zongos* as "strangers' quarters" and the "twin" towns of traders and chiefs. It is also interesting that despite universal insistence today on the fundamental historical oneness of Accra, all of the quarters that represent the triumphant Ga-Akwamu axis of political and economic power (Abola, Asere, Gbese, and Otublohum) were associated with the Dutch in the eastern part of Accra, while the smaller and politically less central quarters that were reportedly of Guang and stranger origin (Sempe, Akanmaje, and Alata) constituted English Accra. The two parts of Accra were physically separated until well into the nineteenth century.

Like several features of Ga verbal culture, the opposition of inland river and outer sea recalls a similar idea in Yoruba culture (Barber 1991: 179). There is undoubtedly a historical connection here, but precisely how it came about I do not know. Ga contact with the Yoruba has probably been continual, though varying in intensity and social form, from the beginning of the migrations, during the migration through Togo, and in every ensuing century; and of course both Ga and Yoruba may have been influenced by ancient contacts with other groups. But however the figure may signify in Yoruba, Ga history has uniquely configured its meaning for Ga. In going to the sea, Korle poised Ga between the people and their languages upstream and the people and languages from over the sea, defining Ga without finally severing it from either. To this day, Great Accra is recalled in Accra's drum appellation, in Akan as traditionally pronounced in Ga, *Nkran Ashiedu Kɛtɛkɛ, odɔm nni amanfo* "Great Accra increases-in-tens, many do not have an old town."

6

Upstream, Inland:
Other People's Languages

Although both widespread polyglotism and societal multilingualism may have been encouraged by the massive assimilation of people who spoke languages other than Ga, they are obviously not a simple result of it. Linguistic assimilation of a population can lead to the elimination of its language as a second language as well as to its maintenance. Many individual descendants of assimilated populations have indeed lost all command of their ancestral community language, and only one of the various languages mentioned in the last chapter, Akan, has in fact taken hold as a second language in Accra. Moreover, Hausa, perhaps the only true lingua franca other than English, did not appear at all. In this chapter, we consider the history of Akan and Hausa as second languages in the Volta basin and why they and not other languages dominate Accra and its hinterland.

Why Akan?

Even more strikingly than Ga, Akan in its Fante dialect has expanded on the coast during the past five centuries, at the expense of Guang to the east and probably to the west as well. West of Shama, it spread at the expense of Ahanta. It is probably impossible to reconstruct old language community boundaries on the Fante coast precisely, for evidence invariably relates to a commercial center, not borders. The precise location where one language gave way to another not only changed frequently but also is usually simply unknown. However, a general pattern is discernible.

Fante is the community language of Cape Coast and Elmina today, but this was almost certainly not always the case. Throughout the sixteenth and seventeenth centuries the people of Elmina are referred to as the Afutu (in various spellings). Afutu today is the name of a Guang language, spoken only in Winneba and Senya Beraku, and its speakers. It has been disputed whether the name implies that Cape Coast and especially Elmina, which is documented much earlier, were originally Guang-speaking. The simplest explanation seems to be that the early population of Elmina, or at least a section of it, was Afutu-speaking but that Fante was already in use as a second language for inter-African trade. This must also have been the case in Komenda and Shama, west of Elmina, which were the major towns of the pre-European state known as Eguafo, a name whose root is also the root of Guang and of the Akan name of Cape Coast, Oguaa. As intensifying trade caused these towns to become more heterogeneous and cosmopolitan, Fante and other Akan-speaking people, such as the Abrem, came to outnumber and otherwise dominate Guang speakers until the latter either gave up their language or moved (or were driven) away. Fante aggression against other coastal states was no doubt a factor. Such a process would explain why no early writers recorded Guang words, even at Winneba and Senya, which are Guang-speaking today, but only Fante, Portuguese, or a mixture of the two.

The Fante first established themselves on the coast in the vicinity of Mankessim and Anomabo, north and east of Cape Coast, before the fifteenth century (McFarland 1985). Their dialect of Akan was not necessarily the only one used on the western coast since the gold traders known historically as Akanist and Abremu no doubt spoke slightly different forms of their own, but as this part of the coast came to be identified politically as Fante, the name was soon applied to coastal Akan in all its varieties.[1] The language was a major second language if not the majority community language on the coast from Elmina to Shama (the "Mina" coast) by the late fifteenth century. If any other language had that status between Cape Coast and Shama throughout the sixteenth and seventeenth centuries, we have no evidence of it.

Beyond Shama, Fante seems to have spread westward fairly slowly. Through the eighteenth and early nineteenth centuries Sekondi and Takoradi, which are now Fante-speaking, were reported to be Ahanta-speaking (Bosman [1705] 1967: 14; Bowdich [1819] 1966; Meredith 1812). As late as 1910 Migeod (1911) claimed that the boundary between Fante and Ahanta, which is now west of Takoradi at Apowa,[2] ran east of Sekondi. If Migeod was right, Ahanta probably disappeared as a community language in these towns when they were developed together as a port and administrative center in the 1920s, attracting large numbers of migrants. Ahanta, like Afutu, was squeezed by other speech communities from both sides, for during the nineteenth century, Nzema—with which it is largely mutually intelligible (Dolphyne and Dakubu 1988: 54)—crossed the Ankobra to encroach upon it from the west. Axim, which Bosman had referred to as "Upper Ante," still spoke Ahanta in the second decade of the century, not Nzema (referred to by Bowdich as "Amanahea"), as it does today. If Christaller (1887/88: 164) is correct that in his day the Gomoa towns of Legu (Dago) and Apam, between Winneba and Anomabo, were or had recently been Guang-speaking, then Fante was still spreading eastward in the late nineteenth century and perhaps into the early twentieth.[3] Nevertheless, by the beginning of the seventeenth century it had already struck an observer as the dominant language as far as and including Winneba (De Marees [1602] 1987: 85).

The growth of Akan as a second language of the Ga—in the usual sense of a language acquired in addition to and after Ga for purposes of communicating with people who do not speak Ga—was affected by both military conquest and trading practices. Different kinds of contact at different periods led to the spread of different dialects of the language. From the earliest period of which we have any knowledge through the eighteenth century, contact was mostly with the speech of the southern Akan, the Fante and the Akwamu. They were encountered in the realms of both trade and war. During the eighteenth century, contact with the Asante-Akyem dialect group increased, mainly through military and political contact, but in trading contexts as well. Since trade in Accra has always depended on relations with the hinterland, second-language practice in Accra has also been affected by developments elsewhere. Before the nineteenth century, much of the evidence for the spread of Akan is indirect, implied by early vocabulary collections and by the linguistic legacy. Later, missionary and imperial concerns provide relatively frequent mention of linguistic practices.

Fante was a major language of coastal trade from the sixteenth century or earlier through the nineteenth. Toward the end of the seventeenth century, Barbot noted that "the Mina Blacks drive a great trade along the Gold Coast, and at Wida by sea" (Hair, Jones, and Law 1992: 382), and such observations recur throughout the history of the coast. The early linguistic "specimens" were collected by traders, who expected them to be useful to other traders. They demonstrate the use of Fante in trade and also provide evidence of local multilingualism.

The first specimen of a language of the Gold Coast, fifteen words noted by the Flemish traveler Delafosse at Mina in 1479 (Escudier 1992), contains at least five identifiable Akan words.[4] The next is a list of eight words collected by the English Captain Towerson in 1555, also from Mina (Hakluyt 1907: 86; reprinted in Dalby and Hair 1964). Four of these words are identifiably Akan, but one, "Cracca Knives," today exists only in Ga as *kakĺa* "knife."[5] It has not appeared on any subsequent word list of Akan. The appearance of the word on Towerson's list surely reflects contact between Ga and the Akan of the western coast in the sixteenth century. Ga are known to have functioned as interpreters on the Mina coast at an early date (Quaye 1972). Perhaps Towerson's informant was one such. De Marees's ([1676] 1987) extensive Mina list at the turn of the century, containing many words and expressions specifically concerned with trade, and Müller's ([1676] 1968) even longer list, collected in the 1660s, that he expressly presented as the trading language of the "Fetu," are further witnesses to the growing importance of the language. A text in what appears to be Akan, collected in 1702, demonstrates that at that time it was the trade language as far west as Assini (Rapp 1955: 229).

Southern Akan seems to have been the main language of the gold trade at Great Accra during this period, although since the Ga and Obutu were important middlemen, their languages were undoubtedly also to be heard. However, the gold was mainly produced by Akan speakers in Ashanti and Akyem (Amoah 1964: 32), and Akan-speaking Akwamu also had an interest in the trade. Today's Akwamu is a subdialect of Akuapem, but at that time the southern dialects, which include both Fante and Akuapem, were not yet strongly differentiated.[6] Ogilby (1670) stated that Akan was the trade language for a hundred miles in each direction from Accra. The political relationship between Akwamu and La also suggests that many of the La must have spoken the Akwamu dialect, as must also many of the Ga at Great Accra.

It is probably safe to say that southern Akan was the most important language of trade—and consequently the most widespread as a second language—on the entire coast from the Ankobra to the Volta, including inland areas wherever trade existed. Nevertheless, there is no reason to think that Akan was a lingua franca during the seventeenth century, in the sense of use between people of different community languages, *neither* of which was Akan. The Akan were dominant in trade and in war and numerous: other people had to communicate with them, and they were in a position to impose their language. Linguistic accommodation was less a psychological than a political matter.

Although substantial texts and word lists of Ghanaian languages appeared in the eighteenth century, observations on the linguistic situation during this period are still few. Johannes Rask's (1754) word list of "Aqvambu" (Akwamu) is a curiosity, for of approximately one hundred items, eleven (mainly names of parts of the body) are Ga, not Akan.[7] Rask visited Akwamu, in the neighborhood of modern Nsawam, from Christiansborg Castle. Like Towerson's list two centuries previously, Rask's mixed list confirms that Ga and Akan were spoken in close association and suggests bilingualism in these languages on the part of informants or interpreters.

In by far the most important linguistic document of the century, Protten (1764) observed that Fante was understood from Axim to the Volta, in contrast to Ga, which was not understood beyond Ningo or "Lay" (Old Labadi).[8] His own repertoire corroborates the statement, for although he had left his native Osu for Denmark at the age of twelve and spent long periods of his life away from the coast, Protten was able to produce good grammars and translations for both Ga and Fante (Reindorf [1889] 1966: 215; Wurm 1874).

At the beginning of the nineteenth century, it was generally agreed that Fante was understood on most of the Gold Coast and that this could be attributed to the trading activities of the Fante people (De Marrée 1817/18: 129; Meredith 1812: 187). In 1821, Hutton, a trader, considered the language sufficiently important, but still little known to the English, to publish a list of eight hundred words and thirteen sentences. Toward mid-century, Beecham claimed that the Accra people understood preaching in Fante and, "Owing to the ascendancy of the Fantee, and the intercourse kept up with it by means of its traders, its language has become the general medium of communication along the coast" (1841: 166). One hundred and fifty years later, Fante is still almost universally spoken (where it is not also the community language) on the coast west of Accra; but the survey results discussed in chapters 3 and 4 indicate that in Accra, among both Ga and others, the Fante dialect (in contrast to other Akan dialects) is not particularly widespread as a second language. This is also true on the Dangme-speaking coast. It is likely that the popularity of Fante began to decrease toward the end of the nineteenth century, after the colonial capital was moved from Cape Coast in Fanteland to Accra, and that this trend was accelerated in the 1950s, when Tema came to rival Takoradi as the country's major ocean port. However, it is also likely that Fante is still widely spoken among sectors of the Ga population not reached by our surveys, particularly fishermen.

Meanwhile, Akan had also been spreading inland, along the Volta valley. It must already have enjoyed a measure of use as a second language among the Guang of

Akuapem, but after the Akwamu defeated the Guang in the seventeenth century, it was imposed on them by force, and the Akyem establishment of the Akuapem state in the eighteenth century, with its capital at Akropong, secured it. The Ga and Dangme states received Akwamu political agents and developed or were given a court system that seems to have involved the use of Akan to some extent; but the Guang on the hills were incorporated into the Akan-speaking state itself and had to use its language in all court contexts (Kwamena-Poh 1973: 10).[9] The Akwamu imposition of their language on the Akuapem Guang has been invoked to explain why the Akuapem towns of the Benkum division other than Larteh (Mamfe, Mampon, Abotakyi, Tutu, Obosomase) are now Akan-speaking rather than Guang; but as Kwamena-Poh points out, the replacement was probably due at least as much to the influx of non–Guang-speaking settlers, particularly Akan and Dangme, who eventually outnumbered the Guang. However, it is surely a major reason why in the early nineteenth century there was a high rate of bilingualism with Akan in the (still) Guang-speaking towns of Akuapem (Christaller 1886: 91, 1887/88: 164).

The Akwamu state had been active in the southern Volta Region and beyond from the beginning of the eighteenth century. The Akwamu army reached Whydah in 1702, and Wilks (1957: 125) has claimed that Whydah and Ardra were within the Akwamu sphere of influence until 1727. After defeat at the hands of Akyem forced Akwamu to move its capital east of the Volta in 1734, it continued to expand as a military and trading power, affecting the Ewe and other peoples to Peki and beyond, and imposing its political forms as it had on the plain (Kea 1969). In 1758, Ashangmɔ, the Ga king at Popo, asked for and got Accra and Akyem assistance in his war against Dahomey, and the Ada-Anlo war of 1769–70 also brought Akan and Ga forces across the Volta. Later in the century, Akwamu and Tafo ("Tuffo") irregular soldiers were to be found operating as far east as Ardra and Dahomey (Dalzel 1793: 6, 34). Early in the nineteenth century, the Ashanti armies defeated the Dahomey at Atakpame and reached Abomey in the 1840s (Wilks 1975: 328). While it is unclear whether these incursions had long-term political or commercial results, they certainly imply a long-standing awareness of, and occasional acquaintance with, Akan as a language of power throughout the lower Volta and southern Togo.

Farther up the Volta valley, Fante traders operated northeast of present-day Ashanti during the nineteenth century, but their numbers seem not to have been large. Ramseyer (1886:73) mentions meeting three in 1884 on the Afram plain, at least two of whom were Muslims. Asante (1886: 21) mentions traders met at Kpandu in 1881 who had come from the coast, and were therefore presumably Fante-speaking, as well as traders from Sierra Leone and from farther north. However, the Volta valley from Peki northward was dominated by Ashanti. Even in the southern area, Anum and Akwamu itself became Ashanti dependencies. It seems to be the Asante dialect (not the Akwamu) that is most widely employed east of the Volta today, especially where Akan is most widely used, north of Eweland.

As in the Accra area, the initial impact of Akan east of the Volta was made by movements of people, first as refugees of various kinds and later as colonists. In some cases refugees adopted another language. Thus, among the Kwahu who fled the Ashanti and settled north of Buem during the eighteenth century, one group shifted to Tem (Christaller 1886:93; Zech 1907:118). More often, however, the Akans moved (or were moved) in sufficiently large groups that they were not assimilated with others but founded Akan-speaking settlements. Such were the groups settled in Buem by Ashanti authorities during the nineteenth century (Marion Johnson 1965). As Johnson points out, the major reason why David Asante (1886: 32) found Asante-speaking children in Adele country was that the Kumasi agent had brought in Asante-speaking colonists and distributed them throughout the district.

There have been several cases of community-language shift to Akan, which were perhaps completed only after the Ashanti invasion of the middle Volta Region in 1869 (Marion Johnson 1965: 33) but must have begun earlier. Atebubu north of Ashanti was originally Guang-speaking but received a relatively large population from the neighborhood of Kumasi (Arhin 1971: 64). It is not clear whether at the time of Ferguson's visit in 1890, the community language of Atebubu was still Guang. He states that "Nkoranza, Atabubu, Gwan, Basa, Yeji, Prang and Abeasi comprise the Brong tribes. They speak a dialect of their own, that is slightly different from Ashanti proper" (Arhin ed. 1974: 9).[10] Since the community languages of Gwan [Dwan], Basa, Yeji, and Prang, immediately east and north of Atebubu, are Guang today, the shift might still have been in progress.

When David Asante (1886: 23) traveled in the Volta Region north of Nkonya, about 1885, the Boro language, once spoken near Worawora and Tapa, was remembered only by a few elders, having been replaced by Twi (Schosser n.d.; Seidel 1898). It has since disappeared entirely, one of the few documented cases in Ghana of true language death (Westermann 1910).[11] To have reached this state, the language must have been declining since well before the middle of the century. It is also clear that in Apesokubi ("Akposo hill" in Akanized Akposo), north of Worawora, there was a shift to Twi from Akposo, which today is spoken mainly in Togo, although as late as the 1950s the shift was not quite complete (Cornevin 1963: 44; Debrunner 1962: 110).

Ramseyer in 1884 and David Asante in 1885 made important exploratory journeys for the Basel mission. Ramseyer went to Brong, Kete-Krachi, and northern Buem, while Asante went farther north to Salaga, then eastward and south through Buem. The country they traveled through was (and is) linguistically and ethnographically very complex. All of its community languages other than the recently implanted Twi—which include a number of forms of Guang of varying degrees of mutual intelligibility, as well as several very diverse languages currently classified in different branches of Kwa (Stewart 1989)—had very few speakers, then as now. It is striking that throughout the area, the presence of Twi (or any other language) as a second language is related not to the number of people speaking a community's language but to contact with outsiders, whether traders or conquerors. Ramseyer found that the area between Atebubu and Nkoranza, which today is very sparsely populated but mainly Akan-speaking (Brong dialect), was still Guang, and although knowledge of Twi was considered widespread, he needed an interpreter for preaching. East of Atebubu was also Guang-speaking, as it is today, with a degree of knowledge of Twi. Farther north, Asante found Twi spoken at Salaga and Grubi, mostly because these towns had quarters of resident Asante. Kpembe (the capital of Gonja, of which Salaga is the satellite traders' town) had been occupied by Ashanti by 1744 (Wilks 1975: 20), but it is not clear to what extent Twi was spoken as a second language there. Similarly, in Kete-Krachi, both observers (and others later) found Twi fairly widely spoken, especially by traders. All of these Guang-speaking towns were market centers on major trade routes, with quarters of resident foreigners.

Farther east, knowledge of the language was less common than it is now. In the 1970s, it was reported that Twi was the main lingua franca and market language in Kpandai, in Nawuri-speaking (Guang) country (Emberson 1979). In the 1980s, the Asante dialect of Akan was widely spoken as a second language in the Gichode-speaking (Guang) area. Thus at the market town of Achode Nkwanta, sellers were Konkomba, Achode, Hausa, and Dagomba, but all spoke Twi to their customers. Since the customers are as diverse as the sellers, the language in this instance qualifies as a true lingua franca.[12] In 1885, a century earlier, Asante could find only three people in this rather isolated region who spoke Twi. A little farther south, in the Adele- and Lelemi-speaking areas, Twi was more widespread. Both had been severely affected by Ashanti invasions: Adele, as mentioned, had been colonized, as had Tapa and Worawora on the northern and western borders of the Lefana-Lelemi area. Farther south still, in the Kebu-, Akpafu- (Siwu), and Akposo-speaking districts, Twi speakers by all accounts were rare (as they still are).

In the 1880s, the Lelemi-speaking district (Borada and vicinity) was approximately the southern limit of Akan as a major second language. A few speakers could also be found in (Guang-speaking) Nkonya because of its use as a trade language farther north (Klose 1899: 291), but Ewe was probably more common (Schreiber 1901). Akan seems to have been little used in Kpandu, the northern Ewe trading town (p. 94).

The flurry of missionary travel writing with an emphasis on language after 1880 was a consequence of the fact that the Ashanti invasions east of the Volta had interrupted the Basel and the Bremen missions in their preparations for northward expansion (Bürgi 1890). A major concern of the Christian missionary observers east of the Volta in the later nineteenth century, such as Asante and Ramseyer for the Basel mission and Zahn and Schreiber for the Bremen mission, was to determine the suitable language for evangelizing this linguistically fragmented hill country (Dakubu and Ford 1988; Heine 1968). The choice was generally conceived to be between Akan and Ewe, in which the Basel and Bremen missionaries, respectively, already had considerable expertise.[13] Their views on how widespread a language was, and hence its value for their purpose, were affected by their vested interests. Thus, when Schreiber (Bremen) said he thought Ewe was better understood than Twi in Buem, an area including the Lelemi-, Akpafu-, Kebu-, and Akposo-speaking communities; and when Schosser (also Bremen) thought Ewe would be more in the interest of the Buem people than Twi, we may suspect they were influenced both by their investment in the Ewe language and by a degree of rivalry between the missions. Similarly, in arguing for the use of Twi as the written language of Buem, Christaller (1895, and in his introductory remarks to Asante 1886) exaggerated Asante's reports of its prevalence. The general picture, however, is clear: toward the close of the nineteenth century, Twi, particularly the Asante dialect, was spreading as a second language in trading centers north of Kpandu and in places that had been colonized or otherwise politically dominated by Ashanti. Yet it was not necessarily the only or the dominant second language.

Mission choices may have affected the fortunes of the languages involved or, rather, of the particular dialect chosen. Although the numbers of non-Akan and non-

Ewe who became literate in Akan or Ewe as a result of missionary teaching were small, school and church use eventually raised the prestige of the chosen language variety. Certainly the fact that the Basel mission used Akuapem Twi—a geographically and politically peripheral dialect with far fewer speakers than either Asante or Fante—and produced major grammars and dictionaries in it (most notably, Christaller 1875, [1881] 1933), as well as a considerable literature, was mainly responsible for the high prestige this dialect long enjoyed, at least among the literate. It also accounts for this dialect's early official recognition as one of the approved languages of primary education. Until the development of an official Asante orthography and to some extent even today, written Akuapem was taught in the schools of other Akan dialect areas, so that for the first half of the twentieth century literate, Christian Akans were often diglossic, speaking their home dialect but reading, writing, and hearing Akuapem at school and church.

Not only was Akan the language of the coastal trading system, of which Accra was a part since its very foundation, and the language of political and commercial access on the plain and in the hills beyond, by the end of the nineteenth century it was also important (though far from universal) as a language of commerce throughout the middle Volta valley; even the southern, Ewe-speaking region had long had considerable contact with it. These areas, and Akanland itself, have been major sources of the Ga population. Today, non-Akan migrants into the Accra area from the northeast are likely to be familiar with Akan as a market language and often speak it at least a little.

Akan is also important in more remote northern source areas. In the territories contiguous to Ashanti and Brong, such as Gonja, and in the multilingual western Brong-Ahafo Region, Akan, especially the Asante dialect, has been a major second language since the nineteenth century and probably earlier (Dakubu 1976). Not surprisingly, Ferguson found Asante to be a language of commerce in the slave-trading center Salaga, although not as important as Hausa (Arhin 1974: 34, 126). Farther north still, Ferguson found Asante spoken only by occasional individuals, except in Chakosi, an island of Anyi speakers whose forebears had come from the south as military aid to Mamprusi several generations previously (p. 75). Even there, the missionaries Martin and Mohr, exploring for the Basel mission in 1906, complained that in Sansanne Mango (the Chakosi capital) no one understood Twi, Guang, or Ewe (*Monats-Blatt der Norddeutschen Missions-Gesellschaft*, vol. 9, p. 86). In distant Dagao, Buluk, and Kusaug, the language has never been widely known except among people who have spent time in the south; but it has been spreading throughout the twentieth century, particularly through the agency of Akan-speaking truck drivers, traders, and shopkeepers (Dolphyne 1977; Rapp 1955). Unlike Salaga and Sansanne Mango, Kusaug, Buluk, and Dagao are clearly outside Ashanti-dominated territory at its furthest extent (Wilks 1993: 203).

Popular Ghanaian linguistic nomenclature classes Akuapem, Akyem, and Asante together as "Twi," and in the survey situation it was not practical to insist on the unfamiliar distinction. We therefore do not have data on which non-Fante dialect is currently most frequently used as a second language in Accra. An educated guess is that many Ga speak Akuapem because of close economic and social ties (including kinship ties) with Akuapem towns and villages. In Ga settlement areas to the west of Accra, it is possible that Fante is more widely spoken than in the groups providing the data discussed in chapter 3. The northern migrant groups, however, who unlike the Ga clearly use Akan as a lingua franca, may be expected to speak Asante. It is also observable that many of these people use what appears to be a pidginized variety of Akan. No further information is available about modern contact varieties of Akan.

Ewe is also spoken by a large population with which the Ga have historic ties, beginning with migration traditions that associate some of the Ga with places important in Ewe tradition and continuing, like the Akan connection, with remembered wars, significant assimilated populations, and a considerable current presence in Accra. Ewe has more speakers than Ga, and if the entire Gbe linguistic group (which includes Fon) is included, it rivals Akan in terms of both size and historical military power. It is mentioned by nineteenth-century travelers as an important trade language in the lower Volta valley: even Christaller (1895) agreed that it was the second language of the Avatime and Logba, and Schreiber (1901) claimed it was more widely understood in Nkonya and even Buem than Twi. Klose (1899: 347), who considered that Twi was the language of commerce and communication in the whole Volta Basin, nevertheless found that Ewe was widely understood in the Adele area. It is still a major second language as far north as Nkonya and the Buem area (Dakubu and Ford 1988: 124; Ring 1981), and some observers consider it to be as widely spoken as Twi as far north as Apesokubi.[14]

Ewe was written as early as Akan, was successfully standardized, and has a relatively large literature (Duthie and Vlaardingerbroek 1981). The first major translation into Ewe, a Roman Catholic catechism of 1658, was almost a century earlier than any comparable work in Akan or Ga (Debrunner 1965: 22; Egblewogbe 1985: 80). The first major grammar, Schlegel's *Schlüssel zur Ewesprache* of 1857, based on the Anlo dialect group, was published a year earlier than Zimmermann's Ga grammar and only slightly later than Riis's (1853) grammar of Twi. In the standard form that developed out of this early work, expanded with material from other Ewe dialects, it has been used in churches and taught in schools in non–Ewe-speaking areas (such as Akpafu-Lolobi, Avatime, and Logba) of the southern Volta Region, reinforcing its status as a second language (Duthie 1988; Ring 1981). In another dialect form (Gen [gɛ̃]) it is one of the two indigenous languages recognized for official use in the Republic of Togo and the lingua franca throughout the Togo-Benin coast (Bole-Richard 1983).

There are also numerous cases of assimilation into the Ewe-speaking community, mainly of groups of refugees from the Akwamu or the Ashanti. The most notable historical cases are perhaps that of the Ga ruling family, which fled Akwamu and founded Glidji in 1663, and the Fante group that arrived from Mina to found Anecho in 1720 (Bole-Richard 1983: 6). The Ga, who became known as the Gen (Ewe for "Ga"), seem to have maintained close contacts with Accra for a time but eventually merged with the Mina, and their dialect of Ewe has become the commercial language of southern Togo and part of the southern Republic of Benin, a situation that Bole-Richard attributes to the commercial dynamism of the Mina, especially the women. Some of the Glidji people returned to Accra about 1730 and founded the Anecho subquarters of Labadi, Osu, and Accra (Reindorf [1889] 1966: 47). The mother of Christian Protten was among them (p. 215).

Dangme-speaking groups, especially Shai, who fled east across the Volta from the Akwamu at the time of the fall of Ladoku early in the eighteenth century, established several communities, most of which eventually became Ewe speaking. One of these, Agotime, now entirely Ewe-speaking, was at least universally bilingual in Ewe by the middle of the nineteenth century (Kropp 1966; Schlegel 1857: viii; Zahn 1870: 34), although Christaller (1895: 6) claimed it was still Dangme-speaking. A few, such as Se-Zogbedji in Togo, have remained Dangme-speaking.

Farther north in Togo, there was clearly a lengthy period of instability caused by pressure on the area from all directions in the early nineteenth century, particularly from slave raiders. The consequent redrawing of linguistic and ethnic boundaries is reflected in the extreme geographical and genetic discontinuity of the linguistic map of the area (Dakubu 1988b: 118). There is good evidence that numerous groups in the area have at various times changed their community language. Some were assimilated into one of the very small language communities; for example, speakers of a language called Simaí were assimilated into the Siwu-speaking Akpafu, and some of the Santrokofi (Sɛlɛ speakers) believe their ancestors spoke a language called Sɛtafi (Debrunner 1962: 114). Others, probably involving more individuals, shifted to Ewe, particularly in the Agu Mountain area (p. 110). Since no knowledge of the earlier languages has remained, it is impossible to say how many languages totally disappeared and how many lost some of their speakers but survive elsewhere.

Despite all this, few Ga in Accra, and even fewer Akan or northern migrants, speak Ewe, and we might well ask, why not? The popular opinion that Ewe is "too difficult" is obviously a consequence of its position in Accra, not an explanation. One reason might be that Ewe is simply farther from the Ga area than Akan, with no shared border. Among the eastern Dangme, especially among the Ada, who are geographically adjacent to Eweland and even more historically involved with it, Ewe is widely spoken (Dakubu 1988a). However, the fundamental reasons are undoubtedly economic and political. The Gold Coast, including Accra, was always richer than the nearest Ewe-speaking areas, which had no gold themselves or in their hinterland. It is recorded that Fante and Ga traders operated on the Slave Coast in the eighteenth and nineteenth centuries, but there is little mention of Ewe speakers trading on the Gold Coast.[15] Ewe never had a presence as a trade language in Accra itself, as Akan did. According to Zahn (1870: 50), most of the African Christians at the Anlo missions in 1856 were Ga, which suggests that there was a class of Ga who considered themselves more "advanced" than the Ewe. Most important, the Ga (not unaided, to be sure) defeated the Ewe in war more than once in the nineteenth century, and the assimilation of Ewe people into the Ga is celebrated in song and oral tradition as the acquisition of captives, not the absorption of equals or former rulers (Dakubu 1981: 29–31, 283, 310). Some arrived as refugees (Marion Johnson 1965: 47). In such circumstances, Ewe institutions that would demand the use of the Ewe language were never adopted by the Ga, because they were never imposed on them. Later in the century, colonial boundaries reinforced the status of Akan and provided an additional barrier against Ewe: throughout the history of the Gold Coast colony and eventually southern Ghana, Akan-speaking lands constituted its core; from 1884 to 1914 the present Volta Region of Ghana, which includes almost all of Ghanaian Eweland, was part of German Togoland, and after 1919 the Ewe lands were divided between Britain and France. Since Ghanaian independence in 1957, the border has been no less a barrier, despite the merger of British Togoland with the Gold Coast following the plebiscite of 1956. Often closed because of political hostility between the two countries, the Ghana-Togo border today splits the Ewe dialect area and separates the Ghanaian Ewe dialects from other very closely related forms, including Gen. It also ensures that within Ghana itself the Ewe are far fewer than the Akan.

Both Akan and Ewe have always had rivals in the Volta Region. Besides Ewe, Hausa has been in use at least as long as Akan in parts of the area; Kotokoli, a variety of Tem, has been significant; and by the nineteenth century, English was important. Nor are the towns of Akanland itself less multilingual than others. It is not surprising that a town with a history of trade and language shift such as Atebubu continues to be multilingual at the community level (Arhin 1971). But even relatively small, geographically central, and historically Akan towns are more multilingual than might be expected. In Takyiman, at the heart of the Brong Akan dialect area, Brempong (1984: 22) found eighty-seven languages (including several Akan dialects) spoken in the population of about 12,000. His survey of 660 households indicated that although the people of the *zongo* were indeed more polyglot than those of the main town (15.5% monoglot versus 44.9%) and virtually everyone spoke Bono (Brong) and/or Asante, in both sections a majority spoke two languages or more and a few spoke several more. The main second languages were Asante, English, and Hausa; Ga was spoken by a mere 2.5%. In Begoro in Akyem, a rural district center, not only is there a *zongo*, or strangers' quarter, but also many (probably a majority) of the Akan inhabitants speak other languages. This is related to the high rate of literacy (so that many speak English) and to the fact that, as in the Accra area, many of the farmers of the district are migrants, especially Dangme, Ewe, and Chamba (Tem speakers) but also Dagomba, Sisaala, Mosi, Hausa, Fulani, Tuareg, and Nzema. Dangme and Ewe people dominate the markets in the nearby villages, and the language of market trade tends to be that of the seller (Ayim 1991: 35).

One might also ask why Ga did not become a major second language. In fact, it was and is widely spoken among neighboring people who have either been dominated by the Ga in the past, particularly the Awutu (Christaller 1887/88), and/or have kinship ties with Ga or frequently attend markets in Accra, such as both Akan and Guang speakers in Akuapem and the Dangme (Dakubu 1988a: 115). On the basis of pre-war experience Rapp (1955: 221) estimated the Ga community at 50,000, with twice that number of second-language speakers. The fact that it does not rival Akan is explained by the combination of community size and historical military, political, and economic might, plus the fact that the Ga themselves have always spoken Akan with outsiders. The languages of all the other important slave-trading people on this part of the coast—Akan, Gen, Fon, and Yoruba—are well represented in the New World; but the only documented appearance of Ga (other than in Oldendorp's (1777) word lists from the Virgin Islands, taken from new arrivals) is from Haiti, where Henrici (1898: 400) collected a vodun song in Ga.[16] This lack of a Ga presence might reflect the relatively small size of the Ga-speaking population in the eighteenth century, together with a tendency of the Ga to sell only imported slaves, but it probably also reflects Ga use of the Akan language in extracommunity contexts.

No other language of the West Coast (that is, other than Akan, Ewe, coast Guang, or Dangme) has been an important second language in Accra or in southern Ghana, but several others have been represented by significant communities at various times, some of which have changed the Ga-speaking community and its language. The Kru community from the Liberian coast tends to be associated today with menial forms of urban labor and with extreme varieties of popular English; but from the sixteenth century to the twentieth the Kru were important to European trading ships as the boatmen who brought landing canoes ashore across the surf and as interpreters, all along the coast to Europe and at least as far south as Loango (Bennett and Brooks 1965: xxxi, 110, 298; Davis 1976: 1), and have made a major impact on West African popular music (Collins 1985).

The Kru seem to have made a strong impression on the Ga in the domain of food, provoking the proverb *Kluunyo hiɛ akwɛɔ ni ajaa lɛ omɔ,* literally "they look at a Kru man's face and give him rice," that is, to each his due.[17] On the Kru coast itself they were historically important suppliers of provisions to ships. Among other things, they are recorded to have sold plantains (Davis 1976: 41). The Ga word for plantain, *amádàá,* is apparently ultimately from the same source as the English "banana." The word is certainly foreign to Ghana, for Dangme and Awutu use similar (but not genetically cognate) forms, but Akan uses a word meaning literally "European yam" (*brɔde*). A very similar word is common in the languages of Senegal, Sierra Leone, and Liberia, and it seems very likely that the word was brought, together with the fruit, by Kru on European ships.

Kenkey, the typically Ga food made from slightly fermented corn that has been ground, formed into balls, and steamed, is commonly called *kɔ̃ŋ* in Ga, contracted from *kɔ̃mì.* The word exists in no other Ghanaian language. Dangme has a different word, *otimi,* which still exists in Ga but is relatively rare. Isert ([1788] 1992: 125) referred to it as "This *kummy* . . . their original type of bread," mentioning that baking ovens were limited to places where Europeans had stayed. The word seems to have originated west of the Gold Coast, also probably brought by the Kru. On his voyage of 1555, in addition to his "Mina" list, Towerson collected a short word and phrase list from a language that has been identified as Kra, one of the Kru languages (Dalby and Hair 1964: 187). Included is *Begge come* "Give me bread." Dalby and Hair interpret the first word as modern Kra *be je* "let see" and do not comment on the second. The similarity to the Ga word is obvious.[18]

Hausa and the Language of Indirect Rule

Although occasional Hausa individuals may have reached the coast at an earlier date, the Hausa community in Accra dates from the middle of the nineteenth century. The spread of Hausa as a lingua franca on the Gold Coast dates from approximately the same period but probably became significant in Accra when the colonial capital was moved there in 1877, a move comparable in its political and linguistic significance to the move of the Ga capital from Ayawaso to Accra two centuries before. As with Akan, it is essential that the expatriate Hausa community be distinguished from the speakers of Hausa as a second language. Within these categories, the resident Hausa community must be distinguished from the itinerant, and second-language speakers using the language mainly for communication with the Hausa themselves must be distinguished from networks of non-Hausa speakers of Hausa as a lingua franca. Yet, as for Akan, though in very different ways, trade and military activity underlie the presence of both community and vehicular Hausa. Quite unlike the Akan situation (in which a resident trading community and second-language use were generally preceded by war), we may say, roughly, that the establishment of a resident Hausa community was everywhere a consequence of trade, while the prevalence of Hausa as a lingua franca in the Gold Coast results essentially from military policy, although not necessarily from war itself, and *not* from trade, as the conventional wisdom as expressed by Zima (1968: 373) or Gil, Aryee, and Ghansah (1964: xxx) would have it. Both had everything to do with British colonial expansion.

The date of the arrival of the first Hausa settler in Accra is unknown. There was a Sarkin Zongo (recognized *zongo* community head) in Accra from 1850, but the first remembered and documented settler was Malam Naino, also Sarkin Zongo, whose title to land (in Ussher Town, presumably at Zongo Lane) was confirmed in 1881 (Odoom 1971). Since Malam Naino is said to have come as a teacher, a community requiring a teacher must have already existed. The Hausa, Bornu, and Fulani communities at this time were closely connected, often interrelated, and apparently were using Hausa as a common language. There has been a Hausa community ever since. It grew considerably during the first half of the twentieth century, so that its establishment and heyday coincided with the period of colonial rule. The 1948 census indicated that the Hausa then constituted the largest single non–Gold Coast ethnic community in the city, at 3.4% of the total population. Forty-one percent of the Hausa were women, rather more than in most migrant groups, and 35% had been born in Accra (Acquah [1954] 1972). In the early 1950s, Rouch (1956) found that unlike children of other immigrants from beyond present-day Ghana, Hausa children born in Accra were not usually sent to their fathers' villages. In 1954, the government recognized three Hausa community chiefs, two for the Fulani, and one each for other communities (Acquah [1954] 1972: 102). Hausa people still constituted the largest community in Sabon Zongo in 1979 (Moser 1979).

By the beginning of the twentieth century, virtually all the towns of any commercial significance at all in what is now southern Ghana had a *zongo*, a resident strangers' quarter usually settled initially by Hausa, and most of them still do. To mention a few from the literature, Dodowa, at the center of the palm oil trade, had a Hausa Town by 1900 (Ardayfio 1977: 28); Odoom mentions Winneba and Swedru (Agona) from the 1930s; and Larteh has a small *zongo* (Brokensha 1966: xvi), as do most Akan towns, including Begoro (Ayim 1991), Atebubu (Arhin 1971), and Takyiman (Brempong 1984), not to mention Kumasi's very large one (Schildkrout 1978). On the lower Volta there are *zongos* at Kpong (Odoom 1971) and Ada. It is commonly taken for granted that Hausa is the lingua franca of these settlements, although in some cases this is not strictly true. For example, Ayim reports that while Hausa is widely spoken, Akan is the main lingua franca of Begoro Zongo, and this is probably true of *zongos* in many Akan-speaking towns. It is also popularly assumed that since most long-distance migrants reside in *zongos*, there is a special relationship between the Hausa language and anyone from north of Ashanti, or at least Brong-

Ahafo. In this context the term "Hausa" tends to be used very loosely and has been since the mid-nineteenth century. Not all of those referred to as Hausa, even by themselves, are historically ethnic Hausa, nor is it necessarily the case that every *zongo* includes Hausa people among its inhabitants, although it seems that most of them do.

The Hausa arrived in Accra initially in pursuit of trade. Since they had been heavily engaged in the slave trade, it might be wondered why they became established so late. The usual explanation is the power of Ashanti, which even in the nineteenth century did not usually allow foreign traders, especially Hausa, south of Salaga. There was no *zongo* in all of Ashanti before 1874, although there were certainly Hausa visitors and even residents in Kumasi then and earlier. For example, the butchering trade in Kumasi is said to have been the province of the Hausa in 1820 (Rouch 1956: 20, after Dupuis [1824] 1966), and Meredith (1812: 158) mentions the presence of a Muslim from "Kassina," presumably Katsina, together with his entourage in the Ashanti party at a durbar near Anomabo (near Cape Coast) in 1802. There seem to be no such notices of Hausa in Accra.

In the whole of the Volta basin our information on the use of Hausa (as for Akan, and for much the same reasons) relates essentially to the nineteenth century, with most of it coming from the period after the British sack of Kumasi in 1874. Although the language had undoubtedly begun to spread early in the century or before, Ashanti military activity in the middle years discouraged the missionary travelers on whose observations we mainly rely and presumably the Hausa traders themselves. After Ashanti power had been somewhat curbed by the British, Hausa penetration was encouraged by both the Germans on the east bank and the British on the west. In 1800 there was said to be only one Hausa speaker in Salaga, the major nineteenth-century slave-trading entrepôt for Ashanti and the Gold Coast (Rouch 1956: 19. By the end of the century, according to Ferguson, Hausa was the major vehicle of commerce there (Arhin 1974: 34). The Hausa and their language also partly replaced the Asante and theirs in Togoland (Marion Johnson 1965: 57).

Farther north, in Dagomba, there was a Hausa presence much earlier, probably by the latter part of the sixteenth century; but although bilingualism in this language is reflected in loanwords and musical usages in Dagbani and many other languages of present-day northern Ghana, it was probably limited to small groups of specialists, particularly in the trades (for example, butchers and fiddle players), and the Muslim literary and religious elite (Benzing 1971: 118). Contact seems to have been with Hausa who were soon assimilated into the Dagomba, and with itinerant traders, who did not form resident strangers' colonies. Hausa traders of Katsina origin went as far west as Wa, almost to the Black Volta, in the 1860s, but here, too, they did not establish a Hausa colony but were assimilated, as in the Dzangbeyiri section of the town (Rattray 1932: 453; Wilks 1989: 63). As in southern towns, strangers' sections, or *zongos*, where Hausa is usually current have since been established in most northern towns, including Wa and Tamale; but as in the south, the language is not particularly current in the host communities, except in the relatively cosmopolitan market centers and then mainly among men (Awedoba 1979; Dolphyne 1977; Rapp 1955: 229). Early twentieth century British officials in the "Northern Territories" were emphatic in their opinion that the Hausa language had never been a lingua franca there (Cardinall 1931b: 79; Rattray 1932: x). Such statements as Smock's (1975: 171), "At one time a Nigerian language, Hausa, was the lingua franca in the northern portion of Ghana" uncritically repeat popular southern Ghanaian opinion. Through most of the nineteenth and early twentieth centuries the major language of commerce in the northern half of the country seems to have been Moore, the language of the Mosi caravans that continued the ancient tradition of trade between the forest edge and the Niger bend (Cardinall 1927: 115; Ferguson in Arhin 1974: 126, 130).

The Hausa caravans were not made up solely of male itinerant traders and their porters. They traveled with their women, children, and household slaves, so that they were in practice mobile colonies (Goody and Mustapha 1967: 614; Rouch 1956: 121). When part of such a group established itself to develop its trading activities in a particular place for an indefinite period, it was already a self-contained community in continual communication with the homeland through arriving caravans and contacts with other colonies. Such a group was not likely to be quickly assimilated into the host community, from which it was also sharply distinguished by religious practice.

By the end of the nineteenth century, many such Hausa colonies had been formed adjacent to towns in the southeastern Volta basin along the routes of the salt, rubber, and slave trades. Travelers mention such colonies at Achode Nyambo (Klose 1899: 438); Kadjebi, Kete (the market town of Krachi), and Kpandu (Kling 1891); Dadaura (Wolf 1891); Atakpame (Schlunk 1910); Kparatau (Foli in Sölken 1939); and there were obviously many others. In the eyes of the missionaries of the North German Evangelical Society, Hausa was essentially a vehicular language in Togo; but it was also one of the country's major languages, exceeded in numbers of speakers only by the Anlo and Gen varieties of Ewe (Seidel 1904). Use of Hausa for evangelization in northern Togoland was seriously considered but ultimately dismissed, mainly because of its association with Islam, although structural distance from local languages was also mentioned.[19]

Ludwig Wolf (1891), whose travels in 1889 were aimed at improving the map of the German colony, noted that recorded names of towns were often the Hausa, not the local, names. (This is still true.) Although the missions (Basel and Bremen and later Roman Catholic) continued to concentrate on local languages, the German colonial attitude was generally Wolf's, that Hausa was the lingua franca of the western Sudan and should be encouraged. The missionary Mischlich, according to Sölken (1939: 52), considered that the Sokoto dialect was the basis of the Hausa of the western diaspora and its trading area.

Several of the published specimens of early twentieth-century Togolese Hausa are of sociolinguistic interest. In 1920/21 the missionary E. Funke published sixteen songs that he had collected shortly before 1914. He remarks that some of the singers and informants were not "true" Hausa but belonged to the so-called "Slave Hausa." These must have been the servants of the Hausa, who were not necessarily themselves of Hausa origin, although they had perforce become Hausaphone. It is likely that this class of speakers—undoubtedly outnumbering the "true" Hausa but having marginal status within the Hausa community and frequently communicating with local communities for practical purposes—were particularly instrumental in spreading the language and contributed heavily to its linguistic character.

Unlike Funke's (1920/21) informants, Bonifatius Foli, who provided the text and the data for the phonetic analysis published by Feyer in 1947, certainly spoke Hausa as a second language. Since he had been born in 1877, he was essentially of the same generation. His personal and linguistic history supports the "Slave Hausa" hypothesis. He was not a northerner but (as his name implies) an Ewe, a speaker of the Gen dialect from the town founded by the seventeenth-century Ga royal refugee colonists. He was no ordinary rural southerner, for he had worked as a cook for several German governors in Togo and had also been a trader, traveling the length of the country in both capacities. As a trader, his servants had been mainly Hausas, and the implication is that they, who may be classed with Funke's "Slave Hausa," were a major factor in his acquisition of the language.

Klingheben (who provided the linguistic notes) recognized that the language of Funke's texts sometimes departed from the territorial Hausa of published descriptions, and he attributed some of these "errors" to innovations in "Slave Hausa" (Funke 1920/21: 260). If they included phonetic deviations, these are unfortunately not reflected in Funke's transcription, which was based on Westermann's orthography. Foli's dialect was described as the dialect "spoken by the 'Hausa' itinerant traders in Togo, Dahomey and on the Gold Coast," and it was noted that most of these traders were not really Hausa but were any inhabitants of the lands bordering on northern Togo, who used Hausa as a lingua franca (Feyer 1947: 109). At the same time, there were sufficient Hausa among them that the language of which Foli's was an example remained fully interintelligible with both "real and pseudo-Hausa." Yet it was not a unidirectional process of "correction," for the language of long-term expatriate Hausa tended to take on characteristics of the vehicular (Sölken 1939: 58). The result, as Feyer pointed out, was a variable code, neither idiosyncratic nor wholly stable—hardly an abnormal situation for a language.

Feyer (1947) treated the language comparatively as the Hausa of an Ewe, specifically a Gen, speaker. For example, she attributed the absence of the ejective and implosive features of the Hausa consonant system and neutralization in the morphological systems to differences between Hausa and Ewe. Although Foli's speech was undoubtedly affected by his first language, this approach is surely inadequate. While it may be true that extraterritorial Hausa existed in several varieties, as it still does, there are constant features (present since the nineteenth century) that cannot be attributed to influence by a particular southern language. Grammatically and phonetically, the Hausa described by Feyer resembles the Hausa spoken as a lingua franca in Ghana today; to this extent Feyer was probably right when she implied a common development. One of the most noticeable phonetic features of this type of Hausa, besides the absence of the highly marked features noted above, is that velar consonants that precede high front vowels, which in Nigerian Hausa are palatalized lightly or not at all, are affricated. Thus, *aiki* "work" and *kīfi* "fish" become [aitçi] and [tçifi], and *gidā* "house" becomes [ʤida] in Ghanaian Hausa and also in turn-of-the-century Togolese Hausa as represented by Foli. Foli apparently did not affricate the *k* of *sarki* "chief," as is common in current Ghanaian Hausa; but in an earlier published specimen of Togolese Hausa, this pronunciation is reflected in the transcription *sarekyi*, following Akan orthographic practice (Groh 1911). I have elsewhere (Dakubu 1977) ascribed this pronunciation to the influence of Akan, in which there has been a regular shift of [k] and [g] to [tç] and [ʤ] (orthographic *ky* and *gy*) before high front vowels, but this now seems as inadequate as Feyer's Ewe influence, for the same reason—that it can account for only one subgroup of speakers, who probably did not acquire the language in sufficient numbers to influence it until the feature was already present. In Akan itself affrication became established only during the nineteenth century. Given the large numbers of slaves acquired by Akan-speaking communities in the course of that century, many of whom either came from an area where Hausa was the major second language or were part of a Hausaphone caravan between the times of capture and sale, one wonders whether the influence could not as well have been in the other direction.

The question, therefore, is where the features of Hausa that are characteristic of vehicular and to a lesser extent of expatriate Hausa in Ghana and Togo first appeared. As a problem in comparative linguistics the question awaits investigation, but the historical and descriptive sources seem to point toward Zugu, in the north of the present Republic of Benin. Zugu (Sugu, or Djougou, which has also appeared in the Krobo migration tradition) is a politically and ethnographically complex area that became the major staging post outside Hausaland for caravans traveling southwestward. According to Funke (1914/15), three languages were known as "Zugu language": Bariba (or Bargu); Kyilinga (or Kpilakpila), also a Gur language; and a Sabarma (Zarma, or Zabarima) dialect whose speakers called themselves Dendi.[20] He thought only Bariba was truly autochthonous. There were also a Mande ruling group with Gurma connections and a major Hausa presence (Sölken 1939: 82–83; Wolf 1891). Sölken gives a text by Bonifatius Foli that discusses the Fulani at Zugu. The Zabarima and Dendi in particular have traditionally had a high degree of bilingualism in Hausa (Nicolai 1980: 59), a fact that, as we shall see, is an aspect of the relationship between Hausa as a vehicular language of trade in the area north of the Gbe linguistic area (between the Volta and the Niger) and Hausa as the language of the colonial army and police on the Gold Coast.

The development of Hausa as the language of communication between the expatriate Hausa, who were Muslim, and their trading associates from the Volta to the Niger seems to account for its association with Islam, but it does not really account for the popular association of Hausa and also Islam with what is now northern Ghana. It is true that many slaves who originated from those areas were sold in the Gold Coast by Hausas or Hausa speakers, but there is no reason to think that many of them were Muslims or that they had acquired Hausa. The freed "Grunshies" around Accra after 1874 were reported to be speaking their own languages and Akan, not Hausa (Christaller 1889).

Neither does the pattern just described explain why Hausa should have become the lingua franca in today's Accra of people who have never been active in trade. We have seen that although the resident Hausa community in Accra has been relatively large, compared to other groups of strangers, it has nevertheless been a very small fraction of the population of the city. Why should its language have been adopted in Accra by networks of speakers who do not necessarily mesh with expatriate Hausa community networks, any more than they do with local Ga networks, in domains that need have nothing to do with trade or Islam?

There is evidence that although vehicular Hausa may have first arrived from the northeast in the context of trade, its present position in Accra, and to some extent elsewhere in southern Ghana, is based on its use in the colonial military. In this context it was brought to Accra not by Hausa and associated people but by troops of mixed origins who already used a vehicular Hausa before they arrived from the east, from Lagos. This initial corps was quickly expanded with people of preponderantly slave and/or northern origins. Their Hausa, like the Hausa of Zugu, must derive from the lingua franca of the forces of Fulani-Hausa military expansion. This seems to point to central-west Nigeria, south of Hausaland but north of Yorubaland, perhaps Nupe, as the area where this group of varieties formally originated and from which it spread west and south.

The Ghana army and police can be traced back to the fort troops of the eighteenth century, many of whom must have been ultimately from outside the Gold Coast.[21] They were on intimate terms with the local populace but not really of them, a pattern that was to continue. When the African Company of Merchants was abolished in 1821 and its possessions, including Cape Coast Castle and James Fort at Accra, went to the Crown as represented by the governor at Sierra Leone, its servants including its African troops were generally retained and the latter were reconstituted in 1822 as the Royal African Colonial Light Infantry. In 1826, it was decided to recruit into the colonial corps from natives and liberated slaves ("those Africans who may have been more recently introduced to the colony") rather than British deserters and culprits from other regiments, as had been the practice.[22] The numbers to begin with were very small, not more than two hundred in 1844, most of whom were said to be "Fante" (Gillespie 1955: 12). This term seems to mean only that they had been recruited around Cape Coast.

The combination of "natives" and "recently introduced Africans" never worked well. The constabulary was reorganized several times during the nineteenth and twentieth centuries in attempts to improve its local status and to militarize sections of it. Problems with local recruiting that arose from perceptions of low status, derived from low pay and associations with slavery, seem to have lasted until independence. In the 1850s there were complaints that the Gold Coast Artillery Corps consisted of "slaves and runaways," and so in 1858 an effort was made to employ literate Africans, but to little avail. When the Dutch gave up Ussher Fort in 1867, the British considered that the existing fort police were too closely connected to the townspeople, and also too old, to be effective. Since in Lagos the use of troops known as "Hausa"— that is, from the middle regions of Nigeria most affected by the military activities of the Hausa-speaking Fulani—[23] was considered a success, twelve men were brought from there in 1871 and more arrived the following year. Gillespie remarks, "Of course, many of the men enlisted were not Hausas, as even today any man from the North is often called a Hausa" (1955: 9). The comment applies to both Nigeria and Ghana.

After 1873, the "Hausa" and "Fante" companies were separated, in a pattern that was maintained throughout the colonial period. A Police Ordinance in 1894 separated the Fante civil police from the Hausa constabulary. The Hausas performed military duties that demanded distance from the local population, such as putting down riots. They provided most of the troops of the Gold Coast Regiment of the West African Frontier Force formed in 1901, which fought in World War I, as well as the Escort Division of the Police that was formed in 1902. The "Fante," who were officially designated the general or civil police in 1889, performed civil duties for which it was considered an advantage to have speakers of the local language. They preserved peace, detected crime, and could arrest people and bring them before the court

(Gillespie 1955: 18). After 1902, "Lagos men" were not to be recruited to the general police, although it seems that lack of willing local recruits meant that this policy was not always followed (p. 51).

Although the "Lagos Hausas" were not all Hausa, they were not southerners. Yoruba troops were briefly employed in Accra around 1880, but they were not considered a success (Gillespie 1955:20). In the same period, recruiting expeditions went to Nupe (in Nigeria) and to Salaga, and the practice of recruiting from the north and among northerners residing in the south continued right through World War II (Killingray 1982). The common sources of recruits are clearly reflected in their "soldier names."[24] Thus, the "Hausas" who pacified the Ewe at Ho and Anlo in 1888 included Sergeant Beliko Fulani and Lance Sergeant Seidu Moshi. Sergeant Imoru Kanjarga won the King's Police Medal for his part in stopping a riot at Mumford in 1923, and Alheri Gurmah served from 1884 to 1926, retiring as a senior superintendant (pp. 24, 56, 64). The first Police Band (formed 1917) was led by Sooquah Grunshie, who had trained for the Regimental Band in England (p. 54). The men of the Gold Coast Regiment that fought for the British in the German African colonies in the 1914–18 war were said to have been recruited from the interior far to the north of Ashanti (Clifford 1920: 9); but the names of the "Native rank and file" who were awarded medals indicate that some also came from Nigeria, both north and south, and the lands between: thus two "Gurmahs" and one "Kotokoli." Clifford remarked that when the Gold Coast Regiment met the Nigerian Brigade in Tanganyika, "Many of the men composing both forces belonged to the same tribes, spoke the same language . . ." (p. 140), which probably reflected both movement between the British West African colonies and the use of Hausa as the lingua franca in both corps.

If Islam and the Hausa language were undoubtedly already characteristic of the Lagos Hausas who served in the Gold Coast in the 1870s and later, their establishment among the Gold Coast forces also owed something to strong encouragement by the British, especially of the language. The British seem to have been motivated partly by stereotyped assumptions about the people they were dealing with and partly by a rationalizing (by categorizing) language and social policy, attitudes that tended to reinforce each other. In 1877, a number of imams were appointed to prepare recruitment notices in Arabic and to send them into the "Hausa country"; we are not told with what success (Gillespie 1955: 20). British officers were encouraged to learn Hausa, and after 1886, when Lagos Colony was separated from the Gold Coast, they were examined in it. To this end, an introductory grammar of Hausa for British officers with the Gold Coast Constabulary was published in 1889 by Joseph Numa Rat, assistant colonial surgeon, a West Indian who had learned the language on the Gold Coast.[25] In the same year this author also published English-Hausa manuals for physical training and for the new ambulance section's stretcher drill.

Further reinforcement of Hausa as the lingua franca of the police and armed forces undoubtedly occurred after 1898, when the Zabarima armies that had controlled much of today's Upper Regions were finally defeated by the French and then the British. The armies dispersed, and many joined the Gold Coast Regiment (Rouch 1956: 23). These Zabarima-led forces had included not only Zabarima but also Mosi, Kasena, Sisaala, Hausa, Fulani, and Jula (Piłaszewicz 1992: 11). The Hausa in particular seem to have played a major part, including leadership. The army (or armies) must have needed a lingua franca, and Hausa was the obvious choice in view of the already widespread use of Hausa in Zabarima and Dendi country. We may draw a parallel with the Hausa-speaking forces of the Fulani in northern and north-central Nigeria.

German policy in Togo also supported vehicular Hausa as a military language, so that in this respect 1914 brought no change to what became British Togoland. According to a reporter in the *Monats-Blatt der Norddeutschen Missions-Gesellschaft* for September 1906, the German officials endeavored to provide themselves with interpreters throughout their highly multilingual territories by recruiting soldiers from every language community and teaching them Hausa along with military drill.

Thus, the Hausa speaker with whom the Akan-, Ga-, or Ewe-speaking Gold Coaster was most likely to come into contact was not the first-language speaker, let alone the man educated in the Hausa literary tradition, but the soldier or policeman (frequently perceived as alien) who spoke a vehicular variety, was illiterate in any language, and represented the colonial power. The greatest concentration of numbers was in Accra almost from the beginning since the headquarters of the Gold Coast Constabulary were moved from Cape Coast to Accra in 1888, but the "Hausa" forces were used to enforce the colonial presence throughout the country. They were frequently pitted against local people, notably in the Anglo-Ashanti wars of 1874 and 1895, in "pacifying" the Ewe in 1888; in driving the Krobo from their mountain in 1892 (Adams 1908); and in the Northern Territories, for example, in the Tongo Fetish campaign of 1912–15. They continued to be used for political purposes in the interwar period, and not surprisingly they were unpopular (Killingray 1982: 84). However, although the use of the "Hausas" in these operations undoubtedly contributed to the generally negative attitude of southern Ghanaians to Hausa, it did not necessarily place barriers to the spread of this class of speakers and their lingua franca. At the time of the 1874 Ashanti war, when Hausa caravans were still excluded from Ashanti, the Ashanti king was raising a "Hausa" force for action against Gyaman by recruiting deserters from the Gold Coast Constabulary, as well as buying them from the Zabarima (Gillespie 1955: 20; Rouch 1956: 23).

The sources of the association of Hausa with marginal social status, the unknown north, and a military-police caste are beautifully illustrated by the story of the sergeant who provided Rat (1889) with a text to illustrate the Hausa spoken by the Hausas of the Gold Coast Constabulary. Because Rat's orthography closely follows Schön's (1876) for Nigerian community Hausa, it provides no information on Sergeant Augustus's pronunciation. Although he was born in Cape Coast, not Accra, his background must have been typical of those in the Gold Coast who, like the "Slave Hausa" of Togo, spoke Hausa as their initial and community language but were not "*echt* Hausa."

When Sergeant Augustus talked to Rat in England in 1888, he must have been a young man in his twenties. His parents were both born in "Bunu" (Bornu?), thus, "almost Hausa," as Rat (1889) translates him (*kusa da Hausa*). They presumably already spoke the language at least a little when they were captured in war, sold, and taken first to Kano and then to Salaga, where they were sold again to Fantes (*Tonawa*) and taken to Cape Coast. There they were both bought by a Cape Coast man (*mutum Gua*), a Mr. Augustus. He freed them, and they married. Since the speaker was a child when his father fought in the Ashanti war of 1874 and he was his mother's eighth born, his parents must have reached Cape Coast well before 1860. His most vivid childhood memory seems to have been the feast that was held to celebrate his recovery from smallpox. After a few years in school, he learned tailoring at the Cape Coast barracks, was subsequently employed at the Elmina pay office, and finally followed in his father's footsteps by enlisting as a soldier. The rest of his "autobiography" is a description of the voyage to England, whither he had been sent for further training. He went with three other sergeants, a drum sergeant, and a drum major, among whom only one, Drum Sergeant Nelson, had a name identified with southern Ghana, and even that name is typical of descendants of nineteenth-century "Brazilian" immigrants to Accra.[26] Sergeant Augustus's own name is obviously that of his parents' Fante patron.

While the Hausa-using masses of Nima and Accra New Town are not for the most part long-distance traders, neither are they preponderantly soldiers and police. The lingua franca of the Gold Coast Constabulary and related organs must have been just that for a long time, the language of the barracks, until the late 1930s and especially the 1940s, when these migrants' suburbs began to grow in earnest. It was pointed out in chapter 4 that there is very little continuity between the northern migrant communities of today and prewar Accra residents from the same homelands. Many of the "migrant" workers of the 1940s, 1950s and 1960s were in fact ex-soldiers who stayed to work in Accra after World War II. The numbers of these ex-servicemen were considerable, for Africans in the armed forces of the Gold Coast totaled 47,000 by July 1945 (Killingray 1982: 83). To the extent that later arrivals found "countrymen" in Accra, they are likely to have been soldiers and former soldiers or police. In addition, the very first settlers in many of the new suburbs, such as Nima and Kanda, had been Hausa and Hausa-speaking Fulani. Thus the Hausa community presence united with the Hausa lingua franca traditions of both trade and the military to ensure that new migrants met a linguistic environment in which Hausa was the key to getting a job, finding a room, and generally surviving in the city.

Observations

Hausa and Manding, the two largest languages of wider communication in West Africa, are spoken in mainly discrete areas that meet in Ghana. They are commonly assumed to be sociolinguistically parallel, and there are indeed a number of similarities in their situations. Historically, both were languages of large Sahelian empires. Both owe their present vehicular use beyond the old territories of those empires to the activities of trading groups that expanded when the empire was already in decline, establishing expatriate colonies, and to use in the rather large armed forces of the colonial power (Calvet 1982). Both are languages of communities with strong trans-Saharan and Islamic cultural and economic connections, but also both expanded greatly during the colonial period (Alexandre 1971: 657). Similar factors underlay the spread of Swahili on the other side of the continent, although Hausa, much less Manding, never received the degree of colonial support enjoyed by Swahili, which unlike Manding or Hausa had never been the language of an empire (Fabian 1986; Whiteley 1969). If we compare Ghana with the Ivory Coast—its neighbor to the west, where a vehicular variety of Manding (Jula) is widely spoken—it also seems to be true in both countries that the language is a trade language in the northern, savannah tier of the country but a lingua franca (independent of the Manding or Hausa community itself) mainly in the towns of the south, especially the capital city. In both Abidjan and Accra, moreover, this is essentially a post–World War II phenomenon. Popular non-Mande use of the term "Dioula" (Jula) in the Ivory Coast closely parallels the popular application of "Hausa" in Ghana: it tends to be applied to anyone from the north, including from beyond the Ivory Coast, and to all Muslims. Like vehicular Hausa in Ghana, vehicular Jula is an urban, extra-"tribal" phenomenon (Tera 1986).

Both languages spread in vehicular forms partly because colonial governments gave them quasi-official status in the armed forces. Before 1914, the French recruited their West African armies mainly from Manding-speaking Mali and Senegal, and their language became the language of command for noncommissioned officers. During the war and after, like the British, they recruited throughout their colonial African empire, but the language remained (Calvet 1982, after Delafosse 1929). The main medium of the spread of the language, of which Ivorian vehicular Jula is a dialect, is said to have been a common, "light" or easy Manding, understood by speakers of any variety (Calvet 1982: 193). One suspects that formally, like Ghanaian Hausa, this variety probably owed as much to the military language as to the community language that gave it its name.

There is even a parallel to the likely precolonial military use of Hausa as the lingua franca of the Zabarima armies in the undoubted use of Manding by the forces of Samory, although unlike the majority of the Zabarima leaders and their men, Samory and the majority of his men were presumably community-language speakers of the language in question.

Despite all this, there are many historical dissimilarities, resulting in important differences in the present sociolinguistic situations. It was pointed out in chapter 2 that the spread of Manding began much earlier, probably by the fourteenth century. It initially spread as much by conquest as by trade, and the occupied territories once extended much further east, including into northern and central Ghana and beyond. Groups of Mande descent (such as the Kantosi, discussed in chapter 4) still exist in Ghana, but the language has not been current as a second language for two centuries at least, having been displaced by Hausa (Crowder 1973; Dakubu 1976; Funke 1914/ 15; Wilks 1968, 1989).[27] Because of this early spread, Manding is a major community language of the northwest Ivory Coast, where it borders Manding-speaking areas of Mali and Guinea, as well as in the linguistic islands of Kong and of Bobo-Dioulasso, which is now in Burkina Faso (Derive 1990). Unlike the Hausa in Ghana, therefore, Mande-speaking communities in the Ivory Coast are not necessarily regarded as expatriate. In non-Manding areas of the northern Ivory Coast, Jula has long been established as a second language, in daily use by most people, and is also associated with conquerors. Neither is the case with Hausa in northern Ghana.

The main difference in the situations of the urban lingua francas arises from the fact that Manding had no strong competition from an Ivorian language, as Hausa did from Akan, so that in this century, Manding (Jula) spread throughout the forest area of the Ivory Coast as the language of traders, a spread that accelerated with the development of towns (Tera 1986: 13). Indeed the spread of Akan in its northeastern

hinterland through military activity, followed by trade and sometimes by colonization, makes a better parallel to the spread of Manding than Hausa does in this particular area. (The spread of Hausa to the south and east of Hausaland is another matter.)

There was no competition from any Ivorian language because no community
was large or powerful enough to impose its language. Around Abidjan, as discussed
in chapter 2, the coast and its immediate hinterland are far more linguistically fragmented than around Accra, and the coast as a whole never produced an economic
equivalent to the Fante. Nor did Abidjan have a strong indigenous structure like
Accra's. Consequently, Jula became the lingua franca not just of migrants from the
north but also of the entire (non-European) city.

The Ga adhere to a tradition of elaborate exchanges of greetings, detailed reports of activities, prayers, and gifts of drink, which has for its primary goal the peace-
ful integration of the community and all who desire to be associated with it into an
explicit and ideally stable structure of authority (Dakubu 1987a). We can see reflected
in this ritual an ideology of hierarchically structured order that maintained the traditional society, although by no means unchanged, until approximately the end of the
nineteenth century. As successive small groups—especially of Akan speakers but
also of Ewe, Sierra Leoneans, northerners, and Brazilians—arrived, they were assimilated into suitable places in the sociopolitical structure of the city in such a way
as not to weaken the host group.

This pattern could not long survive the onset of European colonialism and the
disproportionate numbers of strangers it brought in to serve it. Initially, the "Hausas"
could have had little more impact than the fort soldiers before them, as they lived
apart in barracks and were at least theoretically only temporary residents, but the ever-
increasing numbers that followed and settled on the outskirts of Ga settlements were
quite disproportionate to the Ga community, which ceased to be the "host" community in any practical sense. Even though the migrants formally acquired land from
the Ga, they were ultimately protected by the colonial government, more recently
the national government, and so beyond control. Twentieth-century migrants have
not been integrated into the Ga polity, and indeed it would be suicidal for the Ga
political authority to attempt it, even were the migrants willing, since it could not
cope with the numbers and diversity involved. To recall the tension between Labadi
and Madina, the Akan element as far as the Ga are concerned has long had a place
within the Ga system, but if there is a place for the "Hausa" it is not one that they
care to accept. The ideology of politically stratified order that is enacted at every
formal visit or meeting today serves to define and defend the integrity of the existing
community, not by increasing its strength through the controlled integration of
arriving strangers, but by negotiating the terms of their exclusion.

7

Beyond the Sea:
Exotic Languages

In this chapter we examine the other, more ambiguous source of language meaning, the sea, that is, overseas; the languages that came to Accra and, of course, the rest of the country with seaborne trade. If the lagoon drains a vast continental reservoir of linguistic resources toward Accra, the sea connects it literally with the ends of the earth. The languages that came to Ghana and West Africa with the seaborne gold trade, slave trade, and colonialism are still languages of international economic and political activity, and at least one of them, English, appears to be gaining strength worldwide.

Historically the most significant of these exotic languages have been Portuguese and English, but there was also prolonged contact with Dutch (in both Accra and Elmina), with Danish (in several towns and villages from Cape Coast to Keta), and less intensively with French and German. In the opinion of a number of scholars, the first world trade language to make contact, indirectly, with the Gold Coast was Arabic. The Akan word for "gold, money," *siká*, and Ga *shiká* "money, wealth," are ultimately from an Arabic source, either *'ar-rizqu* "wealth" or *'al-'arzaqu* "profit, means" (from the same root). A reflex is documented as already in use in the neighborhood of Elmina in 1479 (Escudier 1992: 28).[1] Manding-speaking gold traders were active in the vicinity of Elmina before the Europeans arrived, and it is they who must have brought this word (Feinberg 1989: 9; Wilks 1982). The Mande had long been in contact with Arabic speakers and borrowed this word in various forms (for example, *arsikâ* "luck, good fortune").[2]

Any history of the use of European languages on the Gold Coast must begin with Elmina and the Mina coast, where the earliest and for a long time the most intensive contacts were made. Early descriptions of Elmina refer to the area as Mina but to the town as the "*aldea da duas partes*," the town in two parts. As Feinberg (1989: 105) points out, this is suggestive of the historical pattern discussed in chapter 2, according to which an expatriate group of traders normally remained physically separate from the original town and was assimilated into its political structure as a unit, resulting in a twin town consisting of a trader's town and a chief's town. It is likely that this was the situation in fifteenth-century Elmina when the Portuguese arrived and that they did not fundamentally change it, except to replace a variety of Manding with their own language (Baesjou 1988: 49). Evidence includes the word that Delafosse collected for "king," the Manding word *mansa*, not a local word.[3] If it is also true that a Guang language was the community language of a significant section, Elmina at the time of first contact with the Portuguese was a classic case of a trilingual town. The Mande maintained a trading network that covered a large part of West Africa, including southwestern Ghana (Feinberg 1989: 10), which was part of the most far-flung trade system of the time and whose lingua franca was Arabic. A consequence of the Portuguese venture was to be the near eclipse of Arabic by Portuguese as the principal language of world trade and of Manding by Portuguese as the language of long-distance trade on the western Gold Coast. It was also to bring Accra and the Gold Coast more closely into touch with the rest of the world than they had been; but they evidently had contact with it already, however indirect.

The Portuguese and Their Language

For almost five hundred years, the coast of Ghana was known to Europeans as the Gold Coast, for the very good reason that it was an important source of gold, as it still is. This toponym was never a firmly bounded term, but it can usually be understood to refer to that portion of the West African coast that stretches from the mouth of the Ankobra River at 2°20′ west, to the Volta River at about 0°40′ east, not quite the entire coast of modern Ghana. The names Ankobra and Volta are both of Portuguese origin—the Rio Cobra, or Snake River, because it was thought to be winding, and the Rio Volta, or Change River, because of a periodic fluctuation in the direction of the current at its mouth.[4]

The string of forts that lines the Gold Coast is unique in West Africa. The earliest were built by the Portuguese in the fifteenth and sixteenth centuries, primarily for the gold trade but increasingly for slaves, and then seized in the seventeenth by the Dutch or the English and enlarged for the slave trade. Those east of Christiansborg were built by the Danes in the eighteenth century, also for the slave trade (Van Dantzig 1980). By 1864, the British had bought or captured all of them. Many of the smaller buildings that were merely lodges or factories have disappeared, but the major ones are very large and still in use for various purposes.

Portuguese of some kind was certainly spoken in and around these establishments, by both local people and various kinds of foreigners, from late in the fifteenth century until the beginning of the nineteenth. Equally certainly, it is not spoken there now. English, in contrast, is widely known. Given that their speakers all spoke or speak at least one other language, we want to consider the nature of the sociolinguistic systems that have involved these languages and the historical relations between them. Was Portuguese spoken by networks of speakers that can be equated to today's speakers of English in domains comparable to those of modern English? If so, the disappearance of Portuguese and the spread of English are simply aspects of the replacement of one foreign language of external communication with another. The fact that the Portuguese language long outlasted the Portuguese presence, as elsewhere on the sea routes, and that English and other European languages were simultaneously in active use on the coast for more than two hundred years suggests that the history of exotic language use on the Gold Coast (including, of course, Accra) is more complex.

The nature of the code also poses a question. There are no extant texts of the Portuguese of the Gold Coast. Modern writers (Berry 1971; Naro 1973; Spencer 1971) have generally referred to it as Pidgin Portuguese. Contemporary witnesses qualified it by such terms as "the language of the Blacks" (Müller [1676] 1968), or "Negro Portuguese" (Protten 1764). On the whole, the term "pidgin," like the qualifications that preceded its use, seems to signal distinctions among the speakers of a language, not among types of linguistic code. Among speakers of metropolitan varieties of European languages, including linguists both Ghanaian and foreign, it most clearly signals the otherness of the speakers. As with the other languages encountered, we shall assume that Portuguese and English have been locally spoken in more than one variety but that use of the same glossonym normally implies interintelligibility.

Portuguese on the Gold Coast certainly did not originate as the "emergency" language of a mixed population abruptly thrown together, disadvantaged by inadequate access to the target language, nor was the effort at verbal communication one-sided. During the fifteenth and sixteenth centuries, contact with community-language speakers of Portuguese was direct and intimate, and it was the Portuguese who made the initial linguistic effort. Portuguese ships first rounded Cape Three Points in January 1471. Elmina Castle was founded in 1482, to take advantage of the plentiful supply of gold and to keep other Europeans out. Its builder (Diego d'Azambuja) depended on the linguistic skills of a Portuguese captain, who "had been to Mina several times before, knew the African dialect, and was able to act as an interpreter for the official party. Fernando [the captain] arranged for a meeting between the village elders and the Portuguese" (Vogt 1979: 22). At first, therefore, it was the Portuguese who learned the local language, not vice versa. This was not an isolated case, for contrary to some claims, Portuguese traders spoke African languages elsewhere on the Guinea coast, especially the western part (Hair 1992: 18).

D'Azambuja arrived to build the castle with a force of six hundred Europeans (Bartels 1965: 1). They did not remain in such numbers, but throughout the sixteenth century Elmina Castle had a considerable Portuguese staff in addition to its slaves. The first permanent garrison (in 1482) comprised sixty-three men. In 1529 there was a garrison of fifty-five, all of whom had to be Portuguese, including four women who operated the castle bakery (Vogt 1979: 46). There were an additional twelve Portuguese at Fort San Antonio in Axim.

These people interacted with the locals from the beginning, but Africans were not exposed only to an informal, colloquial variety of Portuguese. The Afutu king and many of his people were converted to Christianity,[5] and the king's sons and sometimes wives visited the vicar of the chapel on the hill where Fort St. Jago now stands for instruction in the faith, customs, and (most significantly) the language of the Portuguese. In 1529 a class was organized for this purpose (Vogt 1979: 55). For several years in the 1570s, Augustinian missionaries at Elmina taught mulatto children in the castle and were working as far afield as Komenda and Abakrampa (Bartels 1965: 2). According to a report of 1572, they were teaching catechism and reading, presumably in Portuguese and Latin, and the sight of local youths with books and papers was not unusual (Texeira da Mota and Hair 1988: 77).

A significant number of the early Gold Coast African speakers thus constituted a homogeneous group, many of whom were formally taught by community-language speakers. If a pidgin is defined as a language that originated from abrupt contact, with drastic reduction in form because of the unavailability of an adequate model (Crowley 1992: 262), then Gold Coast Portuguese was not a pidgin. Nor was the Gold Coast particularly unusual in this respect. The first West African speakers of Portuguese seem to have been fifteenth-century captives, taken to Portugal to be taught the language so that they could act as interpreters on ships and in coastal establishments. In the sixteenth century there were also free interpreters, and there were free students from the western Guinea coast in Portugal who renewed the pool of fluent speakers as they returned home (Bradshaw 1965: 7). At least two free students went to Portugal from Afutu around 1513 (Debrunner 1967: 19). Portuguese colonists settled in such places as Cape Verde and what later became Portuguese Guinea in the fifteenth century (Naro 1973: 445); on São Tomé, where a Portuguese "Creole" also took root, in the fifteenth and early sixteenth centuries (LePage and Tabouret-Keller 1985: 28); and the kingdom of the Congo early in the seventeenth century (Bal 1975: 36). It has been suggested that metropolitan Portuguese colonists in Cape Verde and Guiné deliberately used a kind of "foreigner talk," invented in Portugal for communication with Africans, but even if this is true, there was obviously more than one source of Portuguese on the Mina coast and on the Guinea coast generally.[6]

At the same time that Portuguese was being formally imparted, conditions also existed for the development of a lingua franca with a local character. Direct bartering between ships' crews and Africans, although forbidden, was not uncommon (Vogt 1979: 34, 36). Such contact would have encouraged the acquisition of informal varieties. Metropolitan Portuguese itself had as yet no standard form, but in any case, the crews of Portuguese ships were not always themselves community-language speakers of Portuguese, certainly not of an educated variety. Many had been born in West Africa or Brazil. Most significant is the fact that before Elmina Castle was built, long before the Atlantic slave trade became overwhelmingly important, the Portuguese had made themselves middlemen in the intra-African slave trade between the mouth of the Niger and Elmina, via São Tomé, a trade that reached its height between 1510 and 1540 (Debrunner 1967: 20; Rodney 1969: 13; Vogt 1979: 57). Delafosse recorded that when he was at Mina, four hundred slaves arrived from the Slave River (the Niger mouth) and were sold there (Escudier 1992: 32). Some of these people originated from the Benin kingdom, where there was also a Portuguese presence—in 1553, Captain Windam reported that the king of Benin spoke the language, having learned it as a child (Hakluyt 1907: 42)—and from the lower Niger; they were sold to gold merchants who needed to transport goods inland and who would later sell or employ them as farm labor (Wilks 1993: 74). Others were kept as laborers and craftsmen in the castle. The latter must have learned to communicate with Portuguese and local Africans in Portuguese or in Akan or in both. By the time they reached Mina, some may already have been familiar with Portuguese.

From the very beginning of our records, then, we have in the neighborhood of Elmina something like the three-term system of language use that in one way or another frequently seems to characterize African multilingualism: an exotic language for long-distance trade, which apparently shifted from Manding (and indirectly Arabic) to Portuguese late in the fifteenth century; the growing presence of an African language as the language of regional trade and politics, namely Akan; and at least in the early days another language as the language of domestic and cultural life, Afutu.

The spreading local use of Portuguese is attested by the English Captain Towerson's Gold Coast vocabulary of 1555 (Dalby and Hair 1964). Of his eight "Mina" words, two, *bassina* and *molta*, are Portuguese or Spanish.[7] Even if Towerson was mistaken in including them in the same list with his Akan words, that he did so surely indicates that Spanish-Portuguese words were in use among Africans. He also reported numerous conversations in Portuguese with Africans from "Hanta," that is, Ahanta. De Marees, who visited the coast in 1601, means Portuguese when he speaks of the blacks' language and when he mentions *Fetissero* as a word in "their [Africans'] language" ([1602] 1987: 48, 67). The 266 words and expressions of De Marees's Akan vocabulary include 6 Portuguese words.[8] Only one, *adaka* "chest" (from *arca*) is still used in Akan (and many other languages throughout West Africa as well).[9]

The Portuguese built three major forts, at Elmina, Axim, and Shama, but they had lost all to the Dutch by 1642 and never again had a land base on the Gold Coast. Nevertheless, their language remained in local use, as is very clear from the writings of the later part of the seventeenth century. W. J. Müller spent eight years on the Gold Coast in the 1660s as Lutheran pastor of the Danish Fort Frederiksborg at Amanfro, near Cape Coast. Unlike De Marees ([1602] 1987), but like most writers from this period until the middle of the nineteenth century, he uses many words of Portuguese origin for Gold Coast phenomena: *Blanquen* for "Christians," that is, Europeans; *Fitisiken* for local religion; *Cabessirer* and *Grandis* for African officials. Numerous remarks testify to the use of Portuguese between Africans and (non-Portuguese) Europeans. Describing the court of the king ("Day," i.e., *odehe*, modern Akan *odehye*) of Afutu ("Fetu"), he mentions that his interpreter translated from Portuguese into the Fetu language (Müller [1676] 1968: 68). He also explains that when somebody wanted to start trading with Europeans, he would approach a friend who understood Portuguese to act for him.

Müller includes brief specimens of Portuguese as spoken locally, one of the very few writers to do so. He mentions that "we *Blanquen* are called *Filhos de Deos* by them [Africans] in the Portuguese language" ([1676] 1968: 89), and he quotes two sentences in local Portuguese:

Once when I found such an idol basket in the field and wanted to open it one of the foremost men among the Blacks called to me: *O Senor, no abrid, pretto Diabol sta adentro.* (p. 193)
["Oh sir, don't open, a black devil is inside."]

Jan Commè [*nyankɔmɪ] *sta atra forte.* (p. 95)
["God is strong behind," signifying severe thunder.]

Of the 440 words in Müller's Akan word list, 15 are probably of Portuguese origin. Ten of these are still used in Akan.

Another witness to the use of Portuguese was Jean Barbot, a Huguenot trader, whose descriptions of voyages made a few years later, in 1678–79 and 1681–82, were published first in English in 1712. He gives one short specimen, an oath, *Per esta crus de Dios* "by this cross of God." Hair considers Barbot's poor spelling of Portuguese to be evidence that he did not really speak it, but it is better interpreted as evidence that he had found it useful, even necessary, to acquire the language orally on the coast itself. His list of Akan words was obtained through a Portuguese-speaking slave (Hair, Jones, and Law 1992: lxiv).

Bosman, a Dutchman, wrote of his experience on the coast in the 1690s. He, too, speaks of Portuguese as the language of the Africans, for example, "This [day of the week] they call their *Bossum*, or in the Portuguese *Sancte-Day*" ([1705] 1967: 153); "the Oldest and principal wife, here called *Muliere Grande*" (p. 199). As in Müller's German and Barbot's French and English, Portuguese words with local reference abound in Bosman's Dutch: *Rio Cobre, Grenadoes, Remora, Mulatto, Canoas, Fetiche* (for both gold manufactured into objects, and hence adulterated, and local deities), *Caboceer* or *Cabocero* (local dignitary), *Feticheer* (local priest), *Blanks* (whites), *Calabash*, and *Milhio*.

At the end of the seventeenth century, then, Portuguese was still sufficiently established that relatively sophisticated representatives of European trading nations considered it a normal medium for trade, learned it while on the coast, and also adopted words from it into their own languages when reporting on Gold Coast customs and activities. References to "their" Portuguese imply that the language was in use among local Africans and that the variety used had local or at least West African characteristics. Its register range may have been relatively narrow, but it was not reduced to merely the vocabulary of basic bargaining. Indeed, none of the Portuguese phrases given by Müller ([1676] 1968) or Bosman ([1705] 1967) are specifically limited to buying and selling; they mainly concern religion and social customs.

The Portuguese themselves, as well as Portuguese-speaking West Africans and Brazilians, were not in fact absent, despite their official defeat and banishment from the coast. Throughout the seventeenth and eighteenth centuries they were well established at several places on the coast controlled by the Kingdom of Dahomey (then known as the Slave Coast) in what is now the Republic of Benin, where both Europeans and Gold Coast Africans traded with them (Hair et al. 1992: 382). The Portuguese also continued to come to the Gold Coast. When the Dutch acquired the Portuguese possessions on the Gold Coast in 1641, they agreed that the Portuguese could continue to trade there for the next hundred years, provided they paid a 10% duty (Crooks [1923] 1973: 2). Portuguese and Brazilian trading activity increased in the early eighteenth century (Van Dantzig 1978: 152), and during the first half of that century there was a Catholic chapel on the hill facing Elmina Castle (which then belonged to the Dutch) specifically to accommodate the Brazilians trading at Elmina (Feinberg 1989: 80). In 1749, when the British at Cape Coast were dealing only in slaves, instructions to the governor there indicated that he was not to trade with other Europeans *except* the Portuguese because gold and Brazilian tobacco were needed for salaries and other cash expenses (Crooks [1923] 1973: 18).

By 1700, Portuguese seems to have become a true lingua franca on the Gold Coast, used mainly among people who did not speak it as a first language. Its domains had narrowed, and we can be sure its functional goals had correspondingly changed. On the one hand, it was no longer a language of literacy, as far as the Gold Coast was concerned, and its use was associated with the class of Africans involved in European trade. On the other hand, the language was probably present in more than one variety. As Hair has remarked, Barbot's comment—"Many of them [on the Accra coast] can still speak some few words of Portuguese, *and* the Lingua Franca they learnt of their fore-fathers, when the Portuguese had the whole commerce on this coast" (my emphasis)—(Hair, Jones, and Law 1992: 453) is not entirely clear, but it would seem to point to a distinction between an approximation to metropolitan Portuguese and a more radical variety, both of which were in current use.

In the Accra area, the Portuguese and their language were present from the middle of the sixteenth century. The first commercial contacts were made in 1517, when a mission was sent from Mina to Accra (Vogt 1979: 83). Labadi sent a mission to Mina in 1520, and gold traders from Great Accra also visited Mina from about that time. By 1557, trade at Little Accra was sufficiently important that the Portuguese burned and looted it to discourage the Accra from trading with the French and English. Shortly thereafter they built a fortified lodge on a site between the present James and Ussher Forts. Portuguese-Accra relations were never very cordial, for the Accra attacked the lodge around 1570 (Texeira da Mota and Hair 1988: 26) and again, after it had been rebuilt in 1572, around 1578, when they destroyed it and prevented Portuguese boats from landing (Vogt 1979: 126). The lodge was not rebuilt, and the Portuguese had no establishment on the Accra coast thereafter except for the brief period in 1679–82, when a party of Portuguese private adventurers bought Christiansborg Castle from the Danes and occupied it until they handed it back to the Danes.

The importance of the Portuguese language in Accra in the seventeenth century was emphasized by Tilleman, a Danish contemporary of Barbot and Bosman, who spent a total of nine years on the coast. He informed prospective slave traders that in the Kingdom of Acara, trade deals between Europeans and Africans were negotiated only by those who spoke "the country's Portuguese," usually Africans employed or formerly employed at the forts, and that it was necessary to hire such an intermediary ([1697] 1994: 30). He reiterated the advice with respect to the coast at large.

The use of Portuguese in Accra in particular was probably due less to a Portuguese presence in the sixteenth century than to its use throughout the seventeenth and eighteenth centuries by the Danes and by the Dutch, for whom it was the preferred language of trade and contact in the Far East, as well as in Africa (Boxer 1965: 224). Most sailors, traders, and officers in the Dutch service spoke it, and although local varieties developed, they were intercomprehensible (Valkhoff 1972: 94). Negotiations to build a Dutch fort at Accra were underway in 1610, but Fort Crèvecoeur (now Ussher Fort) was not actually built until 1649, although a lodge was built on the site some time earlier (Van Dantzig 1980: xi). Until the destruction of Great Accra, the structure of Accra—with Little Accra and its European establishments on the shore, controlled by Great Accra inland—conformed to the pattern of the dual town of stranger traders and chiefs.[10]

During the eighteenth century, smaller lodges and forts, now mostly vanished, were built at Labadi, Teshi, Tema, and Kpone. The Danish also expanded eastwards—from Fort Frederiksborg at Amanfro (built in 1659 and lost to the English in 1685) and Christiansborg Castle (also built in 1659 at Osu on the site of a lodge erected in 1650, the Danish headquarters after the loss of Frederiksborg; Winsnes in Tilleman [1697] 1994) to forts on the Dangme coast at Ningo (1734), Tubreku (Togbloku?), and Ada (1783)—so that with the building of the English Fort Vernon at Prampram (1745), there was a European establishment and therefore some form of interaction with Europeans at every important Ga and Dangme coastal town. Access to European trade was undoubtedly part of the motivation for the formation of most of these towns.

Despite the scarcity of explicit comment, there is little doubt that the language of this trade and interaction continued to be in Portuguese. There is evidence, for example, that in the eighteenth century, local treaties written in Dutch were orally translated into Portuguese for the benefit of local signatories.[11] All European writers, especially the Dutch, continued to borrow words with specific local reference or signification from this language. Most of our direct information comes from Danish writers, based at Christiansborg Castle. Protten (1764: A3 recto), who had stayed near Popo for a period in the 1730s, as well as at Elmina, stated that "Negro-Portuguese" was spoken by all blacks, along with Fante, as a "general language," in addition to their mother tongues, right from Axim to Eweland and Popo in today's Republic of Benin. Others are less specific, but their writings through the 1780s are compatible with Protten's description. L. F. Rømer (1760), who traded in Christiansborg for many years and published two books about it in the 1760s, gave no word list but used so many Ga words and expressions that he must have spoken the language.[12] In referring to the Fante, however, he used Portuguese words, and even about Labadi and Osu he used quite a number. P. E. Isert, another Dane, who spent three years on the coast in the 1780s and traveled to Akuapem and Anlo, published short word lists of Ga, Asante, and Ewe, as well as quoting local words from time to time, but he also mentioned Portuguese terms as expressions used by the local people in such a way that he was clearly quoting local Portuguese usage. For example, "the Blacks' greeting" at Christiansborg was *Adio ahura* "Good day, sir," evidently Portuguese *a Deo*, with the Ga and Akan title *owura* ([1788] 1992: 28); "what the Black calls *rossar* places," that is, farms, from Portuguese *roçar* "plant" (p. 161); "they say, 'Such and such a *grandee* is *bringar*-ing'" (giving drinks), from Portuguese *brincar* (p. 138). It is clear that Portuguese on the Gold Coast was not a simple market jargon but a language of business *negotiation* and the elaborate social forms that implies.

Portuguese was a worldwide language, the lingua franca (and not only for commercial transactions) of the port towns of Africa, the Far East, and the New World. The Dutch government periodically tried to replace it with Dutch in its Asian possessions, such as Batavia, but without success, for the resident Dutch community, as well as the local and mixed blood community associated with it, preferred to use Portuguese in that context (Boxer 1965: 224). Since African Portuguese-speaking communities are known to have existed in Cape Town and on the Sierra Leone coast,[13] where they have disappeared, as well as in Cape Verde, Senegal, and São Tomé, where

Portuguese is still spoken, the question arises of whether Portuguese was also a community language of Africans (mainly perhaps of mixed blood) on the Gold Coast, particularly at Elmina. There is no direct evidence for such a language community, but there is evidence that by the mid-seventeenth century the mulatto community was politically distinct; and such a group, which was surely bilingual, may well have maintained Portuguese as its community language, reinforced by the castle slave community. According to Feinberg (1989: 89), the Portuguese-Dutch agreement of 1637 made provision for the many Portuguese mulattoes in Elmina to remove to Portuguese-speaking São Tomé if they so wished. Under Dutch administration, mulattoes continued to constitute a separate group in Elmina, known as *Tapooyers*, a Portuguese term of Brazilian origin that implied observance of Portuguese law and custom (Baesjou 1979: 18). All of this suggests a community of Lusophones, or at least balanced bilingualism in Portuguese and Akan. Vestiges of a Portuguese community in Elmina lasted at least through the nineteenth century, notably in the Saint Anthony's Society (Odamtten 1978: 27).

The disappearance of Portuguese from the Gold Coast is related to its replacement by English as the language of trade worldwide,[14] but locally it was a consequence of the abolition of the slave trade by the British in 1807—or rather, of British enforcement of their abolition for everyone else—and the departure of the Dutch and the Danes. Denmark had abolished the trade in 1805, followed by Holland in 1814 and France in 1831. The Portuguese abandoned their fort at Whydah in 1807 (Akinjogbin 1967: 193), but their language died slowly. Brazilians of African descent became the dominant social force in the town, and Portuguese was the language of instruction in Whydah schools until the end of the nineteenth century (Bay 1986: 37). The Atlantic slave trade and contacts with Brazil continued in the area into the 1840s at least (Debrunner 1965: 33–35; Freeman 1844: 245).

An event that might have prolonged the use of Portuguese in Accra, but apparently did not, was the arrival in Accra (as well as Whydah and Lagos) in 1836 and after of the Portuguese-speaking Brazilians, known in Accra as the "Tabon" people (from the Portuguese expression (*es*)*ta bon*? "are you well?"). These were freed slaves sent by the American Colonization Society after Brazil freed foreign-born slaves in 1831 (A. Brown 1927: 196; Debrunner 1965: 37). They were integrated into Ga-speaking society through the Otublohum quarter, and there is no evidence that they maintained the Portuguese language into a second generation, which indicates that it was no longer especially useful. Christophersen (1953: 285) claimed that there were still West Africans "who can speak a little Portuguese, learnt either in Brazil or from parents who had learnt it there," but if such speakers exist in Accra today they must be very few indeed.[15]

Portuguese words continue to recur in nineteenth-century works about the coast, such as Meredith's (1812) and Hutton's (1821) in English and De Marrée's (1817/18) in Dutch, but with gradually diminishing frequency. A few, such as *palaver* and *fetish*, are still current in Ghanaian English, and others in Ghanaian languages. As Bradshaw (1965: 36) noted with reference to the languages of Sierra Leone, there is very little overlap between Portuguese loanwords in Akan or Ga and the Portuguese vocabulary that is characteristic of local use in English, presumably because the objects and concepts new to African and European languages were complementary.

A number of words from the Far East and the Americas that were carried through the medium of Portuguese have been very widely borrowed into both European and Ghanaian languages. Examples are *veranda*, *cacao*, *hammock*, and *guava*. The only such word that is unique to Ghanaian English is *kenkey*. The first citation is De Marees's *Kangues*, or *Kankis*. Its source is either Malay *kañji* or Tamil *kánxi* "cooked rice," one of these being the most likely source of the other (Yule and Burnell [1886] 1903). The Ghanaian food is normally made of maize, but the word was no doubt borrowed (like Ga *kɔmì*) in the meaning "cooked cereal."[16]

There are numerous publications on the Gold Coast dating from the first half of the nineteenth century, mostly in English, but there is no direct reference to the Portuguese language there. The officers and traders most likely to have noted it were based at Cape Coast, where Portuguese was probably never as important, from the English point of view, as at Elmina or Accra. Besides, British interest was turning in-land, away from the coast toward Ashanti, and Portuguese was a coastal phenomenon.

The Spread of English

The Portuguese monopoly of the Guinea trade was broken in the 1540s, as the French and English followed down the coast after the gold. Like the Portuguese, the English at first seized people to train as interpreters. When Towerson made his first voyage to Mina in 1555, his party communicated with local people in Portuguese, but he had occasion to inform the people of one village that their men had been taken to England (by some previous party) to learn the language. He assured them they would return to "be a helpe to the Englishmen in this Country" (Hakluyt 1907: 86). Some of these interpreters, apparently Ahantas, were with him on his second voyage, and he used English-trained interpreters again on his third voyage to Mina in 1577. On this trip he also traded at "the further place of Mina, called Egrand," that is, Accra, in competition with French ships. Use of Portuguese by the Engish on the Guinea coast after the sixteenth century has been questioned—for example, by Spencer (1971: 9)— and with respect to the Gold Coast it is true that it is little mentioned in English sources, although they certainly used it in the Gambia (Dillard 1979: 263). Debrunner (1967: 64) implies that at Cape Coast Castle, use of its own interpreters rather than Portuguese-speaking intermediaries was a matter of Royal Africa Company policy from the 1720s. Nevertheless, in the highly competitive situation on the Gold Coast, where a European trader's activities were not always confined to his own nation's establishment, if the English did not speak Portuguese themselves they must often have found it necessary (like Tilleman) to employ Africans who did.

The English acquired their first land bases in 1618, building forts at Cormantine and Takoradi. These were lost to the Dutch in 1664, but in return the English got Cape Coast Castle, their headquarters for the next two centuries, rivaled in size among European establishments on the Gold Coast only by the Dutch headquarters, Elmina. James Fort in Accra was built in 1673, followed by six others between Accra and Dixcove and another at Whydah on the Slave Coast. Most of these were abandoned early in the nineteenth century. James Fort remained the only English establishment on the Ga-Dangme coast until Fort Vernon was built at Prampram in 1745. Preceded by the Dutch at Fort Crèvecoeur in the 1640s and the Danes at Christiansborg in 1650, not to mention the Portuguese—with the French, the Swedes, and the Brandenburgers not far away—the English in Accra were just one European presence among several. On the one hand, the Portuguese language allowed Gold Coasters to communicate with all of them, just as it allowed Europeans to communicate with all Africans, and there was thus no commercial reason for the English language to spread far beyond the fort's own interpreters. On the other hand, individual Europeans hired local people as servants, both in Cape Coast Castle and in James Fort, and these servants presumably acquired English.[17]

In the eighteenth century, small numbers of free local boys, mainly mulattoes, received an education in the prevailing European language at the major forts, where school was held rather irregularly, depending on the availability and interest of a chaplain. The Dutch restarted a castle school in Elmina in 1643, but it met sporadically except under J. E. Capitein, chaplain and schoolmaster from 1742 to 1746, who had received his education and been ordained after being taken to Holland from the western Gold Coast as a child of seven (Debrunner 1967: 66). Thirteen wards of the Ashanti king Opoku Ware were among Capitein's pupils (Debrunner 1967: 75). Meredith (1812: 85) later mentioned a school at Elmina for both sexes but thought that it had declined in recent years.

In the 1720s, Christian Protten received his elementary education at the Christiansborg Castle school from the Reverend Elias Svane. He and Frederik Pedersen, who adopted Svane's name, continued their education in Denmark, attending the University of Copenhagen. Protten later taught at Christiansborg, for a total of twelve years between 1737 and 1769, and indeed prepared his grammar and catechism for that purpose. School was held in English at Cape Coast Castle in the 1690s when a priest was present (Bartels 1965: 3; Tilleman [1697] 1994: 22) and irregularly thereafter. From 1752 to 1756 the Reverend Thomas Thompson, the first Church of England missionary on the coast, was chaplain at Cape Coast Castle and also taught in Cape Coast town. Through him, three boys, including Philip Quaque [kwaku], were sent to England in 1754 and two more in 1762 (Crooks [1923] 1973).

Others, including the best known Gold Coast scholars of the period, Capitein and Anton Wilhelm Amo, were educated entirely abroad (Debrunner 1967: 66). In 1753 "four sons of prominent men" of Anomabo were taken to France, apparently for education. One of these was a son of Chief John Korante, who had sent another son to be educated in England in 1751 (Matson 1953: 48). John Acqua and George Sackee were educated in England, at the expense of the Royal Africa Company, from 1753 to 1755. One of them was actually being held hostage. This may have followed some kind of pattern, for as late as 1837, two boys (relatives of the king of Ashanti) who had been held hostage at Cape Coast Castle since 1831 were sent to England for education, returning in 1841 (Freeman 1844: 5). Throughout the latter half of the eighteenth century, dozens of African children were studying in Liverpool at the expense of their parents (Anstey and Hair 1976: 5), most of them from the Gold Coast (Debrunner 1967: 65; Matson 1953: 52).[18] Debrunner (p. 70) suggests that the growing ascendancy of the English language during the eighteenth century may have been related to the fact that far more boys were being educated in England than in Holland or Denmark.

Quaque was ordained in England and returned in 1765 to serve as chaplain and teacher at the castle until his death in 1816, but in 1788 the school for mulatto children still had only twelve pupils. The English presence in Accra (that is, James Fort) toward the end of the seventeenth century amounted to a staff of twenty-six, mainly military, most of whom were probably English: a chief merchant, an assistant, a barber, a sergeant, a constable, and a drummer, as well as twenty soldiers plus an unknown number of servants and slaves, which made it the smallest of the three European establishments there (Tilleman [1697] 1994: 25). It remained small throughout the eighteenth century, despite considerable trading and military activity, including the destruction of Dutch Accra in 1782 in pursuance of the war between England and Holland. In 1749 James Fort had only 32 slaves of all types, compared to 367 at Cape Coast, 118 at Whydah, and 63 at Dixcove. In 1789, the company servants in Accra, both black and white (excluding slaves, apparently), totaled 16, and included no writers. There is thus little evidence of either schooling or jobs that required literacy being provided for Accra people.

The situation began to change after 1807. In his report for 1822, Sir Charles Macarthy commended the commandant of James Fort, Captain Blenkarne, and a schoolmaster named Cotton for their recent efforts in the education of young Africans. This school lasted until 1826 and was held again in 1832 and 1837–38; there was also an English school in Prampram in the 1820s (Debrunner 1967: 96). Nevertheless, in all the British establishments on the coast there were only two schoolmasters, three teachers (all Africans), one printer, one female teacher of needlework (at the girls' school in Cape Coast), and one linguist-interpreter (also African). The Cape Coast school had seventy pupils, and the three African teachers also conducted a night school in Cape Coast for adults (Bartels 1965: 7). It was the products of the Cape Coast Castle school who mainly staffed the English schools in Accra and elsewhere (Debrunner 1967: 96). In the same year (1822), the British forts were employing seven writers, of whom three were Africans. The great majority of this staff was in Cape Coast (Crooks [1923] 1973: 147). Most of the Africans involved were of mixed blood.

A few more African literates may have been in private employ outside the forts. In 1828 five British merchants were living in Cape Coast town (increasing to fourteen by 1834) and two in Accra, who with a number of African merchants were potential employers of Africans literate in English. In 1830, the population of the coast is said to have included ten English merchants and "some coloured gentlemen educated in England" (Crooks [1923] 1973: 261).[19] Nevertheless, the number of literate users of English must have remained very small through the first thirty years of the century and heavily concentrated in Cape Coast (Debrunner 1967: 73).

Like the other second languages we have looked at, English spread in more than one range of domains, and like them its spread on the coast was related to its spread elsewhere. In varying degrees, it was spread through formal education, which quickly became the province of the Christian missions; through the military; and by population movements that resulted from events in other places. We shall first consider the expansion of formal education in English in the years before and just after the establishment of colonialism.

With the arrival of the Wesleyan mission at Cape Coast in 1835, a push for evangelization and literacy began, both through the medium of English. Indeed, in the writing of both Cruickshank (1853) and T. B. Freeman (1844: 243), Christianity and the English language are all but explicitly equated, partly in opposition to Catholic (and in Freeman's eyes un-Christian) Portuguese. Cruickshank, anxious to increase the British presence, complained that the use of English at the time was very limited, confined to "a broken conversational dialect," and that the castle school had made little impact. The missionaries seem to have disagreed with this judgment (Odamtten 1978: 40) and employed its products as teachers and interpreters. By the 1850s there were a thousand or more pupils at the Wesleyan schools, so that literate speakers of English were becoming scattered throughout the country and many Fante chiefs had secretaries.

The first Methodist Primary School in Accra (James Town) was founded in November 1838, and by 1840 it had eighty pupils, sixty boys and twenty girls (Bartels 1965: 43). A Methodist Training Institute opened in Accra in 1841 (Debrunner 1967: 145). However, the greater impact on education in the Ga-speaking area was made by the Basel mission, which began mission work at Christiansborg in 1828 and established the first school to solicit pupils who were not mulattoes, referred to by Reindorf ([1889] 1966: 218) as the Government School. This lasted until 1835, when the sole surviving missionary, Andreas Riis, moved to Akuapem. A school for mulattoes was opened again at Christiansborg under a new Danish chaplain, which C. C. Reindorf himself attended. The Basel mission school was reopened by Zimmermann in 1843, aided by a group of Jamaican missionary-colonists, with teaching in English, although the school later switched to Ga. The first postprimary school in Accra was not firmly established until 1855. Disturbances related to the departure of the Danish and the takeover by the British, especially the bombardment of Teshi, Labadi, and Osu in 1854, seem to have been responsible for delays. Zimmermann founded the mission and school at Abokobi, in the Ga interior, in that year. The present Osu boarding and middle schools were founded in 1858, followed by the Basel mission school at Mayera, on Gbese land (Debrunner 1967: 150; Reindorf [1889] 1966: 6ff.).

In 1848, there were about 300 pupils in the schools of Akropong (Akuapem) and Christiansborg combined (Reindorf [1889] 1966: 220). By 1891, Accra (including James Town, Ussher Town, and Christiansborg) had seven schools, teaching 1,130 pupils (5.7% of the population), of whom only 171 were female. By 1952, when fee-free elementary education was introduced, a little under 20% of the Accra population had three or more years of elementary school. In 1955, 86% of all children between six and sixteen years old were in school (Acquah [1954] 1972: 108).

The school language policies of the Methodists and the Basel mission were diametrically opposed. While the Wesleyans concentrated on English and largely ignored Fante and Ga for instruction purposes, although not for evangelizing (Bartels 1965: 22), the German-speaking Basel missionaries taught in Twi or Ga in all their schools. Unlike the North German Evangelical Society schools east of the Volta, they did not teach German in the primary years (see, for example, Schreiber 1901: 84). It was to further this indigenous-language policy that they produced comprehensive grammars and dictionaries of Akuapem Twi and Ga and numerous religious and educational translations within a remarkably short time.

Nevertheless, the Basel schools eventually became important agents in the spread of English. In the syllabus introduced in 1869, English was begun in the fifth primary year and was continued as a major subject thereafter, as was Ga (Debrunner 1967: 151). In 1882, the British colonial government passed an Education Ordinance, stipulating (among other things) that mission schools could be assisted financially on the condition that they taught in English and made religious instruction optional (Odamtten 1978: 211). The Basel mission accepted these grants, although reluctantly. The result was a distinction between government schools that taught in English, in which religious knowledge was an optional subject, and private (mission) schools, among which there was a further distinction—between assisted schools that taught in English, mostly in town, and unassisted schools that continued to teach only in Ga (or Akan), mainly in rural villages. The Bremen mission schools refused government grants until 1902 (Ahadji 1976: 187).

In the ensuing years there have been policy variations concerned with the speed with which English was to be introduced as the language of instruction, reacting to both the perceived value of Ghanaian languages in education and the practical aspect of teaching in a language new to the pupils. In 1925 an Education Ordinance withdrew the English medium of instruction requirement for government grants to private schools, and in 1927 the Report of the (British) Advisory Committee on Native Education in Tropical Africa resulted in official recognition of the use of indigenous languages at the primary level, particularly in the first three years (Boadi 1976: 88; Smock 1975: 174). In 1951, however, the Accelerated Development Plan recommended that English be the language of instruction by the second primary year, and in 1957 the government adopted the policy that English be the medium of instruction throughout elementary education (Boadi 1976: 93). This policy was reversed in 1970, when the local Ghanaian language was again made the language of instruction for the first three years (Smock 1975: 175), a policy that has continued to the present.

Although the mission schools are now for the most part government schools, the nineteenth-century distinction between rural schools that taught mainly in the local languages and urban schools that taught mainly in English has by no means been obliterated. In rural schools, policies favoring an early shift to English have generally not been implemented (Boadi 1976: 95), particularly in Akan-speaking areas. In Accra, the highly multilingual school situation (such as that reviewed in chapter 3) has tended to encourage the early use of English. The Education Review Committee of 1967 recognized this when it said that despite its recommendation that a Ghanaian language be the medium of instruction in the first three years, English could be introduced in this capacity earlier "in the metropolis [Accra] and other urban areas" (p. 94). In any case, government policy on the language of instruction has not affected the private, independent schools, locally known as "international schools," where English is the language of instruction from the beginning of primary school and children's introduction to the language is pushed back to the "international" nursery school.

Educationists and academics tend to favor a longer period of transition to English as the sole language of instruction, but its function in postprimary education has never been seriously questioned, nor has the principle that primary education in Ghana should give everyone a working command of both the written and the spoken language. No matter how uneven the standard achieved—and it is often very poor from an educational point of view—there is no doubt that the schools do indeed serve to spread the language and that most people in Accra look on even a smattering of "book English" as worth acquiring.[20] As Christaller foresaw in 1886, primary education in English has had the effect of favoring the use of English as a written language over Ga, with its relatively small community. Shortly before independence, Rapp (1955) noted that although Ga teachers did not seem particularly enthusiastic about teaching Ga, they would rather teach English in its place than Akan, even though a majority of the Ga clearly spoke Akan. The attitude today is not different.[21]

Although the number of English people in Accra greatly increased with the establishment of colonialism, the social distance between Europeans and Africans increased even more, especially after 1885, when government bungalows and leisure facilities were built in Victoriaborg. Throughout the colonial period, exposure to educated varieties of English was overwhelmingly through church and school, with no very sharp distinction made between them.

Despite less unequal social relations, very few people can have been exposed to the English of its native speakers during the eighteenth century, even in and around the English forts. Apart from a small number of English officials and occasionally their wives, fort workers were mainly African. However in 1781 two foot companies of a hundred men each, mainly convicts and deserters, were raised in England and sent to Cape Coast to fight the Dutch. One hundred and forty-four were killed or wounded in the assault on Dutch Accra in 1782, including sixty "English Blacks," (Crooks [1923] 1973). Convict soldiers were again sent to the Gold Coast in 1783, and two companies of English troops were sent to fight Ashanti in 1823, followed by more in the next two years; but in 1826 all English troops were withdrawn and the practice of recruiting deserters was discontinued, mainly because their low survival and high desertion rates made them uneconomical. By this time there were no white soldiers at Accra, only at Cape Coast. What influence these soldiers may have had on the English of Africans in and outside the forts is hard to judge, but such as it was it cannot have been in the direction of a standard, educated variety.

In 1822, the Africa Company's African troops, with a few additions, were formed into a corps of the Royal African Light Infantry, numbering about 200, of whom 130 were stationed at Cape Coast and 35 at Accra. A militia was formed in Accra in 1823 to police the town, while the Gold Coast Corps was stationed in the forts (Crooks [1923] 1973). In 1844, the corps at the forts was down to 129 and the militia for the whole coast numbered 62, so that the number of such personnel in Accra at this time must have been small (Gillespie 1955). However, they are important because the role of the armed forces in spreading popular English was as significant as their role in the spread of Hausa. Local literate recruits were preferred, especially for the "Fante" civil police, but since they were scarce there were sporadic attempts to teach English within the corps. Classes were started in the 1870s to teach English to noncommissioned officers, but they petered out by 1878. The first native officers were sent to England for further training in 1874–75 (p. 16). From 1902 to 1912 the police school taught recruits a little English and how to tell time, but in 1916 there were complaints that the police manual was not being read because it was in English. Nevertheless, despite the policy that the language of command should be Hausa in the Hausa constabulary and Fante or Ga in the civil police, officers often lapsed into English even when it was not being actively taught and despite the fact that most of the men understood neither the coast languages nor English (p. 51).

The situation suggests the prevalence of limited, nonstandard varieties of English within the forces. A likely contributor, overlaying the early input of English soldiers and following the reorganization of 1822, was the West India regiments. West Indian soldiers were present throughout the nineteenth century, in close association with local soldiers. According to one witness, the British had 5,000 troops in Cape Coast in 1825, including colored regiments from the West Indies (Bennett and Brooks 1965: 139). In 1840, the Royal African Colonial Corps was combined with three companies of the First West India Regiment to form the Third West India Regiment (Crooks [1923] 1973). In 1844, the First West India Regiment at Cape Coast numbered 136 men, plus 10 wives and children. The company was withdrawn in 1850 but brought back in 1860, after the Gold Coast Corps was disbanded for mutiny. In 1902 the West Indian presence was strengthened with additional superintendants of police (Gillespie 1955: 42).

The possible sources of the English of the armed forces thus included partly learned (because haphazardly taught) standard English, uneducated metropolitan colloquial English, and West Indian neo-English. In recent years, the "pidgin" English that resulted has been the language of communication between the army and police, especially the "Hausa" units, and the local populace (Dadzie 1985: 118), a pattern that was probably established very early.

If West Indian creolized English was one likely source of popular Ghanaian English, at least three others were varieties, or groups of varieties, that originated on the West African coast: Krio of Sierra Leone, Kru English, and Nigerian Pidgin English. The people who arrived in Accra from Freetown in the 1840s brought with them an English that had a complex history of its own, beginning in 1772, when the abolition of slavery in England led to the freeing of 15,000 slaves, which in turn led to a repatriation movement (Barbag-Stoll 1983: 34, quoting Fage). In 1787 a group of 400 blacks plus 70 whites were sent to the future Freetown. According to Grade (1892: 366), some were North Americans and some were British soldiers discharged in 1783. They were joined by Nova Scotians, by black British Americans (in 1792), and by 500 Jamaican Maroons in 1800 (Barbag-Stoll 1983: 34). These groups, speaking at least three different dialects of English, formed the host community into which the British brought confiscated slave cargoes after 1807. By the 1830s, the precursor of Krio existed in Freetown in at least two varieties, apparently reflecting dialect differences among the pre-1807 population, and was distinct from vehicular or strictly second-language English ("pidgin") (Jones 1962). As on the Gold Coast, there was also a West Indian presence throughout the nineteenth century. West India regiments were often stationed at Freetown, especially from 1843 to 1874, when the governor of Sierra Leone was in charge of all British interests on the coast.

English was established in Monrovia in 1820, when the first group of free Americans settled there because the British did not allow them to land at Freetown. Many more followed, including Africans recaptured from ships on the high seas and West Indians from the British Barbadoes, as well as liberated Americans (Fraenkel 1964: 11, 17). Liberian English exists in many varieties, among which those of Monrovia are to be distinguished from the lingua franca spoken in the interior and from the Kru English of the coast, also a lingua franca, which closely resembles the Krio of Sierra Leone and may have been acquired from its community speakers (Hancock 1970/71).

The Freetown, Monrovia, and Kru varieties were all introduced into the Gold Coast, especially Accra, in the course of the nineteenth century. The descendants of freed captives who immigrated from Freetown to Accra in the 1840s became Ga-speaking, but they were also English-speaking, as Freeman's meetings at Badagry and Abeokuta indicate, and some of them must have come as community-language speakers of an early form of Krio (Freeman 1844: 222, 229). After 1827, graduates of Fourah Bay College in Freetown taught throughout British West Africa, spreading both a West African variety of educated English and the Krio that most of them spoke out of school (Barbag-Stoll 1983: 52). Lower-level educational institutions in Freetown also contributed their products and their language to the British colonies.[22] In 1871, the Gold Coast police force of 115 men included 25 Sierra Leoneans, as well as 4 West Indians and 1 Kru (Gillespie 1955: 10).

Contact with Kru English began not later than the 1830s, when its speakers had already made a name for themselves as deckhands, boatmen, and traders all along the West African coast (Bennett and Brooks 1965; Davis 1976; Martin 1985). At this time they also began to work on shore as laborers, including on cocoa plantations in Fernando Po. However, the main impact of this variety probably occurred after World War I, when most Kru laborers moved from Lagos and the Oil Rivers to the gold mines of the Gold Coast and then to Accra, Takoradi, and Kumasi. There were 13,000 Liberians in Ghana at the census of 1921 (Martin 1985: 405), and Accra had 1,335 in 1948 (Acquah [1954] 1972: 31). Most were Kru, although at a more elevated economic level there were also contacts with the Monrovia merchant class. Liberian seamen in the port towns of Accra and Takoradi after World War II, and their speech, seem to have made a strong impression on the young (Dadzie 1985: 118). This is perhaps related to the fact that throughout the first half of the twentieth century, and perhaps before, they were important agents in the development and spread of West African popular music (Collins 1985). Although lyrics were generally eventually transmuted into local languages, the songs often spread initially in English. Kru urban laborers were less glamorous than seamen but were nevertheless another group of which local people were very much aware (as noted in chapter 6) and with whom they interacted.

Nigerian Pidgin English became particularly salient in the 1970s, when large numbers of Ghanaians at all social and educational levels went to work in Nigeria and sometimes brought the language back, but its presence in Accra predates this. The ex-soldiers who remained in Accra in domestic and service jobs after 1945 included a considerable number of Nigerians, particularly Ijaw, who hailed from the Niger delta, the present Rivers State of Nigeria. They used Pidgin English among themselves and with other ex-servicemen. The English had been able to exclude other Europeans from the Niger delta area by 1650, so that the English language was established and naturalized there much earlier than elsewhere on the Guinea coast (Elugbe and Omamor 1991). Since the Niger delta was a continuing source of slaves on the Gold Coast and thus, perhaps, of some of the early inhabitants of the Alatas of Accra and its coast, Nigerian Pidgin or its ancestor may have affected the English of Africans at James Fort and Cape Coast by the end of the seventeenth century.

The area in which so-called Nigerian Pidgin English originated and is still strongest has a history of repeated contact with community-language speakers and of formal instruction in English, both locally and in England, dating at least from the eighteenth century (Forde 1956: viii). In the diary of Antera Duke, a wealthy Efik trader, we have a piece of extended writing in a form of this language dating from the 1780s that demonstrates the continuing influence of standard English on a localized variety. For example, the first entry in Forde's edition begins: ". . . so I walk with Egbo men to go for Etutim . . ." (Forde 1956: 78). From a modern point of view, the use of prepositions here is inconsistent. To "go for" a place (that is, Etutim's [house]), is common pidgin today, but the use of the preposition "with" in "walk with" or "to" with the infinitive is not. Duke occasionally used the standard "to" rather than "for," as later in the same entry, ". . . soon after we hav[e] all [the] Egbo men go to Egbo Bush Bush. . . ." The absence of inflexions on verb and noun and of the definite article are common pidgin today, but Duke's use of the connectors "so" and "soon after" and the plural form "men" are not. Duke's total innocence of punctuation is hardly relevant, since many writers who speak English natively have problems with it.

The Nigerian Pidgin English that came to Accra in the twentieth century was probably a descendant of the spoken vernacular on which Duke's written language was based, but it had been considerably affected by Krio in the nineteenth century. For example, the high proportion of people of Yoruba origin among Sierra Leoneans is thought to explain the presence of Yoruba elements in Nigerian Pidgin since few Yoruba spoke the language before the twentieth century (Elugbe and Omamor 1991: 20). Cameroonian Pidgin English was similarly affected by Krio in the nineteenth century, so that it strongly resembles it in the twentieth (Todd 1979).

Unlike Portuguese, English eventually spread beyond the coast. The focal point from which the spread proceeded followed the British headquarters: first Cape Coast and then Accra, although as far as the literate varieties are concerned, the concentration of schools in Cape Coast—including the University of Cape Coast with its Institute of Education—means that the town has remained important up to the present. At various times throughout the eighteenth and early nineteenth century, children and wards of the king of Ashanti were educated at Cape Coast and in England (Crooks [1923] 1973; Freeman 1844). Hutchison in Kumasi with Bowdich evidently conversed with the local people in English (Bowdich 1966: 383). Military confrontation with the British (which involved large numbers of troops, although the majority were Africans) had a linguistic as well as a military impact on Ashanti, for in 1877, at the same time that the Ashanti king was raising a Hausa force, his armies were using the English drill book (Gillespie 1955: 20). Farther north, English was hardly present until well into the twentieth century. Ferguson does not seem to have encountered any local speakers of the language during his travels beyond Gonja in the 1890s, although in the northeast in 1894 he found that a few Muslim traders could speak English (Arhin 1974: 110). His head carrier at Wa spoke it (p. 162), but he was probably not of northern origin.

Many Muslim traders had most likely acquired their English to the south, in what is now the northern Volta Region, where a variety of vehicular English was fairly widespread in the market centers. Some of these traders had in fact been soldiers; Klose (1899: 307) describes one particularly enterprising trader, Abo-Karimo, who had once been a "Hausa" soldier in Accra and had spent time in London. In 1894, Klose found that he had to use Pidgin English at Kete-Krachi and in Nchumuru country and that his servants quickly acquired English in Nkonya (pp. 296–97). In Buem and farther north, in Adele and Achode, he found that the available interpreters were mainly English-speaking traders in rubber and ivory and that most were from Accra.[23]

The language was not yet spreading through schooling, for at that time the Basel mission schools of Nkonya and Buem were teaching only in Akan and local languages (pp. 294–95). The Bremen missionaries who began work at Keta, Peki, and Anlo at mid-century depended heavily on English-speaking interpreters from among the local people (Zahn 1867: 18; 1870: 51, 80).[24]

Is there a distinctive, autonomous code or range of codes that can be suitably labeled "Ghanaian Pidgin English"? Berry (1971: 513) seems undecided. He divided West African pidgins into two types, Liberian and a second spoken in Ghana, Nigeria, and Cameroon (Krio, as a community language, he treated separately). However, his remark that Kru English was "not so widespread as elsewhere" is an admission that it was indeed spoken in Ghana. We have seen that Ghana and particularly the major centers such as Accra have received many varieties of vehicular, creolized, and metropolitan English in the past two centuries. Before that, it is possible but not demonstrated that (as Tonkin 1971 seems to suggest) the English of the servants of the English forts (such as the founders of Nleshi Alata and its equivalent in Cape Coast) was acquired by some of the captives bound for the Americas, so that in the nineteenth century, New World developments of the fort English came back to Freetown and Monrovia and eventually to the Gold Coast.[25] However, it is the twentieth-century imports that are most evident today. With the possible exception of the lower ranks of the post-1970 army and police, speakers of a radical variety of English in Ghana have usually learned it somewhere else. If a specifically Ghanaian variety of West Coast nonliterate, second-language English exists, it will probably be found in the army.

Throughout its history but increasingly during the colonial period, popular and vehicular English in Ghana was exposed to the literary standard and metropolitan colloquial varieties, as well as to numerous West African and West Indian varieties, both educated and otherwise. As early as 1863, one reasonably acute observer thought that "blackman's English" was typical of the West Coast *except* Accra, where the people had learned "better."[26] A result is that to most Ghanaian speakers, the kinds of English that outsiders call "pidgin" have no autonomy. It has been pointed out that what most makes English a desirable acquisition is access to reading and writing and the economic advantages that accompany them (Elugbe and Omamor 1991: 143). Therefore, even when learned strictly "by ear," the variety acquired by an individual is usually the closest to a recognized literate model available and is always subject to revision in that direction. As Berry (1971) pointed out, the "Pidgin English" of the Herskovits's (1937) collection of Asante tales is better described as an attempt at literate English, based on a generalized West Coast vehicular English and contrasts markedly with the language of their Nigerian collection (Herskovits and Herskovits 1931). The few texts from the nineteenth century—which include the short speech by the king of Ashanti's linguist (or the linguist's interpreter?) at Cape Coast in 1824, reproduced by Bennett and Brooks (1965: 139), and Bell's (1893) report of a conversation with his servant, who seems to have been a local man—are mostly (socio)linguistically indeterminate for lack of information about the speakers and because the transcriptions were very likely affected by the unconscious political agendas of the reporters and their imperfect acquaintance with the idiom. But it is noteworthy that Klose's (1899: 371) quotation of his interpreter, whom he referred to as a murderer of Negro English, departs only slightly from "normal" English.[27]

English in Ghana is regarded by most Ghanaians as possessing a very diverse range of styles and register forms, of which some speakers have a broader command than others, although (as with a community language) no one commands all of them. A speaker limited to the less literate varieties is generally regarded as having imperfectly learned the language or perhaps as having learned a class dialect of it. The reverse is not altogether true, for speakers limited to literate varieties are not (at least by themselves) regarded as unfinished learners, although such varieties certainly index class. The distinction Omamor makes between Nigerian Pidgin English and Nigerian speakers' inadequately learned, "broken" English is difficult to apply in Ghana (Elugbe and Omamor 1991: 51), and there is relatively little code switching such as Scotton (1975) describes for Lagos.[28] What does occur seems to be regarded by the participants as switching between class dialects, often for stylistic purposes. Despite speakers' perceptions, however, these varieties are not completely mutually intercomprehensible.

I do not wish to suggest that Ghanaian speakers of English have passively imitated whatever English was presented to them, adding nothing of their own. Probably the most comprehensive examination of Ghanaian English is Sey's (1973), although it deals only with literate varieties. Ghanaian pronunciation is distinctive, and there are differences between the pronunciations of the Ga and the Fante (Criper 1971). Since independence, the target model of the educated variety has been gradually shifting from the British educated standard to a model based on the speech of Ghanaians with a Ghanaian secondary education, on which the noticeable influences from external varieties of English are from North America (especially black America) and Nigeria. Such influences, affecting vocabulary, idiom, and intonation, are promoted by popular music and increasingly by travel between Ghana, Nigeria, and especially the United States, which now has a rather large Ghanaian expatriate population.

One of the most remarked-on developments of the past twenty years has been the student jargon, disparagingly referred to in Ghana as pidgin English, that is used among themselves by most secondary and postsecondary students (Dadzie 1985: 118). In lexicon and syntax this situational style draws heavily on both coastal vehicular varieties of English and Ghanaian languages. Since there is lack of agreement within the education system on standards and models, it is not surprising that students at the university level often have difficulty recognizing sociolinguistic fields in English and orienting themselves among them (Hyde 1994; Odamtten, Denkabe, and Tsikata 1944).

Remarks

It only makes sense to say that Portuguese was replaced by English if it can be shown that Portuguese was used in certain sociolinguistic functions before the nineteenth century and that English was used in those functions afterward by the same people or the same categories of people—the successor networks. The most salient domains are those whose functions involve (or involved) communication between Africans and Europeans. They may be divided into two sets: the interrelated domains of Christianity and literacy and the intertwined domains of the Atlantic trade, specifically the slave trade, trade-related politics, and military command.

Considering the brief and tempestuous nature of the sixteenth-century Portuguese presence, and in contrast to the language history of Elmina, it is unlikely that Portuguese was ever significant as a language of Christianity and literacy in Accra. These domains, however limited at first in scope, were introduced to the Accra coast with the establishment of the Danish, Dutch, and English forts, in their languages. In Elmina, Portuguese was replaced by Dutch when the fort changed hands. In the nineteenth century, Danish and Dutch were replaced in both domain ranges by English, except that the religious domains were shared with Ga (and with Twi in Akuapem).[29] In each case, the language was replaced when the European networks that supported the European side of the dialogue were replaced. This is true even of the introduction of Ga and Akan, for despite eighteenth-century efforts by such men as Capitein (1744) and Protten (1764) and several Danish officers, these domains in their modern forms were largely created for these languages by Germans and Swiss, who spoke them as second languages.

Alternatively, the domain(s) of Christianity may be treated as new subdomains of religion in general. In that case, it is Ga that was partially replaced, first by Danish and perhaps Dutch and English and then more definitively by English, especially within the (relatively) urban networks. Similarly, the Methodist language policy spread the already existing school domain of English in James Town by taking it outside the fort and expanding the network to include more Africans; English replaced Dutch, to the extent that it had ever been used for literacy by Africans in Dutch Accra, but the pre-1882 Basel policy created a new set of domains, of school life and skills, in the Ga of Osu.

Portuguese lasted as the language of commercial negotiation as long as inter-European competition lasted. In a place like Elmina, it is not simply a matter of maintaining the language as before 1642 but for fewer purposes. It appears that the replacement of Portuguese for religion and literacy meant the eventual elimination from the local scene of educated varieties, and the vehicular variety that remained was noticeably different. In the usage of Africans, with which we are concerned, this vehicular Portuguese (and in Accra, Danish, or Dutch) was replaced by several varieties of English, depending on whether the speakers also belonged to the networks that used English in religion and literacy. These in turn were related to the economic level of trade and politics at which speakers operated. In the political subdomain of military command, as the armed forces came out of the forts and expanded, the language of the fort soldiers—which in the English forts was perhaps an early vehicular English and in others perhaps Portuguese—was replaced by a new vehicular English but also by vehicular Hausa. If the kinds of interactions involved are admitted as comparable, then use of vehicular English in interactions between the military and local people represents replacement of the fort troops' use of (probably) Ga or Akan. The use of English not directly addressed by or to Europeans, like the military use of Hausa generally, coincided with the British introduction of new networks of African users into the expanding domain. Beyond the military, code shift in a domain that involved the discourse of Accra's and the Gold Coast's interests in the world beyond the seas has coincided with shifts in the balance of power among European participants in the domain.

8

Flood Control: The Dynamics of Multilingualism

Accra, including inner Accra, Osu, Labadi, and their suburbs to the north and west, obviously does not constitute a speech community in the sense of sharing "rules for the conduct and interpretation of speech, and rules for the interpretation of one linguistic variety" (Hymes [1972] 1986: 54). It rather comprises a great many such communities, most of whose members belong to a community-language network plus at least one other language network, almost always one or more of Ga, Akan, Hausa, and English. It comes rather closer to Fishman's definition of a community "set off by density of communication or/and by symbolic integration with respect to communicative competence *regardless of the number of languages or varieties employed* (1970: 32, emphasis in original). Even by this definition, however, the difference between inner and outer Accra is more obvious than their unity. The problem then is to define the relationship among communities and language networks in such a way as to locate the differences (if any) between the metropolis and the rest of the country. For this I propose a revision of the concept of the speech field.

Accra as a Speech Field

The speech field as defined by Hymes ([1972] 1986: 55), a "total range of communities within which a person's knowledge of varieties and speaking rules potentially enables him to move communicatively," does not characterize a social entity but the actual and potential network membership of the individual, regardless of community membership. However, we may turn it around and say that Accra constitutes a speech field in the sense of a roughly determined but expanding, and so unstable, geographical space, containing a range of communities, also unstable, among which linguistic communication is based on particular ranges of linguistic varieties deployed

162

according to certain kinds of rules. Since the city is spreading spatially and the communities within it are shifting in relation to one another in location, size, and membership, the configuration of the field is inherently unstable. The present study has done little to define the speaking rules, except to show that they must be different in inner and outer Accra. It is important to note that the opposition of "inner" to "outer" Accra is by no means spatially exclusive but is fundamentally a social idea that may be expressed spatially. Madina, for example, might seem obviously part of outer Accra on historical and geographical grounds, but as described in the 1960s its population was preponderantly southern, socially and linguistically more comparable to Adabraka perhaps than to Nima. Since large numbers of people continue to move outward from central Accra, as well as inward from elsewhere, the same is probably true of the vast new suburbs of North Kaneshie and North Achimota. These settlements undoubtedly include members, perhaps in spatial sectors, of both the "inner" and "outer" network complexes.

It is likely that a comparable differentiation exists in all major towns of Ghana. The actual languages involved are not different in the two parts of the city or between the city and the rest of the country, but the degree of overlap (number of shared nodes or bilingual speakers) between user networks of any pair of Ga, Akan, Hausa, English, and any other Ghanaian language—as community plus second language or as two second languages—varies considerably. In both parts of Accra, although to different degrees, there is obviously far more overlap of every community-language network with the Ga network (as second language) than in the rest of the country. This is also true for Hausa in outer Accra and probably for English in both areas, especially in comparison to rural districts and especially with popular varieties of English. It is likely that community-language networks overlap with Akan rather less than they do in the rest of southern Ghana west of the Volta but more than in most of the remainder of the country.

An individual's "communicative competence" in this speech field is clearly enhanced by polyglotism (membership in more than one network), to the extent that the competence of monoglots is suspect. It appears that this has long been so. The nature and distribution of competence in a particular language, including the kinds and ranges of both formal and performance competencies and the definition of appropriacy (Hymes 1972: 281), depend on many factors, including its own and others' expectations of the community, as well as residence, gender, education, and economic factors.

Variation in the competencies people actually acquire locates variation across the speech field in the behavior of individuals. Consistently, those who live and work in inner Accra, whether of Ga origin or not, speak fewer languages than outer residents, regardless of gender, to a degree not accounted for by subtracting the community languages of the outer residents. Ga is still almost universally known and a target of assimilative shift in the old inner city, but it is definitely the least widespread of the four major second languages in the outer city. Akan, Hausa, and even English tend to be spoken more widely (share more nodes with more community-language networks, that is, have larger networks of second-language users) in the outer city, but the difference is dramatic with respect to Hausa, even though that language, like the others, is usually not imported but learned in Accra. Despite the Dagaaba tendency to prefer Akan and English, they belong to the outer city on the criterion of the distribution of Hausa across the community-language network. Yet, not even Nima can be defined as a Hausa speech community, for there are too many long-term residents who do not speak it.

The differences in the rules for multilingual speaking between inner and outer Accra create a difference in what may be called the language of modernity, which expresses the positive value that both subcommunities—in Fishman's (1970) sense of community—place on urban life. It was suggested in chapter 4 that in outer Accra, Hausa is associated by its speakers with modern urban life. On the one hand, many people of outer Accra, especially the young, tend to use Hausa more than their community languages, which they are often accused of speaking badly and mixing with Hausa. This, rather than any association with Islam, seems to be the underlying source of the language's continuing vitality. Inner Accra, on the other hand, favors an urban register of Ga, which appropriates foreign-language material via the speech styles of a wide range of domains and speakers—from thieves, musicians, and drinkers to schoolchildren and fishermen—into a community language that already has a large number of integrated loanwords from all the languages with which it has historically been in contact. The phenomenon is not new, having been noted by Ablorh-Odjidja (1961). Known in Ga as *plashéèle*, apparently from English *pleasure*, the register includes both what we might call urban slang and a kind of disrespectful teasing of outsiders (Tetteh 1990: 7). The range of sources for this register is indicated, for example, by the current *álè* "get out!" from French *allez!*; *náà néé* "well now" from English *now*, with Ga *nɛɛ* "this," and meaning the same thing as the formal Ga *amrɔ tɔɔ néé*; and *tolí* "gossip, story, adventure," perhaps from a pidgin; as well as words from so-far unidentified sources, such as *lɛfɛ* "something."[1]

Like the urban Hausa of the outer city, Ga *plashéèle* tends to be frowned on by the community elders, but as a generation ages, its slang may pass into the general vocabulary. For example, Ablorh-Odjidja (1961) listed *okesé* "fine, grand," a word probably of Guang origin, but it has now largely lost any slangy connotation; and *aréè*, an abbreviation of English *arrangements* meaning "arrangements directed toward financial profit," is now somewhat dated.[2] The strictly Ga expression *etsuɔ fe nɛkɛ̃* "it ripens more than this," that is, "it could be better but is usable, adequate," was attributed by the author of a novella by that name to "juvenile delinquents" (Engmann 1968), but today it is regarded as "proverbial."[3] The principle may extend to whole texts, so that the rude songs of one generation of youth may age into "tradition." One suspects that many of the young women's play songs called *Adaáwée*, with their foreign words and references to cigarettes, mail ships, and lovers, have followed a similar cultural evolution (Dakubu 1979).[4] More generally, the vocabulary of formality and tradition reflects the multilingualism of the past, but the vocabulary of urban activity, that of the present. The continued incorporation of non-Ga material into the expressive language of daily life surely indicates something about the speakers' perceptions of the forces that govern their lives.

A Local Model for Language Spread

It was noted at the outset that Accra communities were not only multilingual but also polyglot and that this invited explanation. One kind of explanation seems to be the way in which different languages have spread. In every case, introduction of a language has been promoted by a group in whose interest it was to maintain it. Both Akan and Ga in Accra originally functioned to impose the political interests of rulers. Even after Ga had become the community language of assimilated Guang and Akan, it was very much in the political and commercial interests of many members of the community to maintain Akan as a weapon (if only defensive) in dealing with the Akan community. Obutu had no such function, but perhaps with other Guang languages it continued to function in religious contexts for a long time, an esoteric prop to the religious authority. Educated Africans are frequently accused of clinging to English as a symbol and weapon of economic and social domination, but it is clear that facility in a generally useful language of European trade and in a major language of literacy have always been regarded as desirable, especially when the two have coincided. The single most important factor in the spread of a language has been the appearance of a resident population speaking it as a community language, supported by economic and political power, *plus* the opportunity (or necessity) for local people to participate in that power. For migrants, while Hausa may not exactly be an avenue to power, unless perhaps in a very local sense, it is certainly an avenue to economic participation.[5] The kind of political and economic participation possible through any one of these languages is circumscribed, but all are available. Therefore, the more polyglot a person is, the more varied the economic, political, and social options. This is not quite the same thing as saying that extreme polyglotism is a condition of communicative competence or a feature of the essential repertoire in Laitin's sense. It rather seems to represent a kind of communication insurance. In a varied, historically unstable, and to some extent unpredictable political environment, it is best not to put all the communication eggs in one linguistic basket. One is reminded of Latevi Awoku at Anecho in 1785, speaking Portuguese, English, and Danish and hedging against the future by educating one son in Portugal, another (George Lawson) in England (Debrunner 1965: 29).

Some models of language spread by domain have categorized language functions and types of spread as horizontal or vertical: vertical spread proceeds through interaction between different social strata, compared to movement along the same stratum in different geographical or ethnic groups (Cooper 1982: 9); or horizontal codes "symbolize social equality and solidarity" and spread "spontaneously," but vertical codes "are used or conceived of as vehicles of vertical mobility" and depend on government language policy for their spread (Heine 1977: 231–32). Both versions of the model treat social groups and the language practices that index them as capable of being arranged along a linear scale of "prestige," from "high" to "low" (following Ferguson's classic 1959 paper on diglossia), and language communities as structurally parallel, so that a language or linguistic practice can spread from group to group and still remain at the same level or the same stratum of sociolinguistic prestige, a notion that disregards a basic principle of the definition of a domain—that it is not a universal given but contingent on a society and a language and the relations between them. The trilingual model of figure 2.1 was fundamentally a crudely hierarchical model of this kind (although displayed horizontally), and it is inadequate to the Accra and West African situations for the same kinds of reasons. I observed that only the L_3, the European language, was adequately served by the model. This is simply because the model is a European one, based on European (and perhaps Near Eastern) notions of hierarchical relations between languages, especially the relationship between written and spoken languages and their relationship to religious practice. *All* the languages of Accra can express solidarity or aid mobility and also index social or economic status, depending on the domain, the community, and the variety used. It is also a fact that formality and social distance can be established in any language.

This is not to say that the spread of community and second languages has not been sensitive to prestige, difficult as that is to define, and solidarity or otherwise. However the expression of these social motives and goals in actual linguistic behavior cannot be crudely categorized. Historically, Akan—which Heine (1977) would class as a "local lingua franca" whose use aims ("horizontally") at social solidarity—has certainly promoted the political status of its speakers, and many Ga and Guang would deny that its use normally expresses intergroup solidarity. It is also clear that many Gold Coasters were motivated to acquire English long before government language policies were imagined, for much the same reasons as they learned Akan, and they continue to be so motivated. Interest in acquiring spoken English must be distinguished from an interest in literacy, which is directly linked to jobs, and thus economic status, through academic certificates. Literacy in English is the most economically useful type. Its acquisition usually entails acquisition of a more standard, "higher" variety of English but not necessarily, and illiterate speakers sometimes manage to acquire "good" English.[6]

I suggest that the parallel stratification model derives ultimately from a literate-illiterate model, which even today is largely irrelevant, and that the Accra situation is better served by a model based on the patron-client relationship, enacted as the relationship between host and guest, that historically pervades economic and political relations and, indeed, can be viewed as embodying the "speaking rules" of a culture area—in a very broad sense, its rules of performance (Arhin 1986; Dakubu 1986). That is, interactions are conducted in such a way as to achieve the ultimate goal of strengthening that relationship, which is in fact a relationship between groups, not individuals; this has been hinted at in references in earlier chapters to the relationship between Madina and the La state.

The key to the relationship is that client approaches patron, not the other way round. It is far from being a relationship of equality: the patron-host as the receiver of the outsider, the client-guest, has the political advantage and the recognized right to direct the course of communication.[7] Thus, as was remarked of Akan towns in chapter 6, a buyer who travels to a farm will expect to speak the language of the seller, the farmer-host. This is the context in which Heine's (1977: 236) remarks on the humiliation of not being able to respond appropriately when addressed in English should be seen. The visitor or client (or employee or subordinate of any kind) who cannot respond in the language chosen by the host loses face, or political ground, a fact that of course can be manipulated by a host who wishes to do so. To avoid this kind of embarrassment, as well as accusations of ill will, intermediary speakers are invariably employed for formal and semiformal interactions in all domains, as well as interpreters if more than one language community is involved, regardless of the language competencies of the individuals present.

Exactly how the languages of the Portuguese and the Akan became languages of the whole coast we cannot prove, but it is likely that in each case other people had to come to them. When the Portuguese were only visitors, they used the local language, but once they were established on their "own home ground" in forts, sellers of gold and slaves (or from another viewpoint, buyers of slaves and manufactures) came to them in their establishments, and then Portuguese was appropriate. For the language to outlast the "hosts," it had to acquire a local base. Müller ([1676] 1968) and Tilleman ([1697] 1994) make it clear that Portuguese became the language of the African merchants or rather, outside Elmina, of their agents, who had to be approached by both Africans and Europeans who wished to participate in the slave and related coastal trade. It seems also to have been in some sense the language of the Dutch forts. It was no doubt in the professional interest of African commercial agents to prolong this situation as long as possible. English displaced Portuguese because the English forced themselves into the role of host-patron not only commercially, by suppressing the slave trade and putting the African agents out of work, but also in a progressively broader political domain. The artist's rendition of a meeting in 1895 between a returned Ashanti embassy to London and the governor at Cape Coast Castle, reproduced by Wilks (1993: 179), with the governor lounging in an armchair while the ambassador stands before him with his interpreter, leaves the viewer in no doubt who is "at home" and who is making the approach.

The course of the establishment of Akan as a second language must have been very similar, except that the Fante, like the Ga, established permanent colonies among the people they overwhelmed, with the eventual result that their language also spread as a community language. Both as sellers of gold and slaves and as military conquerors, Akans generally were in a position to cause others to come to them, and so their language had to be learned. The political situation has changed, but Akan speakers are still largely in command in commercial and in many civil contexts.[8]

The position of Hausa does not obviously fit the patron-client pattern; in fact for the residents of inner Accra it does not fit at all, and so they rarely learn the language.[9] It is possible that the migrants of outer Accra have imported different "rules of speaking" that are related to a different approach to social hierarchy (E. Goody 1971). Nevertheless, the crucial fact is that the ex-servicemen who established the northern migrant settlements at mid-century already spoke Hausa as a lingua franca, and it was appropriate to use it with the ethnically and socially very different Hausa speakers who were already there and to maintain it among themselves. These ex-servicemen were in effect the hosts and patrons of later arrivals, helping them settle and find jobs. Even if a new arrival went first to speakers of his community language, each community was very small and poor and worked most effectively through the wider network of Hausa speakers. The recent migrant could obviously function best by joining the network.

In contrast, few migrants have had to approach the Ga directly. As a group they do not regard themselves as dependent clients of the Ga—hence the relatively low bilingualism in Ga among northern men compared to its relatively high incidence among women, who are more likely to have to deal with Ga women on their home ground. The Labadi quarrel with Madina is essentially an attempt to force the Madina people to act like clients, not to make them act like Ga. Ansre and Berry's 1969 Madina survey figures (published by Apronti 1974: 10) show considerably more second-language speakers of Ga (786) than of Akan (573) or Hausa (459). The predominance of Akan over Ga and English, which had the most second-language speakers of all (832), was entirely a function of the larger size of the Akan community itself. It is possible that the situation has changed in the intervening twenty-five years. Still, as well as undermining Apronti's thesis of a Ghanaian preference for Akan over English, these findings suggest that the La reacted to the size and number of non-Ga communities, not to nonuse of the Ga language by individuals, as the framing of the dispute might suggest. Use of the host's language is a symbol of client status, not a "horizontal" gesture in negation of it.

The "rules" for formal speaking between guest and host ensure that either the host's language will be acquired in more than one domain or that the domain will have to be very broadly defined to include many diverse styles and topics of discourse. That is, a commercial or political transaction may involve (in varying degrees of elaboration) greeting, rhetorical narrative, and prayer, as well as exposition and informal argument. Active participation in some domains may be restricted with respect to age and gender but is rarely truly exclusive or limited to unaccompanied individuals. Even servants and small children may be in a position to observe a formal meeting. Assuming that this has been the pattern for a long time, the cultural context for intergroup communication almost guarantees opportunity for a fairly broad knowledge of a politically or economically valuable language to spread through a relatively extensive network of second-language users.

Such a language system as we have outlined can only be as stable as the political economy within which it exists and as the patron-client relationships that support it. It is not obvious that systemic inertia is a significant factor in prolonging a multilingual configuration (Lieberson 1982: 41), apart from the likelihood that individuals, once having acquired languages, are likely to remember them and continue to take opportunities to use them throughout their lifetimes. There have historically been far more shift and assimilation than were immediately apparent or are recognized in the popular ethnic ideology, which reflects the colonial attitude to "custom," "tribe," and the natural persistence of ethnic and national boundaries. It would be rash to attempt to predict the future, but it is hard to avoid the conclusion that while the social value of Hausa as a second language in Accra may gradually wane (not that there is evidence of this as yet), Akan cannot be expected to replace it and certainly will not replace Ga as long as the country's future remains politically and economically uncertain. In this situation, the value placed on English (any variety) as a second language can only increase. There is every likelihood, therefore, that multilingualism marked by a high degree of polyglotism will be characteristic of Accra for a long time to come.

NOTES

Chapter 1

1. E. A. Adokwei of the Language Centre, University of Ghana, very kindly provided some of the documents on which the following discussion is based and drew my attention to others. His assistance is gratefully acknowledged.

2. Significantly, the Danish writers consistently distinguished Ga *a* and *ɔ*. Danish orthography, which also made the distinction, gave them an advantage. The current English pronunciation of "Labadi" is probably a spelling pronunciation.

3. Reconstruction of the consonant as an alveolar voiced stop also helps to explain the otherwise puzzling -*jīī* plurals, for example, *sajīī* "things," singular *sane*, since they can then be treated as palatalization of **d* before a high front vowel, followed by the regular Ga plural suffix -*i*. This explanation of the plural pattern is most plausible if there was also a change in the final vowel, from nonadvanced nasal **[ĩ]* to advanced nonnasal [e] in the singular and to advanced nasal [ĩ] in the plural (before -*i*), in the final stages of a change from a nine- to a seven-vowel system; see Dakubu (1980).

4. Except where otherwise noted, the following account of Madina is summarized from Quarcoo, Addo, and Peil (1967), especially the first two chapters (by Quarcoo). Additional information on Alhaji Seidu Kardo's life was collected by Mr. M. D. Sulley in 1995, from Alhaji Seidu's eldest son, Baaba Seidu.

5. "Kardo" [kaado], from a Fulfulde term for non-Muslims, is the general name for the Dogon in Accra. Alhaji Seidu was a Dogon from Mali, said to have belonged to a group known there as "Kardo Hir."

6. According to information collected by M. D. Sulley from Alhaji Seidu's son in 1995, most of his original group were Mali.

7. The Reverend A. K. Quarcoo, personal communication. In Senegal and other francophone West African countries, a quarter of a town, usually Muslim and invariably with a major market, is often known as the Medina, from an Arabic word meaning "town." This usage may have underlain Alhaji Kardo's choice, but it is not familiar to Ghanaians. It is said that he chose it because, like the Prophet, he had been driven from his original home.

8. A. K. Quarcoo, personal communication.

9. That is, people recorded as from neither another region of Ghana nor another country (Ghana Government 1972: 198).

10. See "Public Notice by the La Stool on Lands at Madina and Surrounding Villages—Surrejoinder," *People's Daily Graphic*, 5 February 1993, p. 11.

11. As pointed out by the author of the letter to the La *mantse*, La Manheaŋ "La New Town" would be more in accordance with current Ga naming practice than La Hee, but this recommendation seems to have been disregarded.

12. Amartey (1988: 79) recounts the myth that Korle (her formal appellation is Naá Déde Àboóyoo) helped the Ga defeat the Ashanti by appearing as a woman, making *kpekple* the night before a battle and selling it to the Ashanti. It gave them diarrhea, and so they were beaten. *Kpekple* is the Ga ceremonial corn food, prepared like couscous, with the addition of oil and okra. In Labadi, Korle is said to be a wife of the town's senior deity, Lakpaa (I. Odotei, personal communication).

13. The semantic pattern by which *faa* means an extended structure, or "river"—which includes a terminal substructure, *mukpó* "lagoon," but refers primarily to the substructure whenever the contrast between the two is not salient—parallels the situation of *nine* "arm, including hand," which is normally translated "hand" even though *de* "hand, palm" also exists.

14. Therefore, I do not consider the sharp distinction drawn by Romaine (1982: 7) between language structure as the subject matter of linguistics and language use as the subject matter of sociolinguistics to be particularly useful, even as a description of practice.

15. It is true that an act of communication may itself bring into being, that is, be the reason for, another act of communication. But since all animals communicate in some way, we must suppose that nonlinguistic communication, and thus reasons to communicate, historically as well as logically preceded the evolution of human language.

16. Fishman seems to regard the difference between macro- and micro-sociolinguistics as the difference between large- and small-group studies. The difference from the present approach is illustrated by his remark that American students assume the normal situation to be "one man, one language" ([1965] 1972: 16). This I take to be a micro-sociolinguistic formulation, but in Fishman's approach it is probably macro. The equivalent expectation in macro terms in the present definition is "one group (society, nation), one language." One is thought to imply the other, within some shifting definition of the group.

17. It must be noted, however, that Ring compared the scores of linguistic communities, not individuals.

18. This is not the sense in which the term "proficiency" is used by Cooper (1982: 11), who proposed it essentially as a term for what I am calling communicative competence.

19. See Dakubu (1987a) for a description of how this acceptance is recognized and formalized in social encounters among the Ga.

Chapter 2

1. See O'Connor (1983: 300, 301, 319) for a consideration of the "parasitism" of African cities.

2. Contemporary West African fiction often provides vivid images of the hardships and the poverty and dirt of contemporary city life, for instance, in Ben Okri's (1981) portrayal of Lagos or Ayi Kwei Armah's (1968) of Takoradi. Kojo Laing's (1986) novel of Accra does not exclude the hardships but celebrates the "special atmosphere."

3. I use "polyglotism" as a general description of individuals' repertoires, in contrast to "polyglossia," a derivative of the established term "diglossia," which implies a certain kind of distribution of domains and goals within a specified set of language varieties.

4. Compare Cooper's (1982: 24) comments on the spread of Swahili as a trade language, to the effect that learning under such informal circumstances was probably gradual, not the result of a deliberate decision but not subconscious either. I see no reason to suppose that learning a trade language is likely to be a gradual process. It is just as likely that adults who have to acquire it need it in a hurry.

5. O'Connor (1983: 236) remarks that Accra is typical of African cities with respect to its physical planning history.

6. By Hunwick (1973: 51), among others.

7. For provocative discussions on a topic about which there is still much to be learned, see Greenberg (1945, 1960), Hiskett (1965), and Hunwick (1964).

8. But see Hunwick (1973: 28), who quotes complaints of a Maghrebine scholar in fifteenth-century Gao that the Arabic of local scholars was weak, "being chiefly acquired from the surrounding Arab tribes." Presumably the degree of contact with community-language speakers of various types varied from place to place, as does contact with community-language speakers of different varieties of English or French today.

9. The Fulani or Fulbe, speakers of the language referred to as Peul, Fulfulde, or Fula, are traditionally a nomadic, pastoral people. Although they were organized into states at various times, for example, Massina, Futa Toro, and Futa Djallon in the fifteenth century (Levtzion 1973: 97), it would appear that their language became a major language of towns only after the Fulani jihad in the nineteenth century and the development of a class of politically dominant, settled "town Fulani" in northern Nigeria.

10. Malinke is a variety of Manding, generally mutually intelligible with varieties or groups of varieties known as Mandingo, Maninka or Mandinka (literally "Mali language"), Bambara, and Jula (Calvet 1982: 184; Dwyer 1989).

11. Variously spelled Juula, Djula, Dyula, and Dioula, meaning in that language "trader." See note 10.

12. The name of Bobo-Dioulasso (in southwest Burkina Faso) mirrors the situation: "Bobo" refers to the Bwa or Bwaba, an indigenous agricultural people whose language belongs to the Gur group, and "Dioulasso" means "Jula (i.e., traders') town"—all in Jula.

13. This language, too, goes by many names and spellings, partly reflecting ethnic differences among speakers, as well as French versus English orthographic styles: Ligby, Numu, Noumou, Hwela, Huela, Dyogoh, Gyogo, and Dioro (Dakubu 1976; Delafosse 1904; J. Goody 1964; Tauxier 1921).

14. Kulango and Degha belong to different groups within the Gur branch of Niger-Congo. Gonja belongs to the Guang branch of the Comoe language family, to which Akan also belongs.

15. According to Stahl (1991: 256), in some places groups of Gonja-speaking Kuulo (Dumpo) are shifting to Nafaanra (the language of the Nafana), although farther east—where Gonja, not Nafana, are the chiefs—the Gonja language has much higher prestige and this does not occur. The shift pattern is also probably affected by the fact that Nafana and Kuulo are both farmers, but the men among the coresident Ligbi speakers are full-time traders. Ligbi has been the target of shift by populations now known as Hwela (p. 267).

16. The people and their language (Nafaanra) are known in Akan as Fantera, Pantera, and Mfantera (Dakubu 1976; Rapp 1933; Tauxier 1921).

17. Kulango is known in Akan as Nkoraŋ or Nkona.

18. Such systems are not limited to Africa; see the diagram of Functional Specialization of Codes in Indonesia reproduced by Fishman (1970: 69).

19. This observation, of course, amounts to a tautology; if the original speakers wielded no economic or political power, it is difficult to imagine why other, distant peoples would learn their language. But since a persistent pattern of exotic language use cannot be explained without attention to the dependence of language spread on power, it is well to keep it in mind.

20. Briefly, the Guang divisions of the Akuapem state are making serious attempts to secede.

21. Bruce Johnson does consider domains of language use, but he does not effectively distinguish them from communicative goals.

22. For further discussion see chapters 6 and 7.

Chapter 3

1. According to Oti-Boateng et al. (1989: *Greater Accra Region*), the Accra Urban Council area, including Osu and Labadi, had a total population of 867,459. Including Teshi (59,552), Nungua (29,146), and settlements along the Dodowa road as far as the Presbyterian Secondary School, the Accra district had a total population of 969,195. If the Ga Local Council area to the west (136,358) and Tema Urban Council area (190,917) are added, the total area regarded as traditionally Ga had a population of 1,296,470.

2. These estimates are apparently based on Tilleman ([1697] 1994: 26), who estimated that Chorkor could muster 60 guns, Accra 500. He also estimated 300 for Osu, which by the same proportion would give a population of around 2,000 for that town.

3. At least this is the traditional account. As Sanjek (1977: 616) pointed out, there are now many people who have grown up in Adabraka or other suburbs who are not aware of "coming from" any of the seven divisions, or even of their existence. The seven are Abola, Asere, Gbese, Otublohum (which constituted Dutch Accra in the nineteenth century) Akaŋmaje, Nleshi Alata, and Sempe (which made up English Accra) (Reindorf [1889] 1966).

4. Where not otherwise acknowledged, this outline of the spread of Accra is based on maps in Pogucki (1955).

5. The name refers to a well that once existed on the south side of the road, on a site now occupied by the Electricity Department.

6. The name Tudu is Hausa for "hill." The area was at one time known to the British as Railway Hill (Gillespie 1955: 50).

7. The Accra Urban Council area (Accra, Osu, and Labadi) had a population of 347,815 in 1960, 564,194 in 1970, and 867,459 in 1984 (Oti-Boateng et al. 1989: 14). No further breakdown was given for this enumeration area. Another report on this census (Ghana Government 1987) gives the total population for the Greater Accra Region as 1,431,099.

8. Even so, men may be overrepresented: in February 1955, there were only 379 male sellers in Accra markets, out of a total of 5,890, a mere 6.4% (Acquah [1954] 1972: 63). However, the deterioration of the economy may be attracting men into the market.

9. The offspring of an Akan mother and a Ga father therefore has a claim on two "hometowns," but the child of a Ga mother and an Akan father might be said to have a hometown only by concession, not by any accepted right. People in this category can have serious problems in matters of inheritance. Such ambiguities undoubtedly affected our data, so that it is impossible to state absolutely the number of Ga or Akan (or, in principle, any other such group) in the survey groups. This is simply an aspect of the indeterminacy inherent in boundaries among people, pointed out in chapter 2.

10. One could, of course, question the sense in which each parent "had" a language. Since few had any difficulty responding to these questions (in Akan, either *wopapa/mami ka kasa bɛn?* or *wopapa/womami krom kasa yɛ dɛn?*; in Ga *mɛni wiemɔ opapa/omaami wieɔ?*), we assume that there was normally unambiguous association between the parent's cultural allegiance and the language in which the respondent interacted with the parent.

11. Ga resident in Central Accra showed no significant difference from other Ga in the size of their linguistic repertoires in 1989. It was not possible to compute the difference for the 1992 group.

12. It is useful to take an average difference of 0.5 languages as significant since the average number of languages spoken may then be rounded up to 1.0. The difference between an average repertoire of 2.2 and an average of 3.6 is then in practical terms a difference between 2.0 languages, with a few speaking more, and 4.0, with quite a lot speaking less. The difference between 0.5 and 1.0 of a language then reflects how closely the majority of speakers of it approaches 100%.

13. The language situation in Zugu is considered in chapter 6.

14. "Speakers" here includes persons who claimed only a modest degree of passive knowledge, and so could not really be called speakers. However, they were an insignificant minority of those claiming any sort of competence in most languages, with the exceptions discussed below.

15. The glossonym "Twi" in common usage refers to those varieties of the Akan language that are neither Brong, spoken north and west of Asante, nor Fante, in the southeast (Dakubu 1988a: 56). Since far more people claimed to come from or have been born in the Eastern Region than the Ashanti Region (tables 3.2 and 3.3), most respondents who claimed to know "Twi" undoubtedly spoke the Akuapem dialect.

16. The dominant language, or language the respondent claimed to speak best, must be distinguished from the first language learned, or language of initial socialization, since these are by no means always the same. I therefore avoid the term "first language" as potentially ambiguous. Since both must also be distinguished from the language associated with the hometown, or place of cultural allegiance—which moreover may be identified with the respondent's father or mother, depending on the group identified with—I also avoid the term "mother tongue."

17. I recall an incident in which a young man, my research assistant at the time, was relieved of a radio that I had paid for by his father, who didn't see why his son, then about twenty, should have a better radio than he had.

18. Dakubu (1981) gives only the raw data. Expressed as percentages of 121 lineage members, the figures for speakers of each language are Ga, 100.0%; Akan, 68.6%; English, 44.6%; Ewe, 27.3%; Dangme, 3.3%; and Hausa, 9.9%. Fifteen persons (12.4%) then resided in nearby Akan-speaking towns and villages, but even if they are subtracted, more than half spoke Akan.

19. According to the 1970 census, the Manchi enumeration area, which was the farming area of the branches of Ajorkor Okai We studied, was almost 47% non-Ga (Ghana Government 1972: 198). The proportion is likely to have risen since.

20. Locally pronounced *fiele* and named after the first settler.

21. The language policy in the schools is that the local language should be the teaching language for the first three primary years, with English a taught subject. After that, English should be the language of instruction, and the local language taught as a subject. There are numerous problems in implementing this policy, which are obviously aggravated in a highly multilingual urban school.

22. It may be said that these children cannot have learned English in any educationally meaningful sense. However, they have indeed learned a language variety, called "English" by themselves and others, that allows them a degree of communication with other people who use a range of varieties that go by the same name.

23. Acquah ([1954] 1972: 41) seems to indicate that in 1954 Adabraka was relatively middle class, especially the Ga, Akan, and Ewe residents.

24. Because Sanjek was interested in perceptions of ethnic identity, he did not consider English. It would be very surprising if English did not have high salience and a considerable number of speakers.

Chapter 4

1. The word, which also occurs in Akan, seems to be from a Manding word for "slave" (Wilks 1962). The most common public use of the word today is as a name for an infant born after several have died (Dakubu 1981: 141–42).

2. Moser's (1979: 4) survey of 1,010 inhabitants of Sabon Zongo, a migrant settlement area south of Ring Road on the western side of Korle lagoon, enumerated only two "Dagarti" (Dagaaba), one Wala (from Wa), one "Kanjaga" (Bulsa), and no Kusaasi. It is possible, of course, that proportions have changed since then.

3. Chiefs in this context are elected or otherwise appointed community leaders in the urban migrant situation. They do not signify hereditary access to land, nor do they necessarily command the same kind of allegiance. Rouch (1956: 131) remarked that the nature of relations between the chief (or chiefs) in Accra and the chiefs in the homeland varied considerably among migrant communities. I did not collect information on this point.

4. Each survey group is basically a quota sample. In each locality surveyed, interviews were held with as many people as could be conveniently contacted, but the interviewers made sure that all age, sex, and education slots were filled on a grid that allowed for ages fifteen to sixty and over, in five-year age groups, and five degrees of formal education (unless, of course, no one could be found to fill a particular slot, for example, women over sixty who had finished the sixth form). There is obviously much room for subjectivity here, and the judgment of the interviewers is important. Interviews in each language community were carried out by a linguistically sophisticated assistant who was a member of the community and also spoke the community's typical second languages. The interviewers for the Bulsa and Kusaasi groups (James Agalic and Nachinaba Bugri) were experienced fieldworkers, and the interviewer for the Dagaaba (Adams Bodomo) was then a recent graduate in linguistics. Although I cannot claim that the survey groups statistically reflect the populations in general, I believe they are reasonably similar to them.

5. Reported in the *People's Daily Graphic*, 23 November 1990, p. 9.

6. Achimota was listed by Christaller (1889: 108) as a Chala village. It also occurs in a Ga riddle that merits a monograph to itself: Riddle: *afóoo tàtso shí mìfo miŋ mikɔ́* "One doesn't cut bitter-leaf [vernonia, a shrub], but I cut and took it." Response: *atsíi mò ta—odɔŋkɔfó* "One doesn't call anyone by name—slaves" (Dakubu 1981: 164).

7. For a detailed description of the survey group, consult Dakubu (1986).

8. This is presumed to be a function of how the sample was collected, not a characteristic of the settlement areas.

9. For a more elaborate discussion of the area see Dakubu (1983).

10. See note 2.

11. Talni and Nabit, the languages of the Talensi and Nabdam, which also border on Kusaug, I treat as dialects of Gurune, *pace* Hall (1983) and Naden (1988: 19, 1989: 145).

12. Except Bisaa, which is a Mande language, all of these languages belong to the Oti-Volta subgroup of the Central Gur languages. For details see Dwyer (Bendor-Samuel 1989), Naden (Bendor-Samuel 1989; Dakubu 1988b), and Naden and Dakubu (Dakubu 1988b).

13. The Fulani of the Sokoto Caliphate followed a similar policy, with comparable results (Alexandre 1971: 656).

14. It is not unusual for a migrant urban community to be self-defined as linguistically and culturally plural. As Rouch (1956: 37) points out, members of the "Gao" community in

Accra include both Zabarima and Tuareg. From the point of view of the homelands, virtually all such communities are in fact umbrellas, uniting numerous subcultural and dialect groups.

15. Even on URA-Radio, 60% of the broadcast time was recently devoted to "national programs," which presumably means in English (*People's Daily Graphic*, 9 November 1990, p. 7). In Accra, Dagbani and Hausa are still the only "northern" languages used by the Ghana Broadcasting Corporation (GBC).

16. Questions on language use for radio, reading, and writing asked for languages actually used for these purposes at least occasionally. Responses that claimed an ability to read or write that was never actually practiced were discounted.

17. Kotokoli is the Hausa name for a variety of Tem, a language spoken at Sokode in Togo. It belongs to the Gurma branch of the Oti-Volta group and is thus quite closely related to these languages. According to Funke (1916: 128), *kotokoli* merely describes Hausaized peoples, but the term has come to specify the Tem speakers of the Tchaudjo state (see chapter 5).

18. The Dogon of Mali are much better known as original religious thinkers than as Muslims; see, for example, Calame-Griaule (1986). Identification with Islam has been widely noted as a feature of the adaptation of savannah-zone immigrants to urban centers (Grindal 1972: 68; Rouch 1956: 146).

19. They particularly mentioned the German football carried by GBC television on Sundays. Their standard of English comprehension perhaps need not be high to follow the game, but it was high enough that they had a favorite commentator (Alan Thompson). The house had electricity, from a line that passes to a large resort establishment down the road, and it ran a refrigerator, as well as television and radio.

20. My investigation of this group was too brief to allow generalizations, but it may be significant that during three visits I observed that women speaking among themselves used both Fulfulde and Hausa but men seemed to stick to Fulfulde.

21. "Wangara" in Ghana is a term (ultimately from Arabic) that refers to people of Mande origin and their Manding language. However, it seems that at least some of the people so called are of diverse origins. According to Rouch (1956: 24), in the last decade of the nineteenth century Samori sold captives—taken in Ivory Coast, western Burkina Faso, and northwestern Ghana—around Cape Coast, possibly continuing a very old trade (Wilks 1993: 76). These people were not assimilated to the Fante but remained in small "Wangara" communities. There is no reason to expect the descendants of such communities to value the Manding language highly.

22. Interviews were carried out by Mary Bodomo in English, Twi, Fante, Ga, and Hausa, using the same questionnaire as for the Salaga market groups.

Chapter 5

1. According to his son's biographical sketch, Noa Akunor Aguae Azu (1832–1917) was a member of the Krobo royal family and a famous priest and savant before he became a Christian for political reasons about 1857 (see also Wilson 1991: 8). There is no doubt that he is an excellent authority from the royal Manya Krobo point of view. He belonged to the Jebiam clan, whose name means "from Biam."

2. Philip Odonkor, field assistant for the Ghana Institute of Linguistics, Literacy, and Bible Translation (GILLBT) Gichode team, believes that the Chala at Odomi have shifted to Gichode completely (personal communication, 1985).

3. According to Cornevin, this state was created at the end of the eighteenth or beginning of the nineteenth century. Ahadji (1976: 31) seems to think that it resulted from a Gurma invasion (the second in the vicinity) in the eighteenth century. However these authors' dates

generally seem to be too recent. According to Tait (1961), the Dagomba invasions that displaced the Konkomba and the Basare eastward, which Ahadji places in the mid-seventeenth century, probably occurred early in the sixteenth. Benzing's (1971: 214) date for the Ya Na who, according to Tait, was responsible for the invasions, Naa Sitobu, is even earlier—in the mid-fifteenth century. If Ahadji's dates are all more than a century too recent, connections among Tchaudjo, Chala, and Dangme traditions become more likely. It is also possible that the givers of the Chala tradition used the name merely for geographical reference, without implying contact with the historical Tchaudjo state or any particular period.

4. The claim that a group from Podoku near Tema founded Kpeshi is thus mistaken (Field 1940: 85). It probably retreated there, which supports the idea of a preexisting connection.

5. Ghana Government (1960). See also Wilks (1957).

6. The map in Brackenbury (1968) shows Hoomey on the Volta below Bator. This is probably identical to Vume on modern maps.

7. See Dakubu (1972) for a more elaborate discussion. There seems to have been another Bia at the western end of the Gold Coast, probably the same name as that of the Bia River. I do not know the relationship between them, or indeed whether there was any.

8. Reindorf (1834–1917), Azu's contemporary and fellow protégé of the Basel mission, did not have his expertise in traditional lore. His work is a compilation from an impressive range of written and oral sources, unfortunately without close identification of the latter. He mentions his grandmother, apparently from the maternal Osu side of his family, who died in 1860. Both Azu's and Reindorf's accounts would seem to record received tradition of the middle of the nineteenth century, in the brief interval between the transatlantic slave trade and colonialism. Where their accounts coincide, they may very well have consulted, for Azu and Reindorf were both teaching at the Christiansborg school in 1864. Reindorf had also lived in Krobo Odumase for a time (C. E. Reindorf in Reindorf [1889] 1966:9). Most unfortunately, I was not able to consult the first edition of Reindorf's *History*. To judge from Jenkins's (1977) discussion of the differences between the two, this chapter might have benefited if I had, especially on the La, but its conclusions would not have changed.

9. This basin, *ayáwa* in Ga, is presumably the origin of the name of the successor village to Great Accra, *Ayáwasò*.

10. The kings were Ayi Kushi; his son Ayite; Nikoi Malai or Olai, whom some authorities consider to have been a usurping regent (interview with Nii Akwaashong Mantse, head of the Ga Mashi State Council, 16 July 1995); Ayite's son (?) Mankpong Okai; Mankpong Okai's son Okai Koi, who was also preceded by a usurping regent, his mother Dode Akai or Akaibi; and Okai Koi's son Ashangmɔ. According to I. Odotei (personal communication) there is documentary evidence that Okai Koi was still alive in 1661.

11. Among the clans of Glidji, which is now Ewe-speaking, is Tugban, that is, Tungma (Ewe has no [ŋm] sound), the name of the old ruling house of the Ga (Bole-Richard 1983: 7).

12. According to Tilleman ([1697] 1994: 25), the town at the Dutch fort was called Aprag, a name probably related to Kpíà, the hill on which stood the old inland capital, and/or "Apara Hill," whither the Obutu King Wiete was driven by the Ga (Field 1940: 143). In a prayer recorded in 1991, the Densu priest referred to Accra extending from Obutu Apíá to Ada Shwilao (the Volta), but he did not know the relationship between Obutu Apla and Kpla Hill at Ayawaso. The name Acara (Accra) seems to have been reserved for the entire kingdom.

13. Originally, Kɔle was probably the deity of a different branch of the founders of Krobo (Wilson 1991: 29).

14. It is really not clear what Field meant by the name Ga Wɔɔ. She also refers to the "Ga Bone" who certainly could not be meaningfully described as "Ga" until much later.

15. "Mankpong" could mean "great town" or "great state" in southern Guang. "Koi," usually pronounced and spelled "Kwei," is now a name for any third-born male.

16. One of Dode Akaibi's remembered sins is that she unreasonably demanded that houses be thatched with clay. One wonders whether this is not a symbol of the northern strand in Ga-Dangme tradition, which the Ga have generally ignored in favor of the southeastern connection. There is also a strongly antifemale aspect to the story, which might reflect Ga opposition to a matrilineal element in their midst (although the Guang are not matrilineal) and/or changes in the political constitution. At this point one can only speculate.

17. *Akanmaje* is almost certainly from *ákáŋmàiaje "place of vultures." The modern word for "vulture" is *ákpaŋà*, but Protten (1764) gave it as "acambba," that is, *akaŋma*.

18. She stated that Obutu and Kpeshi are similar but not identical and that Kpeshi is the language of Kpele, but she did not indicate the basis for this judgment.

19. It is noteworthy that a Guang language referred to in the literature as "Tschumbuli" is now spoken in Benin north of Shabeh near the Nigerian border; that is, in the area from which the Dangme migrations most probably started (Painter 1966: 43; Stewart 1989: 216). It is apparently the result of a migration east from the Nchumburung (or Nchumuru) speaking area of Ghana, in the heart of northern Guang territory just west of the Gichode-Ginyanga speaking area. It is not known whether there has ever been contact between that community and the Ga-Dangme, but its location is further evidence of historical movement across the area that proto-Ga-Dangme speakers must have traversed, in the opposite direction.

20. The first vowel in [kpele] is weak, so that "Kple" and "Kpele" do not signify different pronunciations. Ga Kpele is culturally comparable to Dangme Klama, but the cults and texts are different.

21. "Ele" is a plausible reflex of "La," reflecting a sound change *ai to ε in Dangme, *a* in Ga (Dakubu 1969b). The prefixed *e-* represents adaptation to Ewe nominal patterns.

22. He also says that the Kpessi people were a combination of refugee groups that arrived at various places, including Kpele, but his date of 1764, following the Ashanti defeat of Akyem, is obviously too recent for Ga history (Cornevin 1963: 61).

23. The Akuapem and Akyem dialects of Akan have no [l] sound; hence the substitution of [d]. However, Wilks's derivation of Ada [adãã´] and (A)Dangme [dãŋme] from La [làa] and Labihi [labíhĩ¯] is dubious. Ada is probably an Akan name.

24. The etymology of "Nungua" as "Small Ningo"—*niŋo-wá* (with the Akan diminutive suffix)—and its relatively late establishment are supported by Tilleman's map, which shows Ningo Minor between Labade and Pissy (Kpeshi, probably where the Naval Academy is today) and Ningo Grande between Pompena (Prampram) and Lage (Old Labadi). Another town called Ningo (Ladoku?), apparently larger than either, is indicated north of Tema. Thus both Labadi and Nungua people had La roots, but the Labadi arrived from Old Labadi or Lai via Ajangote, while Nungua connections were with Ladoku near Kpone.

25. It is intriguing that Le is the name of the Volta River in Nchumuru and of its major tributary, the Oti, in Gichode and Nawuri (Zech and Neuhofen 1907: 116). All are Guang languages.

26. It should be clear that by "Dangme" I here mean merely non-Ga speakers of closely related dialects, not the present-day ethnic group or its language.

27. For a version of the shift with a somewhat different emphasis, see Apronti (1974: 11).

28. According to Field (1940), all the Ga towns had Kpeshi among their original peoples, although no traces of them remain in Osu or Nungua.

29. The list is reprinted and discussed in Dakubu (1987b).

30. Since the La are supposed to have crossed the Volta independently of both the Ga and Dangme and to have been former Guang speakers, it is to be expected that their dialect would have been different. Of course that does not prove that De Marees reported that dialect.

31. Judging from old word lists, Chala, but not its closest relatives Delo and Bago, also originally had a six-base number system (Westermann 1933: 8). The Akan have a seven-day week. Several peoples of the central Togo area have a five-day week (Debrunner 1962: 111), but it seems that shorter weeks only appear further east and north (Benneh 1974: 168).

32. Afutu, spoken on the coast at Senya Bereku and Winneba, is very closely related to Awutu. Prof. D. Akyeampong kindly provided the sentence quoted.

33. Ga has regularly lost all initial vowel prefixes, and nasality of the stem vowel sometimes corresponds to a weakened nasal second syllable in Akan.

34. Note that ŋkraŋ, that is, *ŋ-kranɪ, syllable for syllable corresponds best to akrade [akradɪ], with nasalization added. Both names are remarkably similar to a-kanɪ (e.g., Accany), the name by which some Akan traders were known to Europeans in the sixteenth and seventeenth centuries. Etymologically speaking, they are probably all from one source. The sixteenth-century spelling "Egrand" for Accra perhaps reflects another dialect variant, with the nasality in the stem vowel (*a-krã or *a-grã).

35. According to I. Odotei (personal communication), Akwamu was an important political factor in Nungua only after 1680.

36. De Marees ([1602] 1987) recorded the name *pito* when he visited Mina in 1601, so it cannot have been borrowed from Hausa despite the present association of the drink with northerners. According to Müller this was the Fetu name. The Ardra slaves called it "Ahei," evidently the source of modern Ga *ahai*, a nonalcoholic maize drink.

37. According to Reindorf ([1889] 1966: 39), Akanmaje was founded by Ayikai Osiahene, whom Field (1940: 148) mentions as a Gbese elder. These claims are not incompatible since Field also says Akanmaje was at first a division within Gbese, but it suggests that the origin of the quarter may have been historically Guang but not "pure" Obutu.

Chapter 6

1. For this reason, among others, early lists such as De Marees's ([1602] 1987) may be identified as Southern Akan but not specifically Fante, although they may turn out to be proto-modern Fante.

2. J. B. Abban, personal communication.

3. Although Afutu is still a community language in Winneba, at the present eastern border of Fante, it is under considerable pressure. Bilingualism in Fante is universal among its speakers, and there is a very large proportion of non-Guang migrants from southern Ghana in the town's population.

4. Delafosse's definitely Akan words are *berrenbues*, or people of *Abirem* (Abremu); *chocqua* "gold," modern *siká* "money" (and in Ga, *shiká* "gold, wealth"); *enchou*, modern *nsu* "water"; *berre bere* "welcome!" modern *bra* "come!"; and *dede*, modern *dɛ* "good." *Blaa* ([blɔ]?) or *baa* "white," from Spanish "blanco" or perhaps French "blanc," may be the origin of *buro-* in words referring to Europe, Europeans, and the foreign. *Barbero* "c'est ung enffant" seems to include the Akan item *-ba* "child." Delafosse's word for "egg," *agnio*, is unlike modern *kesua* but recalls De Marees's *ovino*; see chapter 7, note 8.

5. *Pace* Dalby and Hair's (1964) identification of this word with Akan *krante* "cutlass." Almost certainly, *kakla* and *krante* are derived from the same root, *kra-*. Knives were an early article of European trade (Daaku 1970: 40), which might account for the spread of names for them. Towerson's Akan words are *mattea* "their salutation," that is, *mate* "I have heard," a response to a salutation; *dassee*, modern *meda ase* "I thank you"; *sheke* "gold," modern *siká* "money" (as on Delafosse's list); and probably *cowrte*, modern *krante* "cutlass." *Bassina* "basins" and *molta* "much" are obviously Portuguese. *Foco* "cloth" is a problem, to be discussed elsewhere. *Kaklá* is not the only instance of preservation in Ga of an Akan word that

has disappeared from that language. Another is Ga *duadé* "cassava," an Akan compound of *-dua* "tree, stick" and *ade* "yam." A calque of this word appears in the Dutch literature as "Stockjams."

6. Earlier transcriptions indicate that Fante did not develop its characteristic affricates [ts] and [dz] before high front vowels until the nineteenth century. Akuapem had not yet been affected by the Asante-Akyem influx that followed the defeat of Akwamu in the eighteenth century. See note 1.

7. Unfortunately, his illustrious countryman Rasmus Rask (1828) republished this list in his *Vejledning til Akra-Sproget*. Once the Ga component is recognized, it is of interest as the first sample of Akan collected as much as twenty miles inland.

8. Trutenau (1971) produced a new edition of Protten (1764), together with Capitein's (1744) translations into Fante.

9. Sources do not distinguish the sense of "court" that is relevant. We may take it that the legal and political domains are not distinguishable in this context.

10. The Akan dialect of Atebubu is classified as a subdialect of Bron (Dolphyne and Dakubu 1988: 56; Dolphyne 1979), not Asante as would be expected if the original Akan-speaking population was from Kumasi. The history of the implantation of Akan in Atebubu would no doubt bear more investigation.

11. Another is Sikɔ (Debrunner 1962). Its speakers were defeated in war and scattered among several communities. Some were sold to the Ashanti and presumably became Akan speakers. See also Cardinall (1931a).

12. Information on the language situation in Achode from Philip Donkor, personal communication, 1985.

13. Although the administrator Klose, for whom German commercial and political interests were paramount, favored Guang and Hausa (Klose 1899: 295).

14. Katherine Abu, personal communication, 1990.

15. There were a few important indigenous traders on the Slave Coast, notably the Lawson family (Debrunner 1965: 29; Freeman 1844: 279), but the Lawsons were actually Minas of Fante origin (Decalo 1987).

16. In Henrici's transcription, which he admits was from memory, the song goes *ē ē*, *womba dschē*, modern Ga *ee, ee, wɔmba je*, "Eh, eh, we are coming there."

17. Kwei Orraca-Tetteh, personal communication.

18. The gloss "bread" was of course generic for a grain staple dish, nor was it necessarily always made of maize as it is today; see comments on "kenkey" in the following chapter. Samarin (1982: 25) noted a somewhat similar word, of problematic origin, in pidgin Sango, *kɔ́bè* "staple dough, food." In view of the role of Guinea coast soldiers in the formation of central African pidgins (Samarin 1990/91), the word could conceivably have come from this source.

19. Christaller (1895: 6); see also a comment by Daüble in *Monats-Blatt der Nord-deutschen Missions-Gesellschaft*, 1909. German colonial authorities were particularly interested in Hausa because it was also a candidate for lingua franca in their other West African territory, the equally complex northern Cameroun.

20. As linguistic terms, Zabarima and Dendi denote mutually intelligible groups of dialects within Songhay (Nicolaï 1980).

21. English troops arrived on the Gold Coast for the first time in 1782 (Crooks [1923] 1973: vi). At no time were they the majority.

22. There were in fact no white soldiers at James Fort at the time (Crooks [1923] 1973: 227, 238).

23. Compare the discussion of language in Ilorin, chapter 2.

24. The tradition of using an ethnic or place-name or some other appellation not used at home when working in the south is an old one, still strongly maintained.

25. According to Gillespie he was a Trinidadian, according to Hair (1967) a Jamaican, but he also published a translation of the Gospel of St. Mark in the French patois of Domenica and a sketch of the Carib language of the same island country.

26. Zimmerman's unpublished letters as quoted by Dretke (1968: 24) suggest that a number of the Brazilian freedmen who arrived in Accra were Muslims and probably Hausa-speaking. Their use of Hausaized Arabic names, some of which (for example, *Azuma*) are still in use among their descendants, is further evidence of this. (The Brazilian immigration is discussed further in Chapter 7.)

27. Although Foli said that "Mandingo" was understood in Borgu and Sokode (Sölken 1939: 79).

Chapter 7

1. See chapter 6, note 4.

2. See Hair (1969) for discussion of an early linguistic comment that seems to imply the use of Arabic at Mina. Its author (Thevet) may have met Mande people with whom he was able to communicate in Arabic.

3. Delafosse actually said, "Et puis nous prinsmes nostre seüreté du *manse* et *caremanse*, quy sont le roy et vice-roy" (my emphasis) (Escudier 1992: 26). The words are clearly being used as titles, not names, and so cannot be identified with Akan names such as Kăra Mansă (Christaller 1886: 93) or Kwamina Ansa (Daaku 1970: 52). *Mansa* is the Manding title for king. There are several possibilities for *caremanse*. Expressions with *mansa* preceded by *kala* "bow," *ker* "war," or *kale* "white horse with a brown mark on the face," on the model of *ker-tigi* "warrior" (Delafosse 1901: 201) or *kala-tigi* "archer" (Delafosse 1929: 328) are all plausible, although no such title is still current, as far as I know.

4. See for example P. Thonning's map of 1802/1838. Wilks (1993: 15) suggests that the Portuguese gave it this name because at the Volta they turned back, finding no more gold trade. Although it is true that *volta* can mean "return," as well as "alteration," surely they kept going.

5. Apparently on more than one occasion (Debrunner 1967: 18–19).

6. See Bradshaw (1965) and Naro (1973) for conflicting opinions on the significance for Guinea Portuguese of the peculiar speech of Africans in Portuguese literature of the late fifteenth and early sixteenth centuries.

7. See chapter 6, note 5.

8. *Pace* Van Dantzig and Jones (De Marees [1602] 1987), *ovina* "egg" is probably not Portuguese but an obsolete local word, relatable to modern Ga *wɔlɔ* "egg."

9. Note the importance in Portuguese times of the *arca con tres chaves* (Vogt 1979: 58), in which the gold was kept at San Jorge da Mina—hence the very early borrowing of *adaka* and *safē* "key." Other Akan words that are probably pre-1600 borrowings from Portuguese are *dánta* "loin-cloth," from *lamben*, a cloth imported by the Portuguese that the people of the Gold Coast cut and wore wrapped around the waist (p. 67), compounded with Akan *-tā* "cloth strip"; *frɔnɔɔ* "oven" and *páănoo* "bread" from *forno* and *pão*, respectively; and *amrăădo* for a government officer, perhaps from *amarrador* "master of a float" or *morador* "garrison soldier." It has previously been attributed to *almirante* "admiral," but either of the less elevated sources gives a better fit, both phonologically and semantically. *Morador* is definitely known to have been a term in common use on the coast with a local application, which is not true of *almirante*. *Amarrador* is Brazilian.

10. It was actually more complex since Great Accra itself was probably a dual town; see chapter 5.

11. Interpreters occasionally signed treaties to this effect. A. Van Dantzig, personal communication, 1994. The practice of interpreting in Portuguese an agreement written in a European language was reported in some detail by Groben (1694: 82), in connection with the acquisition of land for Gross Friedrichsberg in 1683.

12. A number of Danish traders and governors learned Ga, in which Wrisberg and Schønning published translations.

13. Hair (1978) mentions communities of resident Portuguese and Afro-Portuguese traders, as well as both fully and partly acculturated Africans.

14. French is generally said to have been the "world language" after Portuguese and before English, but it was not significant on the Gold Coast, where the heyday of Portuguese more or less coincided with the heyday of French elsewhere.

15. There seem to be a few relics of nineteenth-century Brazilian Portuguese in Ghanaian English. The current word for illegal gold winning, *galamsey*, is clearly related to the Brazilian term for an independent gold winner, *galimpeiro*, and in the Portuguese of the Algarve, *galampear*, a verb meaning "rob, plunder."

16. Compare chapter 6, note 18.

17. Such servants were quite distinct from the forts' slaves; see, for example, Tilleman ([1697] 1994: 22).

18. However, private arrangements did not always have happy results. Governor Richelieu of Christiansborg (1822–1825), paid by the father of Noi Dowuona to take him to Copenhagen for education, treated the boy as a slave until the Moravian and Basel mission organizations brought his plight to the attention of the king, who put him in the garrison school and arranged his passage home (Rasmus Rask 1828). This same Governor Richelieu is said to have concerned himself with the proper education of the mulatto children at Christiansborg (Reindorf 1966: 217) and personally forwarded a request for Basel missionaries (Bartels 1965: 5; Debrunner 1967: 65).

19. The term "gentleman" in Ghana distinguishes a person perceived to have an English education and life-style, a usage that originated with the English themselves. Witness the metamorphosis of John Aqua and George Sackee from "native youths" or "Two Black Boys" at the time of their arrival in England in 1754, to "Two Black Gentlemen" upon their departure in 1756 (Crooks [1923] 1973: 28, 29).

20. For further discussion of language education policy in the 1970s and criticism of the standard achieved, see Apronti (1974).

21. Another policy that was established very early and lasted at least until independence was the ban on speaking Ghanaian languages on school grounds, often enforced with corporal punishment. According to Bartels (1965: 8) it was decreed in 1824, even before a mission was officially established in Cape Coast, that the English language "under penalty be exclusively spoken in the school." This is of a piece with the contemporary suppression of Welsh and Scots Gaelic in Britain (Trudgill 1983: 145).

22. Joyce Cary's fictional Mister Johnson was probably one such agent of language spread. I owe this suggestion to Dr. David Arnott.

23. He spoke of "the encroachment of the arrogant Ashanti traders from the English territory, especially from Ada and Accra" (p. 309).

24. Several of the Bremen missionaries at Keta in 1853 were actually English (Zahn 1870).

25. It should be clear that Mühlhaüsler's (1986: 110) claim that the West Indian English creoles developed from West African pidgin Portuguese by "relexification," a process supposed to have taken place in Whydah or Benin, makes little historical sense. The cases he cites seem to be describable as code switching and mixing. Nor is there reason to regard any

of the varieties of English of Ghana as genetically unclassifiable "mixed" languages, a concept that hopelessly confuses linguistic and social criteria for classification (Thomason and Kaufman [1988] 1991). Although it is true that Ghanaian English varieties are spoken almost entirely by second-language speakers, not only are they learned *as English* but the same was once true of Ga.

26. R. F. Burton, quoted by Jones (1962: 24).

27. The quotation is "Massa, I think it is better we go at home, it is too dark." Apart from the stereotyped spelling of "Massa," only the expression "go at home" is obviously nonstandard; but it is not "pidgin" either, more likely a hyperform on the model of "stay at home."

28. Actually, speakers' perceptions of the relations of Nigerian Pidgin English and even Krio to English may be more like Ghanaians' than is often assumed (Elugbe and Omamor 1991: 122, 139; Gani-Ikilama 1990: 220).

29. Since Reindorf ([1889] 1966) wrote in German, the more educated domains in the education-religion range were shared in Basel mission times between Danish and German.

Chapter 8

1. I am indebted for much of my information on *plashéèle* to conversations with my late colleague, Kwei Orraca-Tetteh. It is sad that he did not live to bring his material to publication.

2. Kwei Orraca-Tetteh, personal communication, 1992.

3. Nii Adjeitey Adjei, personal communication, 1991.

4. The indecency of the songs still known as *Sibisaba* caused such a furor among the Bremen missionaries in 1910 that one of them, Härtter, collected and translated into German the Ewe texts of twenty-one songs (Bremer Staatsarchiv 7,1025 2 41 Folklore).

5. The geographical sources of recruits to the armed forces, now seen by many southerners as a route to economic and political participation, have changed since 1970. I do not know what this has meant for the spread of Hausa since.

6. I do not mean that only sociolinguists are guilty of this confusion. I have met illiterate and semiliterate Ghanaian speakers who are puzzled by the disjunction between their "high" spoken English and their low job status.

7. I do not mean to oppose the expression of cultural solidarity to reaffirmation of political inequality, for they can certainly coexist as communication goals. But the fact that the latter is clearly primary in language spread is obscured by building the model for spread on the former.

8. The Kwahu in particular are well known as traders in Accra.

9. It seems that the few Ga who convert to Islam learn Hausa as the language of their religious "hosts."

References

Abdulaziz-Mkilifi, M. H. 1972. Triglossia and Swahili-English bilingualism in Tanzania. *Language and Society* 1: 197–213. *Advances in the Study of Societal Multilingualism*, Reprinted in Fishman, Joshua A., ed. The Hague: Mouton. Pp. 129–49.

Ablorh-Odjidja, J. R. 1961. *Thinking about Ga*. London: Macmillan.

Acquah, Ioné. 1954. *Accra Survey*. London: University of London Press. Reprinted, Accra: Ghana Universities Press, 1972.

Adams, W. H. 1908. The tail-girl of Krobo Hill. *Blackwood's Magazine* 1116: 517–34.

Adefuye, Ade. 1987. Oba Akinsemoyin and the emergence of modern Lagos. In Adefuye et al., *History of the Peoples of Lagos State*. Pp. 47–62.

Adefuye, Ade, Babatunde Agiri, and Jide Osuntokun, eds. 1987. *History of the Peoples of Lagos State*. Lagos: Lantern Books.

Agiri, B. A., and Sandra Barnes. 1987. Lagos before 1603. In Adefuye et al., *History of the Peoples of Lagos State*. Pp.18–32.

Ahadji, Valentin A. 1976. Rapports entre les Societes de Missions et le Gouvernement Colonial Allemand au Togo de 1884 à 1918. Universite de la Sorbonne Nouvelle Paris 3, Institut d'Allemand d'Asnieres, Thèse de Doctorat de Troisième Cycle.

Akinjogbin I. A. 1967. *Dahomey and Its Neighbours 1708–1818*. Cambridge: Cambridge University Press.

Akuffo-Badoo, W. S. 1967. The Music of Kpa. Diploma in African Music thesis, Institute of African Studies, University of Ghana.

Alagoa, E. J., and A. Fombo. 1972. *A Chronicle of Grand Bonny*. Ibadan: Ibadan University Press.

Alexandre, Pierre, 1971. Multilingualism. In Sebeok, *Current Trends in Linguistics*. Pp. 654–63.

Amartey, A. A. 1969. *Omanye Aba*. Accra: Bureau of Ghana Languages.

———. 1988. *Ŋmaa Ye Eyɛ*. Accra: Ga Society.

Aminarh, Esther Akusika. 1992. The Multilingual Situation in the Central Ashiedu Keteke Area, and Its Effects on Primary Class 1–3. Diploma Long Essay, Language Centre, University of Ghana.

Amoah, Frank E. K. 1964. Accra: A Study in the Development of a West African City. M.A. thesis, Institute of African Studies, University of Ghana.

Ankrah, E. A. Nee-Adjabeng. 1966. *Agwaseŋ Wiemɔi kɛAbɛi Komɛi*. Accra: Bureau of Ghana Languages.

Anquandah, James. 1982. *Rediscovering Ghana's Past*. Accra: Sedco; Harlow: Longman.

Ansah, S. L. 1974. Oral Literature of the Hill Guang, 2 vols. M.A. thesis, Institute of African Studies, University of Ghana.

Anstey, Roger, and P. E. H. Hair. 1976. Introduction. In Anstey and Hair, eds., *Liverpool, the African Slave Trade, and Abolition*. Liverpool: Historic Society of Lancashire and Cheshire. Pp. 1–13.

Apronti, Eric Ofoe. 1974. Sociolinguistics and the question of a national language: The case of Ghana. *Studies in African Linguistics*, Supplement 5: 1–20.

Ardayfio, Elizabeth A. 1977. Evolution of trade patterns in the Shai area. *Bulletin of the Ghana Geographical Association* 19: 22–32.

Arhin, Kwame. 1971. Strangers and hosts: A study in the political organisation and history of Atebubu town. *Transactions of the Historical Society of Ghana* 12: 63–82.

———. 1979. The Brong. In Arhin, ed., *A Profile of Brong Kyempem*. Accra: Afram Publications. Pp. 9–21.

———. 1986. The Asante praise poems: The ideology of patrimonialism. *Paideuma* 32: 163–97.

———. 1989. West African trading settlement in the Asante hinterland in the nineteenth century. *Research Review* (NS) 5(1): 1–20.

———. ed. 1974. *The Papers of George Ekem Ferguson*. Leiden: African Studies Center.

Armah, Ayi Kwei. 1968. *The Beautyful Ones Are Not Yet Born*. Boston: Houghton Mifflin.

Asante, David. 1886. Eine Reise nach Salaga und Obooso. . . . *Mitteilungen der Geographischen Gesellschaft in Jena* 4: 15–40.

Awedoba, A. K. 1979. Bilingualism and Language Shift in Navrongo. Paper prepared for the Workshop on the Study of Multilingualism in Ghana, Institute of African Studies, University of Ghana.

Ayim, D. C. 1991. A Sociolinguistic Survey of Begoro: A Case Study of the Oboase and Zongo Communities. Diploma Long Essay, Language Centre, University of Ghana.

Azu, Noa Akunor Aguae. 1926. Adangbe (Adangme) history. *Gold Coast Review* 2(2): 239–70.

———. 1927. Adangbe (Adangme) history. *Gold Coast Review* 3(1): 89–116.

Baesjou, René. 1988. The historical evidence in old maps and charts of Africa with special reference to West Africa. *History in Africa* 15: 1–83.

Baesjou, René, ed. 1979. *An Asante Embassy on the Gold Coast*. Cambridge and Leiden: African Studies Center.

Bal, Willy. 1975. À propos de mots d'origine Portugaise en Afrique Noire. In Marius Valkhoff et al., *Misclânea Luso-Africana*. Lisboa: Junta de Investigações Cientificas do Ultramar. Pp. 119–32.

Bamgbose, Ayọ. 1991. *Language and the Nation: The Language Question in Sub-Saharan Africa*. Edinburgh: Edinburgh University Press.

Barbag-Stoll, Anna. 1983. *Social and Linguistic History of Nigerian Pidgin English*. Tübingen: Stauffenberg Verlag.

Barber, Karin. 1991. *I Could Speak until Tomorrow: Oriki, Women, and the Past in a Yoruba Town*. Washington, D.C.: Smithsonian Institution Press.

Bartels, F. L. 1965. *The Roots of Ghana Methodism*. Cambridge: Cambridge University Press.

Bay, Edna. 1986. *Iron Altars of the Fon People of Benin*. Atlanta: Emory University.

Beecham, John. 1841. *Ashantee and the Gold Coast*. London: John Mason.

Bell, Hesketh. 1893. The Fetish-Mountain of Krobo. *MacMillan's Magazine* 405: 210–19.

Bendor-Samuel, John, ed. 1989. *The Niger-Congo Languages*. Lanham, New York, and London: University Press of America.

Benneh, George. 1974. Bawku, une ville marché du Ghana du Nord. *Les Cahiers d'Outre-Mer No.106* 27: 168–82.

Bennett, Norman R., and George E. Brooks, eds. 1965. *New England Merchants in Africa: A History through Documents 1802–1865*. Brookline, Mass.: Boston University Press.

Benzing, Brigitta. 1971. *Die Geschichte und das Herrschaftsystem der Dagomba*. Mersenheim am Glan: Verlag Anton Haim.

Berry, Jack. 1971. Pidgins and Creoles in Africa. In Sebeok, *Current Trends in Linguistics*. Pp. 510–36.

Blaeu, Joan. 1665. *Atlas Maior*. Amsterdam.

Blanc, Haim. 1971. Arabic. In Sebeok, *Current Trends in Linguistics*. Pp. 501–09.

Boadi, Lawrence. 1976. Mother tongue education in Ghana. In Ayo Bamgboṣe, ed., *Mother Tongue Education, The West African Experience*. London: Hodder and Stoughton; Paris: Unesco Press. Pp. 83–112.

Bodomo, Adams Amatus. 1988. A Dagaare Dialect Survey. M.A. Essay, Linguistics Department, University of Ghana.

Bole-Richard, Rémy. 1983. *Systématique Phonologique et Grammaticale d'un parler Ewe: Le Gen-Mina du Sud-Togo et Sud-Bénin*. Paris: Editions L'Harmattan.

Bosman, William. 1967. *A New and Accurate Description of the Coast of Guinea*. 4th English ed. London: Frank Cass & Co. 1st English ed. 1705.

Bovill, E. W. 1968. *The Golden Trade of the Moors*. 2nd ed. London: Oxford University Press.

Bowdich, T. E.. 1966. *Mission from Cape Coast Castle to Ashantee*. 3rd ed. London: Frank Cass & Co. First published 1819.

Boxer, C. R. 1965. *The Dutch Seaborne Empire: 1600–1800*. New York: Knopf.

Brackenbury, Henry. 1968. *The Ashanti War, A Narrative*, 2 vols. London: Frank Cass and Co. First published 1894.

Bradshaw, A. T. von S. 1965. Vestiges of Portuguese in the languages of Sierra Leone. *Sierra Leone Language Review* 4: 5–37.

———. 1966. A list of Yoruba words in Krio. *Sierra Leone Language Review* 5: 61–71.

Bredwa-Mensah, Yaw. 1990. An archaeological investigation conducted at Okai Koi Hill (Ayawaso) and its significance for Iron Age archaeology in Ghana. M.Phil. Thesis, Dept. of Archaeology, University of Ghana.

Brempong, Owusu. 1984. Akan Highlife in Ghana: Songs of Cultural Transition. Ph.D. dissertation, Indiana University.

Brokensha, David. 1966. *Social Change in Larteh, Ghana*. Oxford: Clarendon Press.

Brown, A. Addo-Aryee. 1927. Historical account of Mohammedanism in the Gold Coast. *Gold Coast Review* 3(2): 195–97.

Brown, Susan Drucker. 1975. *Ritual Aspects of the Mamprusi Kingship*. Leiden: African Studies Center.

Bürgi, E. 1890. Durch deutsches und englisches Evheland; eine Missionsreise. Bremer Staatsarchiv 7,1025 4 41, Reiseberichte 1876–1925.

Burrows, Sally. 1987. Statement on Shelter and Community Action in Accra. Prepared for IYSH Trust.

Calame-Griaule, Genevieve. 1986. *Words and the Dogon World*. Deirdre LaPin, trans. Philadelphia: Institute for the Study of Human Issues.

Calvet, Louis-Jean. 1982. The spread of Mandingo: Military, commercial, and colonial influence on a linguistic datum. In Cooper, *Language Spread*. Pp. 184–97.

———. 1988. Dynamique du plurilinguisme; présentation d'une recherche. *Linguistique Africaine* 1: 133–43.

Capitein, J. E. J. 1744. *Vertaaling van het onze Vader, de Twaalf Geloofsartykelen, en det Tien Geboden des Heeren*. Leiden: Jacobus de Beunje.

Cardinall, A. W. 1927. *In Ashanti and Beyond*. London: Seeley, Service.

————. 1931a. A survival. *The Gold Coast Review* 5(2): 193–97.

————. 1931b. *Tales Told in Togoland*. Oxford: Oxford University Press. Reprinted 1970.

Cary, Joyce. 1962. *Mister Johnson*. Harmondsworth: Penguin Books. First published 1939.

Chinebuah, I. K. 1977. The national languages in Africa: The case for Akan in Ghana. *African Languages/Langues Africaines* 3: 60–78.

Christaller, J. G. 1875. *A Grammar of the Asante and Fante Language called Tshi (Chwee, Twi)*. Basel: Basel Evangelical Missionary Society.

————. 1886. Zur Völker-und Sprachenkunde Afrikas. *Mitteilungen der Geographischen Gesellschaft in Jena* 4: 88–96.

————. 1887/88. Die Volta Sprachengruppe. *Zeitschrift für Afrikanische Sprachen* 1: 161–88.

————. 1889. Sprachproben vom Sudan zwischen Asante und Mittel-Niger (Specimens of some Sudan languages). *Zeitschrift für Afrikanische Sprachen* 3: 107–32.

————. 1895. Die Sprachen des Togogebiets. *Zeitschrift für Afrikanische und Ozeanische Sprachen* 1(1): 5–8.

————. 1933. *A Dictionary of the Asante and Fante Language called Tshi (Twi)*. 2nd ed. Basel: Basel Evangelical Society. First published 1881.

Christopherson, Paul. 1953. Some special West African English words. *English Studies* 34: 282–91.

Clifford, Sir Hugh. 1920. *The Gold Coast Regiment in the East African Campaign*. London: Murray.

Collins, John. 1985. *Music Makers of West Africa*. Washington, D.C.: Three Continents Press.

Cooper, Robert L. 1982. A framework for the study of language spread. In Cooper, ed., *Language Spread: Studies in Diffusion and Social Change*. Bloomington: Indiana University Press. Pp. 5–36.

Cornevin, Robert. 1963. *Histoire du Togo*. 3rd ed. Paris: Editions Berger-Levrault.

Criper, Lindsay. 1971. The tones of Ga English. *Actes du Huitième Congrès de la Société Linguistique de l'Afrique Occidentale*, 2 vols. Abidjan: Université d'Abidjan. Pp. 43–54.

Crooks, J. J. 1973. *Records Relating to the Gold Coast Settlements from 1750 to 1874*. 2nd impression. London: Frank Cass. First published 1923.

Crowder, Michael. 1973. *Revolt in Bussa: A Study in British 'Native Administration' in Nigerian Borgu 1902–1935*. London: Faber.

Crowley, Terry. 1992. *An Introduction to Historical Linguistics*, 2nd ed. Auckland: Oxford University Press.

Cruickshank, Brodie. 1853. *Eighteen Years on the Gold Coast of Africa*. London: Hurst and Blackett.

Daaku, K. Y. 1970. *Trade and Politics on the Gold Coast 1600–1720*. London: Clarendon Press.

Dadson, Nanabanyin. 1989, January 7. The story of "Cine" in Ghana. *The Mirror*, p. 12.

Dadzie, A. B. K. 1985. Pidgin in Ghana: a theoretical consideration of its origin and development. In F. O. Ugboajah, ed., *Mass Communication, Culture and Society in West Africa*. Oxford: Hans Zell.

Dakubu, M. E. Kropp. 1969a. Bowdich's "Adampe" word list. *Research Review* 5(3): 45–49.

————. 1969b. A note on "La." *Research Review* 5(2): 27–32.

————. 1972. Linguistic pre-history and historical reconstruction: The Ga-Adangme migrations. *Transactions of the Historical Society of Ghana* 13(1): 87–12.

———. 1976. On the linguistic geography of the area of ancient Begho. In H. M. J. Trutenau, ed., *Communications from the Basel Africa Bibliography*, vol. 14. Basel: Basel Africa Bibliography. Pp. 63–91.

———. 1977. A note on Hausa in Ghana. *Papers in Ghanaian Linguistics* 2: 14–22.

———. 1978. Report on the Sociolinguistic Survey of the Kyerepong Area. Ms. deposited in the Library of the Institute of African Studies, University of Ghana.

———. 1979. Other people's words: An aspect of style in Ga songs. In W. C. McCormack and S. A. Wurm, eds., *Language and Society: Anthropological Issues*. The Hague: Mouton. Pp. 98–110.

———. 1980. The Proto-Ga-Dangme vowel system. *Papers in Ghanaian Linguistics* 3: 31–45.

———. 1981. *One Voice, The Linguistic Culture of an Accra Lineage*. Leiden: African Studies Center.

———. 1983. Survey of Multilingualism and Communication in the Buli-speaking Area: Interim Report. Ms. deposited in the Institute of African Studies Library, Legon.

———. 1986. Sociolinguistic Survey of Northern Communities in Accra: The Dagaaba. Preliminary report. Ms. deposited in the Institute of African Studies Library, Legon.

———. 1987a. Creating unity; The context of speaking prose and poetry in Ga. *Anthropos* 82: 507–27.

———. 1987b. *The Dangme Language; An Introductory Survey*. Basingstoke and London: Macmillan.

———. 1988a. The multilingual environment in the Ada District. *Research Review* (NS) 4(1): 35–44.

———. 1991. A note on Dogon in Accra. *Journal of West African Languages* 21(1): 35–40.

———, ed. 1988b. *The Languages of Ghana*. London: Kegan Paul International.

Dakubu, M. E. Kropp, and K. C. Ford. 1988. The Central-Togo languages. In Dakubu, *The Languages of Ghana*. Pp. 118–54.

Dalby, David, and P. E. H. Hair. 1964. "Le Langaige de Guynee": A sixteenth century vocabulary from the Pepper Coast. *African Language Studies* 5: 164–91.

Dalzel, Archibald. 1793. *The History of Dahomy*. London.

Dapper, Olfert. 1686. *Description de l'Afrique, contenant les noms, la situation & les confins de toutes ses parties. . . .* Amsterdam: Wolfgang, Waesberge, Boom & van Someren. First published in Dutch in 1668.

Davis, Ronald W. 1976. *Ethnohistorical Studies on the Kru Coast*. Liberian Studies Monograph Series No. 5, University of Delaware. Newark, Del.: Pencader Publishers.

Debrunner, Hans W. 1962. Vergessene Sprachen und Trick-Sprachen bei den Togorestvölkern. *Afrika und Übersee* 46: 109–18.

———. 1965. *A Church between Colonial Powers; A Study of the Church in Togo*. London: Lutterworth Press.

———. 1967. *A History of Christianity in Ghana*. Accra: Waterville Publishing House.

Decalo, Samuel. 1987. *Historical Dictionary of Togo*. Metuchen, N.J., and London: Scarecrow Press.

Delafosse, M. 1901. *Essai de Manuel Pratique de la Langue Mandé ou Mandingue*. Paris: Ernest Leroux.

———. 1904. *Vocabulaires comparatifs de plus de 60 langues parlees a la Cote-d'Ivoire et dans les regions limitrophes*. Paris: Leroux.

———. 1929. *La Langue Mandingue et ses Dialectes* (*Malinke, Bambara, Dioula*), 2 vols. Paris: Librairie Orientaliste Pual Geuthner.

De Marees, Pieter. 1987. *Description and Historical Account of the Gold Kingdom of Guinea (1602)*. Albert van Dantzig and Adam Jones, trans and ed. Oxford: Oxford University Press for the British Academy.

De Marrée, J. A. 1817/18. *Reizen op en Beschrijving van de Goudkust van Guinea.* Amsterdam: Gebroeders van Cleef.

Derive, M. J. 1976. Dioula vehiculaire, dioula de Kong et dioula d'Odienné. *Annales de l'Université d'Abidjan* Série H, 9.1.

———. 1990. *Étude Dialectologique de l'Aire Manding de Côte d'Ivoire*, 2 vols. SELAF No. 318. Paris: Peeters.

Dickson, Kwamina B. 1969. *A Historical Geography of Ghana.* London: Cambridge University Press.

Dillard, J. L. 1979. Creole English and Creole Portuguese: The early records. In Hancock, *Readings in Creole Studies.* Pp. 261–68.

Dolphyne, F. A. 1977. Language use in the Upper Region—A pilot study. *Papers in Ghanaian Linguistics* 2.

———. 1979. The Brong (Bono) dialect of Akan. In Arhin, *Brong-Kyempem.* Pp. 88–118.

Dolphyne, F. A., and M. E. Kropp Dakubu. 1988. The Volta-Comoé languages. In Dakubu, *The Languages of Ghana.* Pp. 50–90.

Dretke, James P. 1968. The Muslim Community in Accra (an historical survey). M.A. thesis, Institute of African Studies, University of Ghana.

Dudley, Sir Robert. 1646/47. *Dell' Arcano del Mare.* Florence.

Dumestre, G. 1971. *Atlas Linguistique de Cote d'Ivoire: Les Langues de la Région Lagunaire.* Abidjan: Université d'Abidjan, Institut de Linguistique Appliquée.

Dunn, Ross E. 1986. *The Adventures of Ibn Battuta, A Muslim Traveller of the Fourteenth Century.* Berkeley and Los Angeles: University of California Press.

Dupuis, J. 1966. *Journal of a Residence in Ashantee.* 2nd ed. London: Frank Cass. First published 1824.

Duthie, A. S. 1988. Ewe. In Dakubu, *The Languages of Ghana.* Pp. 91–101.

Duthie, A. S., and R. K. Vlaardingerbroek. 1981. *Bibliography of Gbe (Ewe, Gen, Aja, Xwla, Fon, Gun).* Basel: Basel Africa Bibliography.

Dwyer, David J. 1989. Mande. In Bendor-Samuel, *Niger-Congo Languages.* Pp. 47–65.

Egblewogbe, E. Y. 1985. Trois siècles de litterature Ewe: Problèmes et perspectives. *Actes du Colloque Internationale sur le Passage à la Lecture en Afrique Noire.* Lomé: AELIA, APELA, ORSTOM et Université du Bénin. Pp. 79–90.

Elugbe, Ben Ohi, and Augusta Phil Omamor. 1991. *Nigerian Pidgin (Background and Prospects).* Ibadan: Heinemann Educational Books Nigeria PLC.

Emberson, B. 1979. Language in the Northern Guang-speaking Area. Paper prepared for the Workshop on the Study of Multilingualism in Ghana, Institute of African Studies, University of Ghana.

Engmann, Rev. E. A. W. 1968. *Etsuɔ Fe Nɛkɛ.* Accra: Bureau of Ghana Languages.

Escudier, Denis, ed. 1992. *Voyage d'Eustache Delafosse sur la côte de Guinée, au Portugal et en Espagne (1479–1481).* Transcription du manuscrit de Valenciennes, Traduction et Présentation de Denis Escudier. Paris: Editions Chandeigne.

Ewusi, Kodwo, 1977. Rural-Urban and Regional Migration in Ghana. Discussion Paper No. 1. Legon: Institute for Social, Statistical and Economic Research, University of Ghana.

Fabian, Johannes. 1986. *Language and Colonial Power.* Berkeley, Los Angeles, and Oxford: University of California Press.

Fage, J. D. 1962. Some remarks on beads and trade in Lower Guinea in the sixteenth and seventeenth centuries. *Journal of African History* 3(2): 343–47.

Feinberg, Harvey M. 1989. *Africans and Europeans in West Africa: Elminans and Dutchmen on the Gold Coast During the Eighteenth Century. Transactions of the American Philosophical Society* 79(7).

Ferguson, Charles A. 1959. Diglossia. *Word* 15: 325–40.

Feyer, Ursula. 1947. Haussa als Verkehrssprache. *Zeitschrift für Phonetik und allgemeine Sprachwissenschaft* 1(1/2): 108–29.

Field, M. J. 1940. *Social Organization of the Gã People*. London: Crown Agents for the Colonies.

———. 1961. *Religion and Medicine of the Gã People*. Accra: Presbyterian Book Depot; London: Oxford University Press. First published 1937.

———. 1962a. *Awutu-Bereku*. Bawjiase: Speedwell Press.

———. 1962b. The investigation of the ancient settlements of the Accra Plain. *Ghana Notes and Queries* 4: 4–5.

Fishman, Joshua A. 1970. *Sociolinguistics, A Brief Introduction*. Rowley, Mass.: Newbury House Press.

———. 1972. The relationship between micro- and macro-sociolinguistics in the study of who speaks what language to whom and when. First published 1865. In Pride and Holmes, *Sociolinguistics*. Pp. 15–32.

Forde, C. Daryll. 1956. *Efik Traders of Old Calabar, Containing the Diary of Antera Duke, an Efik Slave-trading Chief of the Eighteenth Century.* . . . London and New York: Oxford University Press.

Fraenkel, Merran. 1964. *Tribe and Class in Monrovia*. London: Oxford University Press.

Frajzyngier, Z. 1968. An analysis of the Awutu verb. *Africana Bulletin* (Warsaw) 8.

Freeman, Thomas B. 1844. *Journal of Various Visits to the Kingdoms of Ashanti, Aku and Dahomey in Western Africa*. London: J. Mason.

Funke, E. 1914/15. Die Sprachverhältnisse in Sugu, Dahome (Franz. Westafrika). *Zeitschrift für Kolonialsprachen* 5: 257–63.

———. 1916. Die Stellung der Haussasprache unter den Sprachen Togos. *Mitteilungen des Seminars fur Orientalische Sprachen* 19: 116–28.

———. 1920/21. Einige Tanz- und Liebeslieder der Haussa. *Zeitschrift für Eingeborenen-Sprachen* 11: 259–75.

Gani-Ikilima, T. O. 1990. Use of Nigerian Pidgin in education? Why not? In E. Nolue Emenanjo, ed., *Multilingualism, Minority Languages and Language Policy in Nigeria*. Agbor: Central Books. Pp. 219–27.

Ghana Government. 1960. *1960 Population Census of Ghana: Maps*.

———. 1972. *1970 Population Census of Ghana, Vol. 2: Statistics of Localities and Enumeration Areas*. Accra: Census Office.

———. 1987. *1984 Population Census of Ghana, Demographic and Economic Characteristics: Total Country*. Accra: Statistical Service.

Gil, B., A. F. Aryee, and D. K. Ghansah. 1964. *1960 Population Census of Ghana, Special Report 'E', Tribes in Ghana*. Accra: Census Office.

Giles, Howard. 1985. Accommodation theory: Some new directions. *York Papers in Linguistics* 9 :105–36.

———. ed. 1977. *Language, Ethnicity and Intergroup Relations*. London and New York: Academic Press.

Gillespie, W. H. 1955. *The Gold Coast Police 1844–1938*. Accra: Government Printer.

Goody, E. 1971. "Greeting," "begging," and the presentation of respect. In J. S. LaFontaine, ed., *The Interpretation of Ritual: Essays in Honour of A. I. Richards*. London: Tavistock Publications.

Goody, J. 1964. The Mande and the Akan hinterland. In J. Vansina, R. Mauny, and L. V. Thomas, eds., *The Historian in Tropical Africa*. London: Oxford University Press.

———. 1967. *The Social Organization of the LoWiili*. 2nd ed. London: Oxford University Press.

————. 1968. Restricted literacy in northern Ghana. In Goody, J. ed., *Literacy in Traditional Societies.* Cambridge: Cambridge University Press. Pp. 198–264.

Goody, Jack, and T. M. Mustapha. 1967. The caravan trade from Kano to Salaga. *Journal of the Historical Society of Nigeria* 3(4): 611–16.

Grade, P. 1892. Das Neger-Englisch. *Anglia* 14: 362–93.

Greenberg, J. H. 1945. Arabic loan-words in Hausa. *Word* 3(1): 85–97.

————. 1960. Linguistic evidence for the influence of the Kanuri on the Hausa. *Journal of African History* 1(2): 205–12.

Grindal, Bruce T. 1972. *Growing Up in Two Worlds: Education and Transition among the Sisala of Northern Ghana.* New York: Holt, Rinehart and Winston.

Groben, Otto Friedrich von der. 1694. *Guineische Reise-Beschreibung.* Murjenwerder: Simon Reinigern.

Groh, B. 1911. Sprachproben aus zwölf Sprachen des Togohinterlandes. *Mitteilungen des Seminars für Orientalische Sprachen* 14: 227–39.

Hair, P. E. H. 1967. *The Early Study of Nigerian Languages.* West African Language Monographs 7. London: Cambridge University Press.

————. 1969. An ethnolinguistic inventory of the Lower Guinea Coast before 1700: Part II. *Sierra Leone Language Review* 8: 225–56.

————. 1978. Hamlet in an Afro-Portuguese setting: New perspectives on Sierra Leone in 1607. *History in Africa* 5: 21–42.

————. 1992. Discovery and discoveries: The Portuguese in Guinea 1444–1650. *Bulletin of Hispanic Studies* 69: 11–28.

Hair, P. E. H., Adam Jones, and Robin Law, eds. 1992. *Barbot on Guinea; The Writings of Jean Barbot on West Africa 1678–1712.* London: Hakluyt Society.

Hakluyt, Richard. 1907. *The Principal Navigations, Voyages, Traffiques and Destinations of the English Nation. Hakluyt's Voyages*, with an introduction by John Masefield. Vol. 4. New York: E. P. Dutton.

Hall, Edward. 1983. *Ghanaian Languages.* Accra: Asempa Publishers.

Hancock, Ian F. 1970/71. Some aspects of English in Liberia. *Liberian Studies Journal* 3(2): 207–30.

————. ed. 1979. *Readings in Creole Studies.* Ghent: E. Story-Scientia PVBA.

Hébert, Père J., et al. 1976. *Esquisse d'une Monographie Historique du Pays Dagara.* Diebougou: Diocèse de Diebougou.

Heine, Bernd. 1968. *Die Verbreitung und Gliederung der Togorestsprachen.* Berlin: Dietrich Reimer Verlag.

————. 1977. Vertical and horizontal communication in Africa. *Afrika Forum* 12(3): 231–38.

Henrici, Ernst. 1898. Westafrikanisches Negerenglisch. *Anglia* 20: 397–403.

Herbert, R. K., ed. 1975. *Patterns in Language, Culture, and Society: Sub-Saharan Africa.* Working Papers in Linguistics No.19. Columbus: Department of Linguistics, Ohio State University.

Herskovits, Melville J., and Frances S. Herskovits. 1931. Tales in pidgin English from Nigeria. *Journal of American Folklore* 44: 448–66.

————. 1937. Tales in pidgin English from Ashanti. *Journal of American Folklore* 50: 52–101.

Hilton, T. E. 1962. Notes on the history of Kusasi. *Transactions of the Historical Society of Ghana* 6: 79–86.

Hiskett, M. 1965. The historical background to the naturalization of Arabic loan-words in Hausa. *African Language Studies* 6: 18–21.

Huber, Hugo. 1963. *The Krobo.* St. Augustin: Anthropos Institute.

Hunwick, J. O. 1964. The influence of Arabic in West Africa. *Transactions of the Historical Society of Ghana* 7: 24–41.

———. 1973. African language material in Arabic sources—The case of Songhay (Sonrai). *African Language Review* 15: 51–73.

Hutton, William. 1821. *A Voyage to Africa*. London: Longman, Hurst, Rees, Orme, and Brown.

Hyde, Faustina Baaba. 1994. Problems of learning English vocabulary in a second-language situation. *Legon Journal of the Humanities* 7: 127–35.

Hymes, Dell. 1972. On communicative competence. In Pride and Holmes, *Sociolinguistics*. Pp. 269–93.

———. 1986. Models of the interaction of language and social life. In John J. Gumperz and Dell Hymes, eds. *Directions in Sociolinguistics, the Ethnography of Communication*. New York: Basil Blackwell. Pp. 35–71. First published 1972.

Iliasu, A. A. 1971. The origins of the Mossi-Dagomba states. *Research Review* 7(2): 95–113.

Isert, Paul Erdmann. 1992. *Letters on West Africa and the Slave Trade: Journey to Guinea and the Caribbean Islands in Columbia (1788)*. Selena Axelrod Winsnes, trans. and ed. Oxford and New York: Oxford University Press.

Jenkins, Ray. 1977. Impeachable source? On the use of the second edition of Reindorf's *History* as a primary source for the study of Ghanaian history I. *History in Africa* 4: 123–47.

Johnson, Bruce C. 1975. Stable triglossia at Larteh, Ghana. In Herbert, *Patterns in Language, Culture, and Society*. Pp. 93–102.

Johnson, Marion. 1965. Ashanti east of the Volta. *Transactions of the Historical Society of Ghana* 3: 33–59.

———. 1977. Census, map and guesstimate: The past population of the Accra region. *African Historical Demography*. Edinburgh: University of Edinburgh Centre of African Studies. Pp. 272–94.

Johnson, Michael Torgbor. 1989. Lamɛi Agbɛi kɛ Sablai (Names and Appellations of the La). Diploma Long Essay, Language Centre, University of Ghana.

Jones, E. D. 1962. Mid-nineteenth century evidences of a Sierra Leone patois. *Sierra Leone Language Review* 1: 19–26.

Kea, R. A. 1969. Akwamu-Anlo relations, c. 1750–1813. *Transactions of the Historical Society of Ghana* 10: 29–63.

Killingray, David. 1982. Military and labour recruitment in the Gold Coast during the Second World War. *Journal of African History* 23: 83–95.

Kilson, Marion de B. 1969. Libation in Ga ritual. *Journal of Religion in Africa* 2: 161–78.

———. 1971. *Kpele Lala, Ga Religious Songs and Symbols*. Cambridge, Mass.: Harvard University Press.

———. 1974. *African Urban Kinsmen, The Ga of Central Accra*. London: C. Hurst.

Kingsley, Mary. 1982. *Travels in West Africa, Congo Français, Corisco and Cameroons*. 4th ed. London: Virago Press. First published 1897.

Kling, Hauptmann. 1891. Aus dem Schutzgebiete Togo: Reise der Hauptmanns Kling von Lome über Salaga nach Bismarckburg im Sommer 1891. *Mitteilungen aus der deutsche Schutzgebiete* 5.

Klose, Heinrich. 1899. *Togo unter deutscher Flagge*. Berlin: Dietrich Reimer (Ernst Vossen).

Koelle, Sigismund. 1963. *Polyglotta Africana*. Graz: Akademische Druck- und Verlagsanstalt. First published 1854.

Köhler, O. 1964. Gur languages in the Polyglotta Africana. *Sierra Leone Language Review* 3: 65–73.

Kondor, Daniel. 1989, May 31. The Nafana and the Ligbi, An ethnological account. *People's Daily Graphic*.

———. 1990, November 14. The Challa Society. *People's Daily Graphic*.

————. 27 February 1991. Installing a Chief in Ga, with reference to La. *People's Daily Graphic.*

Kropp, M. E. 1966. The Adampe and Anfue dialects of Ewe in the Polyglotta Africana. *Sierra Leone Language Review* 5: 116–21.

Kwamena-Poh, M. A. 1973. *Government and Politics in the Akuapem State 1730–1850.* London: Longman.

Laing, Kojo. 1986. *Search Sweet Country.* London: William Heinemann.

Laitin, David D. 1991. *Language Repertoires and State Construction in Africa.* Cambridge and New York: Cambridge University Press.

LePage, Robert B. 1992. What can we learn from the case of Pitcairnese? In Rosemarie Tracy, ed., *Who Climbs the Grammar-Tree?* Tübingen: Max Niemeyer Verlag. Pp. 143–55.

LePage, R. B., and Andrée Tabouret-Keller. 1985. *Acts of Identity: Creole-based Approaches to Language and Ethnicity.* Cambridge and New York: Cambridge University Press.

Levtzion, Nehemia, 1968. *Muslims and Chiefs in West Africa.* Oxford: Clarendon Press.

————. 1973. *Ancient Ghana and Mali.* London: Methuen.

Lieberson, Stanley. 1982. Forces affecting language spread: Some basic propositions. In Cooper, *Language Spread.* Pp. 37–62.

Little, Kenneth. 1973. *African Women in Towns: An aspect of Africa's social revolution.* London: Cambridge University Press.

Martin, Jane. 1985. Krumen "down the coast," Liberian migrants on the West African coast in the nineteenth and twentieth centuries. *Journal of African Historical Studies* 18(3): 401–24.

Matson, J. N. 1953. The French at Amoku. *Transactions of the Gold Coast & Togoland Historical Society* 1: 7–60.

Mauny, Raymond. 1961. *Tableau Géographique de l'Ouest Africain au Moyen Age.* Dakar: Institut Français d'Afrique Noire.

McFarland, Daniel Miles. 1985. *Historical Dictionary of Ghana.* Metuchen, N.J. and London: Scarecrow Press.

Meredith, Henry. 1812. *An Account of the Gold Coast of Africa.* London: Longman, Hurst, Rees, Orme, and Brown.

Migeod, F. W. H. 1911. *The Languages of West Africa*, 2 vols. London: Kegan, K. Paul, Trench, Trubner.

Milroy, Lesley, and James Milroy. 1992. Social network and social class: Toward an integrated sociolinguistic model. *Language in Society* 21: 1–26.

Moser, Rex E. 1979. Sociolinguistic Data Concerning the Sabon Zongo of Accra. Mimeographed paper prepared for the Workshop on the Study of Multilingualism in Ghana, Institute of African Studies, University of Ghana.

Mühlhaüsler, Peter. 1986. *Pidgin and Creole Linguistics.* Oxford: Blackwell.

Müller, W. J. 1968. *Die Afrikanische auf der Guineischen Gold-Cust Gelegene Landschaft FETU.* Graz: Akademische Druck- und Verlagsanstalt. First published 1676.

Naden, Tony. 1988. The Gur languages. In Dakubu, *The Languages of Ghana.* Pp. 12–49.

————. 1989. Gur. In Bendor-Samuel, *Niger-Congo Languages.* Pp. 141–68.

Naden, Tony, and M. E. Kropp Dakubu. 1988. Mande languages. In Dakubu, *The Languages of Ghana.* Pp. 155–62.

Naro, Anthony J. 1973. The origin of West African pidgin. *Papers from the Ninth Annual Regional Meeting of the Chicago Linguistic Society*, Chicago. Pp. 442–49.

Nicolaï, Robert. 1980. Remarques sur la diversification dialectale et la propagation des innovations phonetiques en Songhay. *Etudes Linguistiques* (Niamey) 2(2).

O'Connor, Anthony. 1983. *The African City.* New York: Africana Publishing.

Odamtten, Helen, Aloysius Denkabe, and I. Enyonam Tsikata. 1994. The problem of English language skills at the university level: A case study of first year Law and Administration students at the University of Ghana. *Legon Journal of the Humanities* 7: 95–125.

Odamtten, S. K. 1978. *The Missionary Factor in Ghana's Development up to the 1880s*. Accra: Waterville Publishing House.

Odoom, K. O. 1971. A document on the pioneers of the Muslim community in Accra. *Research Review* 7(3): 1–31.

Ogilby, John. 1670. *Africa*. London.

Okri, Ben. 1981. *The Landscapes Within*. London: Longman.

Oldendorp, G. C. A. 1777. *Geschichte der Mission der Evangelischen Brüder aus den Caraïbischen Inseln, S. Thomas, S. Croix, und S. Jan*. Barby.

Oppong, Christine. 1974. *Marriage among a Matrilineal Elite*. London: Cambridge University Press.

Oti-Boateng, E., S. E. Quarshie, R. Malikzay, and S. Amoafo. 1989. *1984 Population Census of Ghana: Demographic and Economic Characteristics*. Accra: Government of Ghana.

Ozanne, Paul. 1964. Notes on the later prehistory of Accra. *Journal of the Historical Society of Nigeria* 3(1): 3–23.

———. 1965. Ladoku, An early town near Prampram. *Ghana Notes and Queries* 7: 6–7.

Painter, Colin. 1966. *Linguistic Field Notes from Banda*. . . . Collected Language Notes No. 7. Legon: Institute of African Studies.

———. 1980. Hill Guang. In M. E. Kropp Dakubu, ed., *West African Language Data Sheets*. Vol. 2. Leiden: African Studies Center.

Persson, A. M. 1980. Language Use in Brawhani. Ms. deposited in the Institute of African Studies Library, Legon.

Piłaszewicz, Stanisław. 1992. *The Zabarma Conquest of North-West Ghana and Upper Volta*. Warsaw: Polish Scientific Publishers.

Pogucki, R. J. H. 1955. *Gold Coast Land Tenure, Vol. 3: Land Tenure in Ga Customary Law. Vol. 4: Land Tenure in Ga Customary Law, Map Supplement Accra 1826–1954*. Accra: Gold Coast Lands Department.

Posnansky, Merrick. 1979. Archaeological aspects of the Brong-Ahafo Region. In Arhin, *Brong Kyempem*. Pp. 22–35.

———. 1987. Prelude to Akan civilization. In Schildkrout, *The Golden Stool: Studies of the Asante Center and Periphery*. Anthropological Papers of the American Museum of Natural History, Vol. 65, Part 1, pp. 14–22.

Pride, J. B., and Janet Holmes, eds. 1972. *Sociolinguistics, Selected Readings*. Harmondsworth, Eng.: Penguin Books.

Protten, Christian. 1764. *En nyttig Grammaticalsk Indledelse til tvende hidindtil ubekiendte Sprog, Fanteisk og Acraisk*. . . . Copenhagen: Kisel.

Quarcoo, A. K., N. O. Addo, and M. Peil. 1967. *Madina Survey: A Study of the Structure and Development of a Contemporary Sub-urban Settlement*. Legon: Institute of African Studies.

Quaye, Irene. 1972. The Ga and their Neighbours, 1600–1742. Ph.D. thesis, University of Ghana.

Ramseyer, F. 1886. Eine Reise im Norden von Asante, und im Osten vom Volta, von Okwawu nach Bron, Krakye und Boem. *Mitteilungen der Geographischen Gesellschaft in Jena* 4: 69–87.

Rapp, E. L. 1933. Die Nafana-Sprache auf der Elfenbeinküste und auf der Goldküste. *Mitteilungen des Seminars für Orientalische Sprachen* 36(3): 54–66.

————. 1955. Zur Ausbreitung einer westafrikanischen Stammessprache (das Twi). In J. Lukas, ed., *Afrikanistische Studien*. Berlin: Akademie Verlag. Pp. 220–30.

Rask, Johannes. 1754. *En kort og sandferdig Reise-Beskrivelse til og fra Guinea*. Troskjem.

Rask, Rasmus. 1828. *Vejledning til Akra-Sproget, med et Tillaeg om Aqvambuisk*. Copenhagen: Møller.

Rat, J. Numa. 1889. *The Elements of the Hausa Language, Or a Short Introductory Grammar of the Language*. London: Waterlow & Sons.

Rattray, R. S. 1932. *The Tribes of the Ashanti Hinterland*, 2 vols. Oxford: Clarendon Press.

Reindorf, Carl Christian. 1966. *The History of the Gold Coast and Asante*. 2nd ed. Accra: Ghana Universities Press. First published 1889.

Riis, H. N. 1853. *Elemente des Akwapim Dialects der Odschi Sprache*. Basel: Detloff.

Ring, James Andrew. 1981. Ewe as a second language: A sociolinguistic survey of Ghana's central Volta Region. *Research Review* 12(2/3).

Robertson, Claire C. 1990. *Sharing the Same Bowl: A Socioeconomic History of Women and Class in Accra, Ghana*. Ann Arbor: University of Michigan Press.

Rodney, Walter. 1969. Gold and slaves on the Gold Coast. *Transactions of the Historical Society of Ghana* 10: 12–28.

Romaine, Suzanne. 1982. *Socio-historical Linguistics, Its Status and Methodology*. Cambridge and New York: Cambridge University Press.

Rømer, L. F. 1760. *Tilforladelig Efterretning om Kysten Guinea*. Copenhagen: Ludolph Henrich Lillies Enke.

Rouch, Jean. 1956. *Migrations au Ghana (Gold Coast)*. Paris: Société des Africanistes, Musée de l'Homme.

Ryder, A. F. C. 1969. *Benin and the Europeans 1485–1897*. London: Longmans Green.

Samarin, William J. 1982. Colonization and pidginization on the Ubangi River. *Journal of African Languages and Linguistics* 4: 1–42.

————. 1990/91. The origins of Kituba and Lingala. *Journal of African Languages and Linguistics* 12: 42–77.

Sanjek, Roger. 1977. Cognitive maps of the ethnic domain in urban Ghana: Reflections on variability and change. *American Ethnologist* 4(4): 603–22.

Schildkrout, Enid. 1978. *People of the Zongo*. Cambridge and New York: Cambridge University Press.

Schlegel, J. B. 1857. *Schlüssel zur Ewesprache*. Bremen.

Schlunk, Martin. 1910. *Die Norddeutsche Mission in Togo 1: Meine Reise durchs Eweland*. Bremen.

Schneider, Gilbert L. 1967. *West African Pidgin English: An Historical Overview*. Athens: Ohio University Center for International Studies.

Schön, J. F. 1876. *Dictionary of the Hausa Language*. London: Church Missionary Society.

Schønning, C. 1805. *De ti Bud, det apostoliske Symbolum og Fader Vor, oversatte i det Accraiske Sprog*. Copenhagen: Schubart.

Schosser, Hermann. n.d. (1890?). *Akpafu*. Bremer Missions-Schriften Nr. 21.

Schott, Rüdiger. 1970. *Aus Leben und Dichtung eines westafrikanischen Bauernvolkes*. Cologne and Opladen: Arbeitsgemeinschaft für Forschung des Landes Nordrhein-Westfalen.

Schreiber, A. D. 1901. *Ein Besuch auf dem Missionsfelde in Togo*. Bremen.

Scotton, Carol M. 1975. Multilingualism in Lagos—What it means to the social scientist. In Herbert, *Patterns in Language, Culture, and Society*. Pp. 78–90.

————. 1976. The role of norms and other factors in language choice in work situations in three African cities (Lagos, Kampala, Nairobi). In A. Verdoodt and Rolf Kjolseth, eds., *Language in Sociology*. Louvain: Editions Peeters. Pp. 201–31.

————. 1982. Learning lingua francas and socioeconomic integration: Evidence from Africa. In Cooper, *Language Spread.* Pp. 63–94.

Sebeok, Thomas A., ed. 1971. *Current Trends in Linguistics, Vol. 7: Linguistics in Sub-Saharan Africa.* The Hague and Paris: Mouton.

Seidel, A. 1898. Beiträge zur Kenntniss der Sprachen in Togo. *Zeitschrift für Afrikanische und Ozeanische Sprachen* 4: 201–86.

————. 1904. *Togo-Sprachen. Kurze Grammatiken, Vokabulare und Phrasensammlungen der drei Hauptsprachen in Togo: Anglo-Ewe, Anecho-Ewe, und Haussa.* Dresden and Leipzig: Koch.

Sey, K. A. 1973. *Ghanaian English.* London: Macmillan.

Smith, Robert S. 1969. *Kingdoms of the Yoruba.* London: Methuen.

Smock, David R. 1975. Language policy in Ghana. In David R. Smock and Kwamena Bentsi-Enchill, eds., *The Search for National Integration in Africa.* New York: Free Press; London: Collier Macmillan. Pp. 169–88.

Sölken, Heinz. 1939. Afrikanische Dokumente zur Frage der Entstehung der Hausanischen Diaspora in Oberguinea. *Mitteilungen der Auslands-Hochschule an der Universität Berlin* 42: 127.

Spencer, John, ed. 1971. *The English Language in West Africa.* Harlow: Longman.

Stahl, Ann. 1991. Ethnic style and ethnic boundaries: A diachronic case study from Ghana. *Ethnohistory* 38(3): 250–75.

Stewart, John M. 1989. Kwa. In Bendor-Samuel, *Niger-Congo Languages.* Pp. 216–45.

Syme, J. K. G. 1932. The Kusaasi: A Short History. Ms. deposited in the Library of the Institute of African Studies, University of Ghana.

Tait, David. 1961. *The Konkomba of Northern Ghana.* Jack Goody, ed. London: Oxford University Press.

Tauxier, Louis. 1921. *Le Noir de Bondoukou.* Paris: E. Leroux.

Tera, Kallilou. 1986. Le Dioula Vehiculaire de Cote d'Ivoire, Expansion et developpement. *Cahiers Ivoiriens de Recherche Linguistique* 20: 5–33.

Tetteh, Victor Ashiteye. 1990. Plasheele yɛ Ga mli (Slang in Ga). Diploma Long Essay, Language Centre, University of Ghana.

Texeira da Mota, A., and P. E. H. Hair. 1988. *East of Mina: Afro-European Relations on the Gold Coast in the 1550s and 1560s.* Madison: University of Wisconsin, African Studies Program.

Thomason, Sarah Grey, and Terrence Kaufman. 1991. *Language Contact, Creolization and Genetic Linguistics.* Berkeley, Los Angeles; Oxford: University of California Press. First published 1988.

Tilleman, Erick. 1994. *En Kort og Enfoldig Beretning om det Landskab Guinea og dets Beskaffenhed (1697); A Short and Simple Account of the Country Guinea and its Nature.* Selena Axelrod Winsnes, trans. and ed. Madison: University of Wisconsin, African Studies Program.

Todd, Loreto. 1979. Cameroonian: A consideration of "What's in a Name." In Hancock, *Readings in Creole Studies.* Pp. 281–94.

Tonkin, Elizabeth. 1971. Some coastal pidgins of West Africa. In Edwin Ardener, ed., *Social Anthropology and Language.* London and New York: Tavistock Publications. Pp. 129–55.

Trudgill, Peter. 1983. *Sociolinguistics: An Introduction to Language and Society.* Rev. ed. Harmondsworth, England: Pelican Books.

Trutenau, H. M. J., ed. 1971. *Christian Protten: Introduction to the Fante and Accra (Gā) Languages 1764 and J. E. J. Capitein's 1744 Fante Catechism.* London: Afro-Presse.

Valkhoff, Marius F. 1972. *New Light on Afrikaans and "Malayo-Portuguese."* Louvain: Editions Peeters.

Van Dantzig, Albert. 1978. *The Dutch and the Guinea Coast 1674–1742.* Accra: Ghana Academy of Arts and Sciences.

———. 1980. *Forts and Castles of Ghana.* Accra: Sedco Publishing.

Verdon, Michel. 1983. *The Abutia Ewe of West Africa.* Berlin, New York, and Amsterdam: Mouton.

Vogt, John. 1979. *Portuguese Rule on the Gold Coast 1469–1682.* Athens: University of Georgia Press.

Ward, W. E. F. 1967. *A History of Ghana.* 4th ed. London: George Allen and Unwin. First published 1948.

Westermann, Diedrich. 1910. Vier Sprachen aus Mitteltogo. Likpe, Bowili, Akpafu und Adele nebst einigen Resten der Borosprache. . . . *Mitteilungen des Seminars für Orientalische Sprachen* 13: 39–57.

———. 1932. Die heutige und die frühere Bevölkerung Togos. *Koloniale Rundschau* 9/12: 1–7.

———. 1933. Drei Dialekte des Tem in Togo, nach Aufnahmen von A. Mischlich. *Mitteilungen des Seminars für Orientalische Sprachen zu Berlin* 36(3): 7–33.

Whiteley, Wilfred H. 1969. *Swahili: The Rise of a National Language.* London: Methuen.

Wilks, Ivor. 1957. The rise of the Akwamu Empire 1650–1710. *Transactions of the Historical Society of Ghana* 3(2): 99–136.

———. 1959. Akwamu and Otublohum: An eighteenth century Akan marriage arrangement. *Africa* 29(4): 391–404.

———. 1962. The Mande loan element in Twi. *Ghana Notes and Queries* 4.

———. 1968. The transmission of Islamic learning in the Western Sudan. In J. Goody, *Literacy in Traditional Societies.* Pp. 161–97.

———. 1975. *Asante in the Nineteenth Century.* London and New York: Cambridge University Press.

———. 1982. Wangara, Akan and Portuguese in the fifteenth and sixteenth centuries 1. The matter of Bitu. *Journal of African History* 23: 333–49.

———. 1989. *Wa and the Wala: Islam and Polity in Northwestern Ghana.* Cambridge and New York: Cambridge University Press.

———. 1993. *Forests of Gold, Essays on the Akan and the Kingdom of Asante.* Athens: Ohio University Press.

Wilson, Louis E. 1991. *The Krobo People of Ghana to 1892, A political and social history.* Athens: Ohio University Center for International Studies.

Wolf, Ludwig. 1891. Aus dem Schutzgebiete Togo: Dr. Ludwig Wolf's letzte Reise nach der Landschaft Barbar (Bariba) oder Borgu. *Mitteilungen aus den Deutschen Schutzgebieten* 4.

Wrisberg, P. W. v. 1826. *Jesu Bjærgprediken oversat iden akraiske Sprog.* . . . Copenhagen: Schubart.

Wurm, P. 1874. Anfänge der Basler Mission auf der Goldküste. *Evangelisches Missions-Magazin* neue Folge 18: 129–50, 195–208, 238–50.

Yule, Henry, and A. C. Burnell. 1903. *Hobson-Jobson: A Glossary of Anglo-Indian Words and Phrases and of Kindred Terms, Etymological, Historical, Geographical and Discursive.* New ed. London: John Murray. First published 1886.

Zahn, F. M. 1867. *Von der Elbe bis zum Volta, Sechs Jahre Missions-Arbeit in Westafrika.* Bremen.

———. 1870. *Vier Freistätten im Sclavenlande* [sic]. Bremen: E. Hilgerloh.

Zech, Graf Julius von. 1907. Land und Leute an der Nordwestgrenze von Togo. *Mitteilungen von Forschungsreisenden* 17, Band 3.

Zima, Petr. 1968. Hausa in West Africa: Remarks on contemporary role and functions. In Joshua A. Fishman, C. A. Ferguson, and J. Das Gupta, eds., *Language Problems of Developing Nations*. New York, London, Sydney, and Toronto: Wiley. Pp. 365–77.

Zimmermann, J. 1858. *A Grammatical Sketch of the Akra or Ga Language including Vocabulary of the Akra or Ga Language with an Adanme Appendix, and Specimens from the Mouth of the Natives*. Stuttgart.

NEWSPAPERS CITED:

Madina today. Madina, Accra.

The People's Daily Graphic. Accra: Graphic Corporation.

The Mirror. Accra: Graphic Corporation.

Monats-Blatt der Norddeutschen Missions-Gesellschaft. Bremer Staatsarchiv 7,1025 51/3.

INDEX